FIFTY KEY FIGURES IN ISLAM

If you would like to learn more about the Muslim culture, people and its teachings, then this is the perfect resource for you. Roy Jackson explores the lives and thoughts of fifty influential figures in Islam and surveys a heritage which spans 1500 years. *Fifty Key Figures in Islam* could not have come at a more interesting time in history. Fully cross-referenced, for each key figure, the book provides:

- biographical details
- presentation and analysis of their main ideas
- an account of their impact and influence within and, if appropriate, beyond the Islamic tradition
- list of major works and further reading

Roy Ahmad Jackson has been a lecturer and writer on religion and philosophy for over fifteen years. He has lectured in Islamic Studies at various universities, including the University of Durham and King's College London. He has previously written books on Nietzsche, Plato, Islam and the philosophy of religion.

D1616125

ALSO AVAILABLE FROM ROUTLEDGE

Religion: The Basics
Malory Nye
0-415-26379-4

Fifty Key Christian Thinkers
*Peter McEnhill and
George Newlands*
0-415-17050-8

Eastern Philosophy:
Key Readings
Oliver Leaman
0-415-17358-2

Fifty Key Jewish Thinkers
Dan Cohn-Sherbok
0-415-12628-2

Key Concepts in Eastern
Philosophy
Oliver Leaman
0-415-17363-9

Fifty Eastern Thinkers
*Diané Collinson, Kathryn Plant
and Robert Wilkinson*
0-415-20284-1

Gurdjieff: The Key Concepts
Sophia Wellbeloved
0-415-24898-1

Who's Who in Christianity
Lavinia Cohn-Sherbok
0-415-26034-5

Who's Who in Jewish History
*Joan Comay, new edition revised by
Lavinia Cohn-Sherbok*
0-415-26030-2

Who's Who in the New
Testament
Ronald Brownrigg
0-415-26036-1

Who's Who in the Old
Testament
Joan Comay
0-415-26031-0

FIFTY KEY FIGURES IN ISLAM

Roy Jackson

Routledge
Taylor & Francis Group

LONDON AND NEW YORK

First published 2006
by Routledge
2 Park Square, Milton Park, Abingdon, Oxon, OX14 4RN

Simultaneously published in the USA and Canada
by Routledge
270 Madison Avenue, New York, NY 10016

Routledge is an imprint of the Taylor & Francis Group, an informa business

Typeset in Bembo by Taylor & Francis Books
Printed and bound in Great Britain by MPG Books Ltd, Bodmin

British Library Cataloguing in Publication Data
A catalogue record for this book is available from the British Library

Library of Congress Cataloging-in-Publication Data
Jackson, Roy, 1962–
    Fifty key figures in Islam/Roy Jackson.—1st ed.
    p. cm.
    Includes bibliographical references and index.
    1. Muslims—Biography. I. Title.
    BP70.J34 2006
    297.092'2—dc22
                2005032377

ISBN10: 0-415-35467-6   ISBN13: 978-0-415-35467-7 (hbk)
ISBN10: 0-415-35468-4   ISBN13: 978-0-415-35468-4 (pbk)
ISBN10: 0-203-00138-9   ISBN13: 978-0-203-00138-7 (ebk)

To my wife Asmi for her remarkable patience during the writing of this book

CHRONOLOGICAL LIST
OF CONTENTS

ALPHABETICAL LIST
OF CONTENTS

PREFACE

Recent years have witnessed a number of historical turning points in the Islamic world, some of which have had a significant impact on the non-Islamic world. I can recall quite vividly the events in Iran in early 1979 as the pro-Western Shah fled and thousands in the streets of Teheran greeted Ayatollah Khomeini. I remember the events, but I also recall being confused and, frankly, astounded by my own ignorance of Islam and the Muslim world at the time, for I was only a teenager who had no Muslim friends or any connection with Islam at all. No doubt I bought in to the newspaper rhetoric of the time: of the 'mad Mullahs' who preferred apparent oppression, disorder, poverty, the veil and backwardness rather than the luxuries, technology, and freedom of the Western world. It took maturity and a number of years of getting to know the Muslim world, people and its teachings before I understood what a simplistic picture was presented by much of the Western media at that time. People do not choose to live in poverty and people do not choose to be oppressed. There are risks involved in any revolution as history has so often demonstrated for we can never be sure that our icons will deliver on their promises. It has taken some time for me, and many others, to attempt to understand why a people should choose to rebel against the apparent utopia of Western values and goods and, perhaps the main reason is that, as the Western world itself is beginning to realise, it is no utopia either. What the Iranian Revolution did was to show the West once more the idea that there are alternatives, and Iran is all the more fascinating in that it is still in the process of self-examination as to what those alternatives can be. More important is the view that there are Islamic alternatives as entries such as Ayatollah Khomeini, Ali Shariati and Abdul Karim Soroush in this book demonstrate. These Iranians themselves are part of a much greater tradition that looks to Islam for the answers rather than to other '-isms'. This is one thing that virtually all the entries in this book have in common, if very little else! In 1980 came the Iran–Iraq war which lasted eight years, at the cost of a million deaths and, in the following year, in 1989, Khomeini issued the fatwa against Salman Rushdie over his supposedly blasphemous novel *The Satanic Verses*. With these events came terms that many non-Muslims were unfamiliar with: 'ayatollah', 'Shi'a Islam', 'fatwa', and so on, yet these are now commonly understood (or commonly misunderstood) terms.

The 1980s, then, were a time when Islam, and Iran especially, was rarely out of the news. During the same decade, of course, another Muslim nation was also a regular news feature as Russian troops strived to control Afghanistan. In that conflict the United States allied themselves with Muslim nations in providing arms and military training to the mujahedin: a legacy that now has come back to haunt them. But by the 1990s the communist world was in decline and Islam was now the new kid on the block. Muslims remained in the news during the 1990s: the conflict in Bosnia-Herzegovina; the Gulf War and the arms inspection crisis in Iraq; civil strife and violence in Algeria; famine in Sudan; the Israeli-Palestinian conflict; the rise in power of the Taliban in Afghanistan, and so on. However, no doubt the biggest turning point so far as relations between Muslims and non-Muslims are concerned is when on September 11, 2001, the twin towers of the World Trade Center were attacked and destroyed. Blame was quickly attributed to Osama bin Laden and the US policy since then has been the 'war against terror' which has seen air strikes on the Taliban and the overthrow of Saddam Hussayn in Iraq.

What should be evident if only from the tail end of the twentieth century is that Islam is important. Love it, or hate it, but you cannot ignore it. I have grown to love Muslim people and the nations they inhabit. The people are, on the whole, kind, sincere and generous. Those of a political bent display a genuine concern for the planet and for humanity as a whole, and they probably have good reason to. There is a concern among many Muslims that there is a growing civilisational conflict between Islam and the West. As one of the entries in this book, the Tunisian Rachid Ghannoushi, has said:

> The West as a concept of civilisation has seen its centre of gravity move from Western Europe to America to Eastern Europe. Israel represents the projection of this centre into the East to wipe out its specific character, its spiritual wealth, and humankind's hope for a new renaissance.[1]

Rather than being presented with the theological view of Islam as a member of the same family as the Judaeo-Christian tradition, we have conflict and difference. Such a perception, of course, does not lie only with Islamist commentators. Many Western writers are just as guilty, if not more so, of portraying Islam as an 'Other'. The late Edward Said's well-known study, *Orientalism*,[2] has recounted how images of the Other have often been created to confirm one's own sense of racial and cultural superiority, or to provide justification for the conquest and abuse of other people's territory. Since the eighteenth century, when the West was at its economic and military apex, Islam has been perceived, not as a threat, but as decadent, irrational, inefficient, lazy, barbaric, false and Satanic. Therefore, the Others became 'objects' that were defined not by their own discourses, but by a discourse imposed upon them by the West. The results, of course, were a grossly biased view of Islam that still continues to reverberate in contemporary discourse. Said's later study, *Covering Islam*,[3] provides an incisive account of Western media treatment of Muslims and Islam following the Iran hostage crisis of 1979–1980 and it is certainly still not too difficult to detect similar media treatment in the Western press of the twenty-first century.

The mistrust and misunderstanding between Muslims and non-Muslims have a long history. Charles Lindholm rightly states that:

> Contemporary Western enmity . . . is not simply a consequence of modern conflict. It is a reflection of the thousand-year rivalry between the Muslim Middle East and Christian Europe for economic, political and religious hegemony over the Western hemisphere and beyond – a contest dominated until recently by Islam.[4]

Initially, through the encounters of the Crusades, the Western reaction to Islam was the fear of a Muslim invasion and a return to the days when Islam spread as far as Spain and southern France. The Ottoman challenge that, in 1529, led to Suleiman's (also an entry in this book) army at the gates of Vienna, was a genuine concern and fear for the world of Christendom, and this was reflected in the Western literature at the time. A series of events in the seventeenth century, however, proved to be important turning points in the Western view of Islam. In 1606, the Sultan deigned to treat a European power as an equal by signing a treaty with the Hapsburgs that ended a costly 150-year stalemate on the Danube. In 1683, a quarter of a million Ottoman soldiers besieged Vienna, but the over-confidence and slowness of the Turkish general to press a military advantage allowed the Christians to prepare and gather resources, resulting in the besieging army being routed and chased down the Danube all the way to Belgrade. The sixteen years of war that followed were a series of military disasters for the Ottomans, leading, in 1699, to the Treaty of Karlowitz which effectively exposed the weakness of the Ottoman Empire.

Until the nineteenth century, the military (as distinct from the commercial) advance of the West into the Islamic world was limited to the areas of the Balkans and along the northern and eastern shores of the Black Sea. The further turning point came with the occupation of Egypt by Napoleon Bonaparte in 1798: 'the first armed inroad of Europe on the Arab near East since the Crusades'.[5] The event is significant in that it began the period of Western intervention in the Islamic world and completely shattered any remaining illusions of the superiority of Islam: 'The great Ottoman Empire, which had aspired to convert the world to Islam, now was obliged to look to the West for inspiration; instead of being Europe's nemesis, it soon would be its "sick man".'[6]

The psychological impact for the Muslim world of such a decline cannot be overestimated and must be a factor in the residual collective memory of the contemporary Islamic world, especially considering the confidence, wealth, efficiency and technology that the Ottoman Empire possessed compared with the frightened, fragmented and superstitious Europe. Further, the seemingly 'natural' triumph of the West over Islam must contribute to the justification of Orientalism as a concept. It is not surprising, therefore, that Islam refers to its own Golden Age as its justification for the 'natural triumph' of Islam over Jahiliyya – the unbelievers. The fact that Islam has suffered under the Western dominance also, for many, brings into question the validity of Islam as superior to other civilisations and ideologies. This collective memory on both sides (the Muslims versus the Christians) continues to be evident in contemporary events, most recently following the events of September 11, 2001, with the attacks on the World Trade Center and the Pentagon. Similarly, the concern that Islamic 'fundamentalism' is a threat has its basis in the fear that was prevalent in Western Europe during the sixteenth and seventeenth centuries.

I for one do not uphold the 'clash of civilisations' thesis. Regardless of religious differences – and there are many, despite the belief in the 'one' God – Muslims do not differ from anyone else: they are human beings and they bleed when cut. As I hope these entries will demonstrate, Muslims are really not that different from non-Muslims and there has always been a constant interaction of ideas between these civilisations.

Structure of the book

Regarding the entries in this book, the reader may note a certain 'imbalance'. In the early period of Islam, where little is known about the lives of the figures, more space has been devoted to their ideas, whereas in the later period, where a great deal more is known, more space may be devoted to that person's life, especially if it proves to have been a colourful one. Sometimes, especially during the early period of Islam, little accurate information is available on an Islamic figure. However, in such cases, rather than omit them, I have taken the opportunity to place the figure in the context of the historical events and movements at the time, thus providing what hopefully will prove to be valuable contextualisation. The number fifty is, of course, somewhat arbitrary. There are not a convenient fifty figures that all scholars of Islam would agree upon. In my discussions with colleagues, in which we drew up our own private lists and engaged in some heated discussions, we generally came up with an agreed thirty or so, whereas the other twenty – the 'outer circle' – were far more contentious. Ultimately, decisions as to who to include and who to omit had to be made. Some readers will approve of my choice and some will not. The difficulty was not in finding fifty figures, but rather in limiting it to fifty. The problem in writing this work was stopping at fifty when there were so many more that could have been included. Perhaps inevitably with a work like this, attention will be paid to omissions rather than inclusions. For this, I can offer no apology other than to say that it is a book on fifty figures, and the publisher would not have been too pleased if I had attempted to 'sneak in' another ten or so. Second, everyone has their own axe to grind. Put a collection of Islamic scholars in a room and no two will agree, especially if involved in the difficult task of making a list of fifty important figures. Let me, then, pre-empt the cries of 'Why isn't so-and-so in the book?' by stating that there are a number of other figures that could be included, but at the sacrifice of certain others and I wanted to present to the reader as broad a sweep of the Islamic world as possible. This is not a work of merely 'thinkers', but figures, whether they are philosophical, political, artistic, or, in some cases, morally 'dubious'. That relates to another point; I am not making any moral assertions here. This is an analysis of people who have had, in some way or another, an impact upon Islam, whether that be good or bad in the eyes of the reader. If I am giving morally dubious characters publicity, I do apologise but, in most cases, they have been dead for quite some time now. And that neatly relates to another point: how many dead figures compared with how many living? I confess that it was probably the struggle to limit the number of living figures that I found most difficult, but I did have to keep in mind that I am dealing with a phenomenon that has existed historically for fifteen hundred years and many have an important legacy. It is often difficult to tell, and something of a gamble to know which living figures will survive the test of time.

In addition, the reader will be confronted here with a plethora of technical terms and a brief Glossary of common terms used in Islam is provided, with the words indicated in bold italic on their first occurrence. For a more complete account, I would recommend Colin Turner's *Islam: The Basics* which 'does as it says on the tin'. My cross-references to other key figures are indicated by the name in bold.

Finally, if the reader wishes an easy introduction to Islam, I can do no better than recommend Karen Armstrong's *A Short History of Islam*. She does what all we Islamic scholars wish we could do: sift through the many volumes available and then provide a succinct, lucid and entertaining overview for the casual reader.

References

Armstrong, Karen, *Islam: A Short History*, London: Phoenix Press, 2000.

Hunter, Shireen T., *The Future of Islam and the West*, Washington, DC: The Center for Strategic and International Studies, 1998.

Lewis, Bernard, *The Arabs in History*, 2nd edn. Oxford: Oxford University Press, 1993.

Lindholm, Charles, *The Islamic Middle East: An Historical Anthropology*, London: Blackwell, 1996.

Said, Edward, *Orientalism*, London: Penguin, 1978.

———, *Covering Islam*, London: Routledge, 1981.

Turner, Colin, *Islam: The Basics*, London: Routledge, 2005.

Notes

1 From a speech, in Hunter (1998, p. 13).
2 Said (1978).
3 Ibid.
4 Lindholm (1996, p. 3).
5 Lewis (1993, p. 183).
6 Lindholm (1996, p. 4).00

FIFTY KEY FIGURES
IN ISLAM

PROPHET MUHAMMAD (c. 570–632)

The Prophet Muhammad led a remarkable life. At the age of 40, he received the first revelation from God (al-lah, 'the God') which was to be a major turning point both in his own life and in the subsequent lives of millions. As the Prophet of Islam, Muhammad, against great opposition, unified the disparate Arab peoples into a community (the *umma*) under one leader and one belief system. After his death, this new movement spread until it became the largest empire since the Roman era and enjoyed hegemony for a thousand years. Today there are around one billion people who call themselves Muslim and look to Muhammad as the model to follow in their lives.

According to traditional dating, Muhammad was born around 570. There is little reliable information, and much hagiography, concerning his family background and early years although it is known that he was a member of a powerful tribe from Mecca in Arabia known as the Quraysh. His particular clan, the Banu Hashim, were not as powerful, though highly respected nonetheless. His father, Abd Allah, died before Muhammad was born and his mother, Amina, died when he was only 6 years old. Consequently, he was entrusted to the care of his grandfather, Abd al-Muttalib who died when Muhammad was 8 years old. His upbringing from then on was in the hands of his uncle and leader of the clan, Abu Talib.

Leaving the myths aside, Muhammad had a relatively uneventful upbringing. As was the practice of the time, he spent some years as a child among the bedouin as it was believed that their moral fibre was stronger than what existed among the urban environment of Mecca. Mecca, by this time, was the centre of trade and relatively prosperous and Muhammad himself turned his hand to trade. He obtained a reputation for being hard-working, modest and trustworthy, hence his nickname al-Amin ('the Trustworthy'). When he was in his twenties, he entered the service of a wealthy widow called Khadija as the manager of her trade caravan and he impressed her so much with his managing skills and character that she proposed marriage to him. At the time Khadija was 40 years of age, compared to Muhammad who was 25, but she managed to produce four daughters and two sons, although the sons did not survive childhood.

Muhammad and Khadija became business partners and it seems that they continued to enjoy financial success, although Muhammad started to become more reflective and spiritual, becoming increasingly concerned over what he saw as the low level of moral and social ethic in Mecca where society seemed to be permeated by class distinctions, poverty and the accumulation of wealth among a small elite. As an orphan himself, Muhammad felt particular sympathy for children who had lost their parents as well as disgust for the practice of infanticide that existed at the time. He spent more time in spiritual practices and engaging in dialogue with the various followers of faiths that came to Mecca to trade. He also would go on short retreats into the nearby caves at Mount Hira where he would be isolated from others, and – denying himself food and drink – he would engage in meditation and prayer.

It was on one such retreat when Muhammad was 40 years old that a vision came to him. It was of an angel, the biblical angel Gabriel, who commanded Muhammad to 'recite' the word of God:

> Recite in the name of your Lord who created – created man from clots of blood.
> Recite! Your Lord is the most Bountiful One, who by the pen taught man what he did not know.
> Indeed, man transgresses in thinking himself his own master: for to your Lord all things return.
>
> (sura 96:1–5)

Here Muhammad is being given a mission and told to make this mission public. Tradition states that Muhammad was illiterate and protested that he was hardly the person to take on such a task, but the angel was insistent and here begins the prophetic era of Arabian history when Muhammad began to receive the revelations from God. Muhammad was, in this sense, no super-human, but a man of average means who acted as the vessel for God's word; words that could be, and were, uttered at any time or place during the rest of Muhammad's life. These revelations became the verses of the *Qur'an*. The God that introduces Himself in this verse is both creator and teacher, and there are already here important themes that will be constantly re-iterated in revelations during the early prophethood of Muhammad, such as the day of judgement, resurrection and of mankind 'transgressing', a reference specifically to some of the people of Mecca who, at this time, were largely pagan and more concerned with material wealth than spiritual matters.

After this initial call to prophecy, in which Muhammad engaged in considerable psychological trauma, doubted his own experience and mission and even considered the possibility that he had gone insane, he received no new revelations for what may have been as long as

4

two years. Certainly it was some considerable time before revelations resumed, with the next revelation possibly being the following:

> You that are wrapped up in your cloak, arise and give warning. Magnify your Lord, purify your garments, and keep away from uncleanness.
> Bestow no favours expecting gain. Be patient for your Lord's sake.
> The day the Trumpet sounds shall be a hard and joyless day for the unbelievers. Leave to me the man whom I created helpless and endowed with vast riches and thriving children. I have made his progress smooth and easy: yet he hopes that I shall give him more. By no means! Because he has stubbornly denied Our revelations, I will lay on him a mounting torment.
>
> (sura 74:1–17)

Muhammad here is told to 'rise and warn', and so there is obviously something he must give warning about, which again seems to be a reference to the people of Mecca who have become rich yet ignored God and, if they do not repent, hell at the day of judgement can be expected. Khadija was the first to become a Muslim and proved to be an important comfort and support until her death in 619. Her cousin, Waraqa ibn Nawful, who was either a Christian or an indigenous monotheist, had some familiarity with Christian and Jewish scriptures and so was able to contextualise Muhammad's revelations for him, tell him who the angel Gabriel was and, from that, that this God is the same God of the Jews and Christians, and Muhammad, therefore, was a prophet in a long line of prophets.

It is unclear who was the first male to become a Muslim (a submitter to the one God). Certainly, one of the earliest was his cousin and son-in-law, **Ali ibn Abi Talib**, who was later to become the fourth *Caliph* as well as the first *Imam* of the branch of Islam known as *Shi'a*. Another early Muslim was **Abu Bakr**, who became Muhammad's father-in-law and also succeeded him as leader of the Muslims after Muhammad died. In the early years, the number of Muslims was small, but when Muhammad began attacking the wealth of the Meccan merchants as well as the gods they worshipped, he encountered a great deal of hostility. While Muhammad's uncle, Abu Talib, was alive the Prophet was protected by his clan (although a number of other Muslims did suffer persecution). But, in the year 619, Abu Talib died and his brother and successor Abu Lahab took the side of the prosperous merchants. Abu Lahab withdrew his protection from Muhammad and now the prophet had to look else-where for protection, in the meantime living on the outskirts of the town in constant danger of his life. However, an agricultural settle-ment nearly three hundred miles north of Mecca called Yathrib (later to be named Medina from *madinat al-nabi*: 'city of the prophet') sent a delegation to Muhammad and invited the Muslims to stay in their town. The main reason for this seems to be that they were aware of Muhammad's organisational talents and leadership qualities and also that he no longer had ties to any one tribe but was effectively the leader of his own tribe of Muslims. Such qualities were useful for the tribal leaders of Yathrib at that time, for they had been engaged for years in civil strife and they needed an independent arbiter to act as a peacemaker. They had nothing to lose but much to gain.

And so, in 622, Muhammad and his followers migrated from Mecca to Medina. This is known as the **Hijra** ('emigration') and marks the beginning of the Muslim lunar calendar. Its importance rests in the fact that it was the beginning of the Muslim community, the *umma*, with Muhammad as its leader. Muhammad settled in Medina as their new arbiter, purchased some land and built the first mosque which was also to be his home. At this stage, Muhammad was by no means the ruler of Medina. This would take time and he would have to prove his leadership qualities. Not all 'submitted' (lit-erally, *islam*) to Muhammad as Prophet of God, even though Muhammad emphasised that he was a Prophet of the same God of the Jews and Christians; an important consideration given that Medina had a large population of Arab Jews.

We have few descriptions of what Muhammad looked like or other personal details. According to his cousin Ali, he was neither tall nor short, had neither curly nor flowing hair (although it was, apparently, red) and he was neither fat nor thin. He ate little and led a modest life. Even when he was leader of thousands, he would still mend his own sandals and engage in other chores and shunned any luxuries. A generous spirit who did not believe in acts of vengeance and loved children especially, he stands as a model for all Muslims. After the death of Khadija, he took a number of wives, his favourite being Aisha, who was to live long after Muhammad's death and became a notable figure in Islamic history in her own right as well as recounting a number of **hadith** (sayings of Muhammad).

Muhammad's main problem on his arrival in Medina was how to support his new-found tribe. Whereas most of the other tribes of the city survived through agricultural means, the Muslims were not only lacking in these skills but also had purchased land that was largely unsuitable for farming. Muhammad put his skills and knowledge of trade and the trading routes of Mecca to good use, however, by choosing the financial option of raiding the trade caravans en route from Mecca. While this proved to be financially beneficial and increased Muhammad's popularity among most of the people of Medina who engaged in the raiding and shared in the booty, it obviously angered the people of Mecca. In addition, the Jewish tribes of Medina, who had rejected Muhammad's religious authority as a prophet, also had trading links with Mecca and were not willing to take part in the raiding. Muhammad had been at great pains to stress his faithfulness to the one God and his links with the Jewish prophets, and, at first, the direction of prayer for Muslims was towards Jerusalem. However, as time went on, relations with the Jews became more difficult as they sided with the Meccans to the extent of treachery. This resulted in the expulsion of the Jewish tribes from Medina and, in one case, the men of one Jewish tribe were executed for treachery.

There followed a series of 'battles' between the Medinans and the Meccans. The Battle of Badr in 624 was a great success for the outnumbered Muslims and gave them confidence, although the Battle of Uhud in 625 was a setback. Nonetheless, after a series of battles in which Muhammad and the Muslims were largely successful, Mecca's prestige and confidence waned as more Arabian tribes joined this new *umma* to share in its success. Muhammad had become the undoubted leader of the people of Medina and other tribes and the revelations of the Qur'an during this period reflect this with a concern more with practical political and legal matters. Muhammad was not a prophet in the strict religious sense but a political and military leader. The Muslims now prayed towards Mecca as their holy city and recognised the **ka'ba**, a cube-like structure in the centre of Mecca, as the home of God, built by Abraham and Adam before him. It was only a matter of time before the people of Mecca also yielded to Muhammad's authority, for financial if no other reasons, and this they did, with some (but little) opposition, in 630. All the pagan idols inside the *ka'ba* were destroyed and the people submitted to the one God with Muhammad as the Prophet.

After the conquest of Mecca, the submission of other tribes began, and most found it beneficial to accept Muhammad's leadership. In March 632, he gave his farewell sermon, reciting God's words: 'Today I have perfected your religion for you, and I have completed My blessing upon you, and I have approved Islam for your religion' (5:3).

7

In June of the same year, Muhammad died in the arms of his favourite wife, Aisha. By this time, all Arabia was united under one belief system and leader. It was a remarkable achievement.

See also: **Umar ibn al-Khattab**.

Major works

There is of course no autobiography by Muhammad. The main sources are the Qur'an which, although it contains little on Muhammad specifically, helps the reader gain a picture of the world of the time and the main themes of the teaching. There are good translations (or 'inter-pretations' as many Muslims prefer to call them) by, for example, Yusuf Ali and N.J. Dawood. Second, there are many *hadith* (sayings of Muhammad) that are now available in English. The selection by Thomas Cleary is a good introduction to some of the Prophet's best-known *hadith*.

References

The Wisdom of the Prophet: The Sayings of Muhammad (Shambhala Classics Library), trans. Thomas Cleary, Boston: Shambhala Publications, 2001.

Further reading

Many biographies of Muhammad are available, each with their own parti-cular perspective. For example, Armstrong comes from the perspective of someone who was once a Catholic nun, who maintains a deep spiritual and mystical attachment that comes through, whereas Rodinson is an atheist Jewish Marxist, who adopts an ideological approach.

Armstrong, Karen, *Muhammad: A Biography of the Prophet*, London: Weidenfeld & Nicholson, 2001.
Lings, Martin, *Muhammad: His Life Based on the Earliest Sources*, London: Islamic Texts Society, 1983 (the oldest but still the best in terms of rigor-ous research).
Rodinson, Maxine, *Muhammad*, trans. Anne Carter, London: Penguin, 1996.
Rogerson, Barnaby, *The Prophet Muhammad*, London: Little Brown, 2003 (the most recent here, but not always the most accurate or sympathetic).

ABU BAKR (*c.*570–634)

Originally a rich merchant of Mecca, Abu Bakr succeeded the Pro-phet **Muhammad** as leader of the Muslim community. Abu Bakr ruled for only two years until his death in 634. He is the first of the four 'Rightly-Guided Caliphs' (**Rashidun**) who ruled the Muslim community from 632 until 661. Although in only two years not much could be expected of any leader, Abu Bakr is important as he acted as a stabilising influence for a community that was still in a very fragile state.

Although the Prophet died suddenly after a brief illness, he had been unwell for at least three months preceding this and his imminent death was expected. Despite this, it seems the Prophet made no provisions as to who should succeed him as leader of the nascent Muslim community. According to the **Shi'a** tradition, Muhammad had designated his cousin and son-in-law **Ali ibn Abi Tatib** to be the next leader, although the majority of Muslims, now known as the **Sunni**, reject this. It seems that Muhammad left the decision of his successors up to his followers, or perhaps he thought that there should be no successor at all. In addition, Arab conceptions of leadership were not authoritarian and it was thought that leaders would emerge due to their own charisma and merit, so even if Muhammad had designated a leader, he might well not have been accepted by the Arabs, despite Muhammad's own status. It is now accepted tradition that there was to be no prophet of God after Muhammad and so any leader who would emerge could not claim legitimacy through prophethood. It is interesting to speculate as to whether Muhammad believed that Islam was to die with the Prophet and, in fact, it could quite easily have done so.

Very little is known of Abu Bakr's early life, except that he was around the same age as Muhammad and one of the first, if not *the* first, male to convert to Islam. His original name was Abdul Ka'bah ('slave of the Ka'ba') Ibn Abi Quhafah, although he took on the name Abu Bakr ('father of the maiden') after the birth of his daughter Aisha. He was also referred to as *al-Siddiq* ('the truthful'). According to Sunni tradition, after the emigration to Medina, he was considered one of the principal leaders of this new Muslim tribe, which was made stronger when Muhammad married Aisha. Abu Bakr was Muhammad's chief adviser and was given some of the central religious positions such as leading the congregation in public prayer during Muhammad's illness. Some Sunni traditions state that Muhammad appointed Abu Bakr as his deputy while he was alive, although Shi'a tradition rejects this.

Already at the time of Muhammad's death a number of tribes in Arabia were getting restless and attempting to break away from the nascent Muslim community, the **umma**. It was quite possible that with the death of the Prophet the tribes would return to the old system of rule by a council of tribal leaders and the old tribal ties and way of life would return once more. Just as likely was the possibility that the powerful tribe of the Quraysh in Mecca might take control once more. Consequently, with such real concerns, the succession was decided on the day of Muhammad's death. Abu Bakr emerged as the acceptable candidate largely because he was not a member of a prominent tribal group, hence possessing vested interests, and he was a close **Companion** of the Prophet as well as having the useful knowledge of intricate tribal relationships.

Abu Bakr was given the title *Khalifat Rasul Allah*, which means 'Deputy (or Successor) to the Prophet of God', although at the time it was not altogether clear what the duties and powers of this role would entail. Certainly he would not have the same powers as the Prophet for his rulings were not derived directly from God and so his religious authority was limited. Rather, he was to keep the precepts, the *sunna* (tradition) of the Prophet and what had been revealed by God. He ruled from his quarters in Medina and his main task was to keep the status quo and hold on to the gains made during Muhammad. This was not an easy task, for rival prophets had arisen and different factions were battling for power. A number of tribes broke away from the fragile *umma*, refusing to pay the tax. One such large tribal group was the Hanifa in Central Arabia which formed its own alliance of surrounding tribes under the prophet Musaylima, but this federation was very loose and was easily quashed at the Battle of Aqraba in 633. This battle was led by the general Khalid b. al-Walid who often acted independently of Abu Bakr and was ruthless in his tactics. Significantly, the defeat of the Hanifa meant that Khalid was now in charge of a large victorious army let loose on the borders of the wealthy Sassanian (Persian) empire and Khalid went on to raid these border territories for booty. This remit went beyond Abu Bakr's role of keeping the status quo, but it is possible that Khalid engaged in these acts without Abu Bakr's permission.

Nonetheless, it was as a result of Abu Bakr's determination to at least keep what Muhammad had gained in terms of a commonwealth of Arabian tribes and his swift actions to form a military force often against the advice of others that kept the Islamic vision alive. Other rival factions, such as the prophet al-Aswad al-Ansi in Yemen, were also quashed. These *ridda* (apostasy) wars were perhaps regarded by Abu Bakr as unfortunate but necessary. For Abu Bakr's part, he followed the example of Muhammad by not exacting revenge against his enemies (the same could not be said of General Khalid). For example, after the revolt in Yemen was crushed, their leader al-Aswad al-Ansi's life was not only spared but he was set free and even married Abu Bakr's own sister.

While General Khalid often acted independently of Abu Bakr, the Caliph would have been aware of the economic necessity of raiding the wealthy borders, an activity that had been going on for many years previously. The importance of the raids was accentuated by the fact that Arabia was in severe financial difficulties, for what was effectively a civil war between Muhammad and the non-Muslims of Arabia had severely affected trade, and this was not helped by the ensuing *ridda* wars. If the new united Arabia was to survive, then raiding outside its borders was an economic necessity. In fact, in 634, Abu Bakr agreed to a new expedition of troops, but this time into Byzantine territory in southern Palestine. Arabia had the wealthy and powerful Sassanian Empire to the east, and the equally wealthy and powerful Byzantine Empire to the West. However, this force arrived in Palestine only to be faced by a well-prepared military force and it was only when General Khalid and his men joined the army and assumed leadership that they defeated the Byzantine force at Ajnadayn.

Apparently Abu Bakr, who had not authorised Khalid to take control of the army, died before news of the victory reached him. Abu Bakr did not always agree with other tribal leaders in the community, and it was not an easy task to keep so many divergent vested interests satisfied. So long as the rewards from the raids beyond the borders kept coming in, however, then the Caliph retained his legitimacy. Where Abu Bakr differed from some other leaders was in his attitude towards the rebels of the *ridda* wars. As already mentioned, Abu Bakr did not take brutal reprisals against them, whereas General Khalid was criticised for doing so. Where both Abu Bakr and General Khalid agreed, however, was that those who had opposed the Muslims (or, rather, the Medinan alliance) should not be trusted as equals even after they had embraced Islam. The rebels were required to pay a tax and were not allowed to take part in battles beyond the borders and, hence, could not share in the booty. This raised future potential problems as there effectively existed two classes of Arab Muslims, as well as denying the Caliph the supply of a large number of troops should this be necessary, as was almost the case in Palestine. At the time of Abu Bakr the raids along the Sassanian and Byzantine borders were sporadic and incidental and so raised little need for a large number of troops as there were no long campaigns, and most probably Abu Bakr saw this as always being the case.

He had reigned for only two years but they proved to be a vital two years. The Arabia that Muhammad had left was just as liable to break up and return to its own tribal ways, yet Abu Bakr not only brought back the breakaway tribes into the *umma* but also gained their pledge of loyalty to Islam. For the first time, the Arabians were united in a common cause, although that common cause was largely the need to gain booty. While this might be seen as being a failure on Abu Bakr's part that he was not able to re-establish the old trade links that had existed before the civil war, the result was that the Arabian people needed to conquer new territory due to economic survival. Without this need, the Islamic faith might not have spread beyond its own borders, remaining a local and strictly Arabian religion. The success of the wars gave Abu Bakr greater authority, although he was far from being an absolute ruler and poor communications required the necessity of others to act independently, as in the example of General Khalid. This poor communication network together with what proved to be a rapid spread of Islam beyond the Arabian borders, would prove to be a problem later on. Nonetheless, the fact that the experiment of the political position of caliph continued after Abu Bakr's death demonstrates that people on the whole were at least satisfied with the system.

See also: **Umar ibn al-Khattab**.

Further reading

Abu Bakr himself did not write anything and there is little information available concerning his early life. Nonetheless, there is an abundance of material concerning these two years of his reign and, in fact, the Hodgson, Hourani and Lapidus are all excellent histories of Islam.

Hodgson, Marshall, *The Venture of Islam: Conscience and History in a World Civilization,* vol. 1 of *The Classical Age of Islam*, Chicago: University of Chicago Press, 1977.

Hourani, Albert, *A History of the Arab Peoples*, London: Faber and Faber, 2002.

Lapidus, Ira M., *A History of Islamic Societies*, Cambridge: Cambridge University Press, 2002.

Shaban, M.A., *Islamic History: A New Interpretation: A.D. 600–750 (A.H. 132)*, vol. 1, Cambridge: Cambridge University Press, 1976.

UMAR IBN AL-KHATTAB (*c.*581–644)

Umar was the second of the four Rightly-Guided Caliphs (**Rashidun**) who reigned over the burgeoning Islamic community during the period 632 until 661. Unlike his predecessor, **Abu Bakr** (*c*.570–634), who reigned for only two years, Umar was to enjoy ten years of rule. It was under Umar's leadership that Islam made its largest and fastest expansion. During his reign, Muslim forces conquered Syria, Jerusalem, Egypt, Libya, Iraq, and the armies of Persia.

Umar was born in Mecca around 581 to the Adi clan of the Quraysh tribe. He belonged to a family of average class, but he nonetheless was able to read, and was well known for his physical strength, becoming a champion wrestler. Before converting to Islam he was known to have a fiery temper and was prone to alcohol. He regarded Islam as heretical and was even intent on killing Muhammad. He was stopped on his way to Muhammad's house, however, with news of his sister's conversion to Islam. Umar was initially angered by the news, but after reading some of the **Qur'an** that his sister had kept hidden he was apparently converted on the spot by the beauty of the language and, rather than killing Muhammad, he determined to accept Islam. Consequently he is sometimes referred to as the 'St Paul of Islam' due to his rapid conversion. Little is known of his life before conversion, apart from the fact that, like so many of Mecca, he had been a merchant, probably of barley and other cereals, and, unlike many of his contemporaries, was able to read and write and, in fact, was skilled in poetical oratory. He had four or five wives and, in all, he married nine wives and divorced three. He fathered nine boys and four girls.

Although he was not one of the very first to convert, Umar was part of the first emigration to Medina (see **Muhammad**), and became an important *Companion* of the Prophet Muhammad. He participated in all the Muslim battles against the Quraysh. He has been described as fair-skinned with some reddishness, tall with a large build, fast-paced, and a skilled fighter and horseman. On the death of Muhammad in 632, it was generally accepted that a successor should belong to the emigrants; the first Muslims to convert to Islam and who migrated to Medina from Mecca with the Prophet. Of the emigrants, Abu Bakr and Umar were considered the best contenders for they were both fathers-in-law of the Prophet, both his intimate friends and confidants, and both highly regarded by the majority of believers. Abu Bakr, then 62 years old, was the senior by eleven years and had previously led the public prayer while Muhammad had been ill and so he was favoured. It is reported that, upon his selection as the Caliph, Umar was the first to shake Abu Bakr's hand and to pledge his allegiance.

He kept his promise of allegiance, acting as his chief and loyal adviser and showing no signs of jealousy or resentment. He was the supreme judge (*qadi*) under the Caliph and always had Abu Bakr's ear. With the death of Abu Bakr in 634, the two leading Muslims were Umar and General Khalid (see **Abu Bakr**). Abu Bakr had designated Umar as his successor and, although they were not in any way obliged to accept the Caliph's designation, his qualities of leadership during the first Caliph's reign had been demonstrated and he would have been his natural successor, regardless of Abu Bakr's recommendation. More important was the decision to maintain the institution of the Caliphate, given that it had only been a two-year experiment so far. General Khalid remained the chief campaigner in the continuing raids into foreign lands, and Umar gave himself the additional title of 'commander of the believers' (*amir al-mu'minin*). Subsequently, the titles 'Caliph' and 'Amir' were used interchangeably.

Umar's first act as Caliph was to reverse his predecessor's policy towards the ex-rebels of the *ridda* wars. The hierarchy of the 'two classes' of Arab Muslims – whereby the rebels had not been allowed to engage in the raids and therefore enjoy in the spoils – was abandoned and, in fact, the ex-rebels were positively encouraged to take part in the raids through active recruitment. This was a momentous step for now what it meant to be Muslim was synonymous with being Arab: none were excluded from this. In addition, it meant that there was greater Arab unity and an additional force of willing fighters. It seemed that a return to its old trading status was considered unrealistic, whereas the wealth gained from the raids of the Sassanian (Persian) Empire especially had proven far more fruitful. However, the Sassanians only tolerated the raids for so long and, at the Battle of the Bridge in 634, the Persian army, sitting upon their elephants, defeated the over-confident Arab forces. At the same time the Byzantines began to mobilise their own forces against the new Arab enemies. The Byzantines and Sassanians were two great world empires and things must have looked rather uncomfortable for the Arabs at this time.

However, Umar's skills lay in his knowledge of the inter-tribal trading links of Arabia and, with the added factor of the prestige of his clan, the Quraysh, this allowed the Caliph to muster a large force. He appointed a military leader of, previously, no great distinction, Sa'd b. Abi Waqqas, to lead the Sassanian front. He set out from Medina with 2,000 men, many of them from Yemen, but on his way this number grew to at least 7,000. During the battles that ensued they overcame their fear of the elephants and learnt some new tactics to defeat their enemies, leading to the Battle of Qadisiyya in 637 where the Sassanians were defeated. At that time, Waqqas had around 10,000 men, the Persians six times as many. Now all Iraq West of the River Tigris was in Muslim hands. The Persian forces fled across the river, leaving behind the likes of treasure Arabs had never seen before in their lives. If there had been any doubt concerning the need for raids in foreign lands before then, these now vanished. Soon the capital of the Persians, Ctesiphon, fell into Arabs hands.

On the Byzantine front, the Arabs continued to hold their ground in Palestine after the victory of Ajnadayn under Abu Bakr in 634. General Khalid had been in charge of that victory, but many were critical of his brutal methods, not to mention jealous of his fame and admirers. This led Umar to accuse Khalid of keeping too much of the booty for himself and he relieved the General of his position, replacing him with Abu Ubayda al-Jarrahin in charge of the whole Byzantine front. Khalid, from then on, seems to have had an inferior role as a co-ordinator of the generals and this act is an example of just how much power a Caliph could wield. Abu Ubayda, for his part, defeated a large Byzantine army at the Battle of Yarmuk in 637, leading to the conquest of Syria and, from there, also Egypt fell in 640. Many of the population of Syria were of Arab origin and, though Christian, perceived the Muslim invaders as just one of many of the varied Christian sects that existed at the time. On the whole, the Syrians were not hostile to the new invaders and, in many cases, were welcoming, hoping for better treatment under their fellow Arabs than what they had received from the Byzantines.

The achievements of the Muslims under Umar are remarkable. In the space of ten years the little-known people of Arabia had destroyed one of the two great world powers, Persia, and stripped the other, Byzantine, of some of its richest territory. These wars on foreign soil were conceived of by Abu Bakr as a necessary means of financial survival rather than perceived as some religious crusade or world conquest. Indeed, although Abu Bakr agreed to this need, it is doubtful that he was always able to control events. These wars continued in the reign of Umar but, as territory grew in size at remarkable speed, the role of the generals has as much to do with the success as that of the Caliph, if not more so. The ex-merchant Umar, from his quarters in Medina, could only marvel over the staggering amount of wealth that was being accumulated from booty, and while he laid the framework of government for the ever-growing empire, much of the administration was by necessity at local level and left to the original inhabitants, with Arabs as overseers. Umar was very conversant with Islamic law, however, and – like Abu Bakr before

15

him – he always ensured that justice was meted out to those conquered rather than enact revenge.

Umar was murdered in 644 by a Persian slave who was angered by a personal quarrel with Umar, stabbing the Caliph six times as he led prayers in the mosque. Umar died two days later, and is buried alongside Muhammad and Abu Bakr. Prior to dying, he appointed a council of six men to elect his successor from among themselves, choosing Uthman ibn Affan. Umar was the first Caliph murdered in Islam, although his two successors were to meet the same fate. Although much of his reign was dominated by military conquest, for Sunni Muslims Umar is regarded as a pious, frugal person who strongly believed in God and in Muhammad's model of what a good leader should be. He is held in less regard by many mystical Muslims, the *Sufis*, for being too 'worldly', while *Shi'a* Muslims regard Umar as usurping the position that belonged to Muhammad's cousin and son-in-law, **Ali ibn Abi Talib**.

Further reading

Umar himself did not write anything and there is little information available concerning his early life. Nonetheless there is an abundance of material concerning these years of his reign and, in fact, the Hodgson, Hourani and Lapidus are all excellent histories of Islam.

Hodgson, Marshall, *The Venture of Islam: Conscience and History in a World Civilization*, vol. 1 of *The Classical Age of Islam*, Chicago: University of Chicago Press, 1977.

Hourani, Albert, *A History of the Arab Peoples*, London: Faber and Faber, 2002.

Lapidus, Ira M., *A History of Islamic Societies*, Cambridge: Cambridge University Press, 2002.

Shaban, M.A., *Islamic History: A New Interpretation: A.D. 600–750 (A.H. 132)*, vol. 1, Cambridge: Cambridge University Press, 1976.

ALI IBN ABI TALIB (*c*.596–661)

Ali was the cousin and son-in-law of the Prophet **Muhammad**. He holds an illustrious place in Muslim history as an intimate **Companion** of the Prophet Muhammad and as the fourth and final of the Rightly-Guided (**Rashidun**) Caliphs who ruled the Muslim community after the death of the Prophet, in 632, until 661 when Ali was assassinated. For the *Shi'a* Muslims he is the first **Imam** and rightful heir to the leadership after the death of the Prophet as they believe that Muhammad passed on his religious authority to Ali. His life is shrouded in myth and legend and he is widely acknowledged, even by critics, as a pious and devout individual as well as a just and well-meaning leader.

During the second Caliph **Umar**'s reign, the people of Mecca and Medina had, on the whole, grown incredibly wealthy from the spoils of war. Tribal leaders outside these cities were also growing in power and wealth and beginning to identify themselves more with their locality than with Mecca or Medina. Umar did not designate a leader to succeed him but, rather, appointed a council of six eminent individuals to choose a successor. Their choice narrowed down to two: Uthman b. Affan and Ali b. Abi Talib. Uthman was a member of the powerful Umayyad clan of the Quraysh tribe, and the husband of two of the Prophet's daughters.

Ali was born some thirty years after the birth of the Prophet Muhammad. His father, Abu Talib, was the Prophet's real uncle. Abu Talib cared for Muhammad when he was an orphaned child and, when Abu Talib felt he could no longer look after Ali, Muhammad took him into his household and treated him like the son he never had (his own two sons died in childhood). According to tradition, Ali, then aged 10, was one of the first, if not the first, male to convert to Islam and he subsequently risked his life for the Prophet by pretending to be the Prophet asleep in his bed while the latter fled to Medina in the **Hijra** of 622. Ali himself then set off for Medina where he married Muhammad's daughter Fatima. During the first battles that the Muslims fought against the Meccans, Ali proved to be a loyal and courageous fighter, possessing a sword with a forked tongue (the *Zulfiqar*, now ostensibly lodged in the Topkapi Museum in Istanbul). He was subsequently entrusted with a number of important missions by Muhammad and also acted as one of his scribes. Among Ali's other important contributions during the life of the Prophet was the destruction of the idols in the **ka'ba** when Mecca fell to Muhammad.

While there is little dispute regarding the loyalty and importance of Ali, not to mention his affection and closeness to the Prophet, there is considerable controversy over his role in the subsequent succession after the death of Muhammad. It seems unlikely and against Arab custom for someone so young, being only in his mid-thirties at the time, to be preferred over an older Companion to be the new leader of the community and, according to *Sunni* tradition, Muhammad left no clear instructions as to who should lead after his death, although he had plenty of opportunity to do so. Abu Bakr was chosen to be the first Caliph but, according to Shi'a tradition, it is believed that Muhammad had explicitly designated Ali to be his successor. The Shi'a believe that the tribal leaders effectively implemented a coup while Ali was preoccupied with the funeral arrangements for the Prophet. However, Ali and his followers chose not to challenge the succession, arguing that to do so would result in needless factionalism at a time when unity was required.

Instead, Ali adopted an attitude of political ambivalence, preferring to concentrate on theological and scholarly issues. His knowledge of the Qur'an and the **Sunna** (tradition of Muhammad) proved invaluable to the first three Caliphs who preceded Ali and some Shi'a traditions recount that Ali's compilation of the Qur'an – which is used by Shi'a Muslims to this day – is both longer (it has references to Ali) and different from that compiled and authorised by the third Caliph Uthman. Ali would not take part in the ensuing *ridda* wars (see **Abu Bakr**) and withdrew his support in political matters of the caliphs, arguing for a more egalitarian *umma* (the Muslim community) in opposition to what was developing into an elite.

After the death of the second Caliph Umar, it seems that the council offered the post to Ali on the condition that he continued the policies of the two predecessors. Ali, however, refused this condition, stating that, as Caliph, his role was not a conditional one. As a result, the post was then offered to Uthman who readily accepted the conditions. This made not only Ali, but also his supporters, who saw in Ali the opportunity to return Islam to the time of Muhammad's rule, very angry. Already there was a feeling among some Muslims that the religious aspect had been sidelined and the people were more preoccupied with military and financial success.

Uthman, on the other hand, was seen as a safe option in that he was quite conservative in outlook. However, as a member of a powerful tribe, he had his own vested interests and had lived most of his life in Mecca, belonging to the Umayyad clan, one of the last to accept Muhammad's rule. Ali, on the other hand, had been a close friend of Muhammad and one of the first Muslims to convert. Being only 9 years old when Muhammad took on the mantle of Prophethood, Ali spent his formative years among Muhammad's family and in Medina. All members of the council were Meccan and, by choosing Uthman, there were concerns that they were not reflecting the interests of the Medinans.

Uthman ruled for twelve years in all, from 644 until 656. He began his new career quietly and quite successfully, initially following the policies of his predecessors as promised. However, as time went on, he felt it necessary to assert greater authority over the increasing independence of Muslim territories. He gained control over the provinces by appointing his own relatives as the governors. In Syria, Uthman's kinsman **Mu'awiya**, was already governor. However, he appointed his foster brother as governor of Egypt, his cousin as governor in Kufa, and another cousin as governor of Basra. On the whole, these were competent administrators, but the accusations of nepotism were nonetheless unavoidable. This was not helped by the fact that Uthman, a generous man anyway, gave much of his wealth to these relatives. However, there were also religious reasons why Uthman was unpopular, for he decided to authorise an official version of the Qur'an. This may have seemed sensible enough, for there were a number of Qur'ans that varied in minor details. However, by authorising an official Qur'an, Uthman was asserting a religious authority that many believed the Caliph should not possess.

While many of Uthman's decisions may have been well meant, they were not interpreted that way and opposition to his rule grew. In 656, a deputation of a few hundred tribesmen from Iraq and a similar number from Egypt arrived in Medina to demand redress for grievances. They virtually besieged Uthman's house and the situation got out of control, resulting in Uthman being butchered by the angry group, with no Medinans prepared to protect the old man.

The murder of the third Caliph obviously came as something of a shock and Ali was the natural choice as successor, although Ali, for his part, expressed some reluctance, bearing in mind the intimidating circumstances. Nonetheless he was persuaded to take up the role if only to avoid possible chaos. There was some opposition, however, notably from Muhammad's widow Aisha. She was also the daughter of the first Caliph, **Abu Bakr**, and, like a number of other opponents, felt that the role of Caliph should not be any greater than Abu Bakr's was and certainly should not have the same religious authority as possessed by her late husband. Aisha, together with two members of the original council of six who had selected Uthman, whipped up military support and the two forces met at the Battle of the Camel (named after the camel that Aisha rode) in 656 in Basra in which Aisha was defeated and sent back to Medina.

Ali's main task was to reassert the authority of the Caliph, and the Battle of the Camel was the first step in this direction. He next set up camp outside Kufa in Iraq to establish his power. He also chose another governor for Egypt to replace Uthman's cousin, but he was less successful when it came to Syria. Mu'awiya, as cousin of Uthman, refused allegiance to Ali until Uthman's death was investigated and avenged. In 657, Ali recruited an army of reputedly 50,000 men, mainly from his residence in Iraq and the two armies – Iraqi Muslims and Syrian Muslims – stood face to face on the plains of Siffin on the West bank of the Euphrates. There followed weeks of skirmishes and the deaths of thousands. At one point Ali seemed to be winning the war when Mu'awiya ordered five hundred copies of the Qur'an to be placed on the tip of their lances and called for neutral Muslims to arbitrate between the rivals on God's word. At this point Ali, who was aging and tired, consented. Sources are vague concerning the issues discussed at arbitration but Ali's decision to compromise on a number of key issues resulted, as Mu'awiya undoubtedly foresaw, in a haemorrhage of support for the fourth Caliph. Those who left disillusioned became known as the **Kharijites** (from kharaja, 'going out'). Many felt that Ali had not only given away victory but subsequently demeaned himself. In fact, it was over a year before the arbitrators finally met and even then came to no decision for it no longer mattered: support for Ali had deserted him and a Kharajite assassinated Ali in a mosque in Kufa in 661. He was buried in an unmarked tomb for fear of desecration. It was subsequently discovered and developed by the **Abbasid** Caliph **Harun al-Rashid**, who built a sanctuary around which grew the town of Najaf. His eldest son, al-Hasan, succeeded him but he soon abdicated. To all intents and purposes, the caliphate now belonged to Mu'awiya and the house of Umayyad.

Ali's importance lies not only in his own writings, compiled after his death in *Nahj al-Balaga* (*The Road to Eloquence*), but perhaps more importantly in the interpretations of his life by subsequent followers. It resulted in a theological schism that exists to this day between the Sunni and the Shi'a Muslims. Despite his unsuccessful career as Caliph/Imam, his legacy is one rich in myth, metaphor and theological significance. His position in the popular imagination is second only to Muhammad himself and, among more extreme Shi'a, his position is equal, if not superior, to that of the Prophet, with some sects ascribing divinity to him. In mainstream Shi'a thought, however, he is regarded as the lawful successor to Muhammad, whose authority was usurped. He is the repository of the Prophet's knowledge, infallible and purified and the first in a line of divinely guided Imams.

Major works

Some of Ali's writings can be found translated into English.

Haeri, Shaykh Fadhlalla (ed. and trans.), *The Sayings and Wisdom of Imam Ali*, London: Muhammadi Trust of Great Britain and Northern Ireland, 1999.

Further reading

All the books below provide a good study of Islamic history not only during the time of Ali, but before and after. In addition, for a Shi'a view, check out Momen.

Hodgson, Marshall, *The Venture of Islam: Conscience and History in a World Civilization*, vol. 1 of *The Classical Age of Islam*, Chicago: University of Chicago Press, 1977.

Hourani, Albert, *A History of the Arab Peoples*, London: Faber and Faber, 2002.

Lapidus, Ira M., *A History of Islamic Societies*, Cambridge: Cambridge University Press, 2002.

Momen, Moojan, *An Introduction to Shi'i Islam: History and Doctrines of Twelver Shi'ism*, New Haven, CT: Yale University Press, 1987.

Shaban, M.A., *Islamic History: A New Interpretation: A.D. 600–750 (A.H. 132)*, vol. 1, Cambridge: Cambridge University Press, 1976.

MU'AWIYA (c. 602–680)

Mu'awiya was one of Islam's early political and military leaders and founder of the great **Umayyad** dynasty (661–750) of Caliphs. He battled against the fourth Caliph, **Ali ibn Abi Talib**, seized Egypt and assumed the caliphate after Ali was assassinated in 661. Mu'awiya's contribution to Islam lies mainly in restoring unity to the Muslim empire, by no means an easy feat. He made Damascus the capital of the Umayyad caliphate and he reigned from 661 until 680, during which time Islam attained its widest geographical expansion.

While the year 661 marked the end of the reign of the so-called 'Rightly-Guided Caliphs' (the **Rashidun**) in Medina and the rise of the mighty Umayyad dynasty in Damascus, the importance of its first Caliph Mu'awiya has sometimes been overlooked. Much of this is likely due to the history books of the dynasty that succeeded the Umayyads, the **Abbasid** dynasty who underplayed the role of the Umayyads and, indeed, emphasised what they regarded as the lack of fidelity on the part of that preceding dynasty. Mu'awiya's role in usurping the authority of the fourth Caliph, Ali, has also brought into question the Umayyad Caliph's motives. While, as a political ruler with considerable power, Mu'awiya can hardly be considered unblemished so far as political intrigue is concerned, he has been regarded by many as a sincere and faithful Muslim who did much to ensure that the Muslim world did not split into warring factions which would have, perhaps, led to the premature end of Islam as a potential world religion. Nonetheless, the need for such unity always results in the sacrifice of certain principles, hence the despair of the minority **Shi'a** community towards the hegemony of the **Sunni** Umayyad. More recent historians, however, have sought to rehabilitate him.

The fourth Caliph, Ali, was the first cousin of the Prophet **Muhammad** as well as the husband of the Prophet's favourite daughter Fatima and the father of his only two surviving grandsons, Hasan and Husayn. Ali's father, Abu Talib, cared for the Prophet when he was orphaned. Also, Ali was one of the earliest converts to Islam. Mu'awiya, by contrast, was born into a clan ('Abd Shams) that rejected the Prophet in his home city of Mecca and continued to oppose him on the battlefield after Muhammad had emigrated to Medina (the **hijra**). Mu'awiya himself did not become a Muslim until the Prophet had conquered Mecca when he then became a scribe in Muhammad's service. Mu'awiya and Ali, incidentally, were roughly the same age.

With the murder of the third caliph, Uthman, in 656 (see **Ali ibn Abi Talib**), a power struggle resulted leading to a series of civil wars (fitnah) which plagued Ali's entire reign (656–661). When Ali became the Caliph, he set about replacing the governors that Uthman had appointed, most of whom were members of the third Caliph's own family. This included Mu'awiya who was governor of Syria although, to be fair, he had actually been appointed by the second Caliph Umar and so Uthman, while confirming his continued governorship, could not be directly accused of nepotism in this particular case. Ali's reluctance to produce the murderers of Uthman resulted in Mu'awiya's resistance to his legitimacy as Caliph. Ali marched to the Euphrates border of Syria and engaged Mu'awiya's troops at the famous Battle of Siffin (657). Mu'awiya persuaded the enemy to enter into negotiations that ultimately cast doubt on the legitimacy of Ali's caliphate and alienated a sizable number of his supporters. When these former supporters, the **Kharijites**, rose in rebellion against Ali, Mu'awiya took advantage of Ali's difficulties in Iraq to send a force to seize control of Egypt. Thus, when Ali was assassinated in 661, Mu'awiya held both Syria and Egypt and, as commander of the largest force in the Muslim Empire, had the strongest claim to the caliphate. Ali's son, Hasan, was persuaded to remove himself from public life in exchange for a subsidy, which Mu'awiya provided. According to a number of historical accounts, Hasan preferred his harem to the government and retired to a life of relative luxury in Medina where he died at the age of 45 after some one hundred or so marriages. His death was probably due to poisoning. Hasan's brother, Husayn, was to prove far more troublesome, however.

In fact, it was some months prior to the death of Ali that Mu'a-wiya had already been proclaimed caliph by his aides. His political acumen was well acknowledged. As governor of Syria for twenty years, he had made the province the most prosperous and progressive in the Muslim world. He had turned a somewhat disorganised military organisation into a trained and disciplined body modelled on the Byzantine army. Many of his recruits were Christian Syrians and Yemenite Arabs but he ensured their loyalty by paying them handsomely and regularly. He is also responsible for building a sizable navy, the first of its kind in the Islamic Empire. In terms of government, Mu'awiya was likewise resourceful, although there already existed an efficient government machine inherited from the Byzantines. Under Byzantine influence he developed the bureau of registry (*diwan*) and initiated the first postal system in Islam.

After the death of Ali, Mu'awiya's authority was largely acknowledged in the east, that is Iraq and Persia, although this did not mean that he did not encounter regular insurgencies among Ali's supporters. In the case of Mecca and Medina, support was mostly for Hasan's brother and Ali's son Husayn, because of his blood relationship with the Prophet. During Mu'awiya's reign, there was no attempt to challenge his authority and when Husayn finally did summon up a force against Mu'awiya's son Yazid, after Mu'awiya's own death, Husayn was defeated and killed at the Battle of Karbala in 681. The death of Husayn is commemorated by Shi'a Muslims to this day and signifies the belief that the true Islam, the Islam of the Prophet and his family, was hijacked by the Umayyads and their descendants.

As Caliph, Mu'awiya is reported as saying:

> I apply not my lash where my tongue suffices, nor my sword where my whip is enough. And if there be one hair binding me to my fellow men I let it not break. If they pull I loosen, and if they loosen I pull.[1]

Instead of resorting to force against his enemies he preferred the art of persuasion, whether that be through words or bribes. Mu'awiya did not employ Christians in a military and governmental capacity, but his favourite wife, the mother of his successor, Yazid, was a Syrian Christian, as were the court poet and his personal physician.

After the relative pacification of the Muslim world, Mu'awiya turned his attention to the Christian West, to the crumbling but nonetheless potent and wealthy Byzantine Empire. Mu'awiya, even before becoming Caliph, had made numerous naval raids against Cyprus, Rhodes, Crete and other islands in the Aegean and eastern Mediterranean waters, but nothing that proved to be too permanently damaging for the Byzantines. In 668, however, an Arab army reached the capital of the Byzantine Empire, Constantinople. Under the generalship of Mu'wayah's son and Caliph-in-waiting, Yazid, they laid siege to the capital, but the attempt failed. In 674, they attempted once more as a two-pronged attack on land and sea. This siege lasted for seven years but also failed. The city did not fall to the Muslims until the Ottoman Turks came in 1453.

More successful were Mu'awiya's incursions into Byzantine North Africa. Under the generalship of Uqbah ibn-Nafi, conquests included Libya and Tunisia and he set up a capital of Muslim Africa in Carthage. The city developed into a flourishing religious and cultural centre with tendrils that stretched to Morocco and Spain. Uqbah was killed in battle in 683 and his tomb-mosque is considered the oldest Muslim architectural monument in Africa as well as a national shrine.

Under the rule of Mu'awiya the concept of the caliphate was transformed and it had come a long way since the time of the first Caliph, **Abu Bakr**, when it was considered a part-time post of limited power. Mu'awiya adopted a Byzantine approach to kingship, in which he sat upon a throne and declared that his son was to succeed him as ruler. Such a system was against traditional Arab forms of leadership and was not popular with everybody, leading to the unsuccessful revolt by Husayn. Yazid could hardly be considered the best person for the job, for he was a drunkard and his military expeditions had proven largely fruitless. Mu'awiya, however, had not relinquished his Arab and Muslim heritage, preferring to keep Islam Arab and discouraging conversions. Although initially the regime relied upon Christians, the positions were gradually filled by Muslims.

Mu'awiya did not rule as an absolute monarch, although he probably laid the foundations for such, and he maintained his leadership through the Arab custom of first among equals. Most importantly, Mu'awiya put an end to the civil wars that were destroying Muslim unity and this could not have been achieved without the use of force and strong, uncompromising leadership. However, he had to allow some degree of autonomy among the fiercely independent tribal leaders and his leadership required knowing when to assert authority and when to withhold it. Pacification was no doubt helped by the expansionist wars and the resultant booty that expanded the coffers of the governors.

Mu'awiya might not, in many people's eyes, have been a caliph of the calibre of those during the **Rashidun**, but he was nonetheless a devout Muslim who strived to maintain the unity of the Muslim community. Biographers refer to Mu'awiya as *hilm* – an Arab term difficult to translate but encompassing such valued qualities as self-control, tolerance and magnanimity. He remained a model of good leadership as he maintained a stable regime during his lifetime, although the fact that the dynasty began its collapse after his death is an indication that his example was not followed by his successors on the whole. He made no claim to religious authority, not wishing to be in the same awkward position as Ali, but he nonetheless encouraged the building of mosques and, especially, the development of the conquered Jerusalem as an important Muslim centre, although this may well have been to prevent pilgrims from focusing on Mecca. While the Shi'a elements in Iraq were largely pacified, there were, as mentioned, occasional rebellions which led to Mu'awiya arresting and executing seven ring-leaders. Although this may have been effective in the short term, it only exacerbated the suspicions and concerns of people of the east. In addition, the choice of his son as successor – while making a certain degree of political sense – was nonetheless seen as asserting too much authority on the part of the Umayyad.

Further reading

All the books below provide a good study of Islamic history not only during the time of Mu'awiya, but before and after.

Hodgson, Marshall, *The Venture of Islam: Conscience and History in a World Civilization*, vol. 1 of *The Classical Age of Islam*, Chicago: University of Chicago Press, 1977.
Hourani, Albert, *A History of the Arab Peoples*, London: Faber and Faber, 2002.
Lapidus, Ira M., *A History of Islamic Societies*, Cambridge: Cambridge University Press, 2002.
Shaban, M.A., *Islamic History: A New Interpretation: A.D. 600–750 (A.H. 132)*, vol. 1, Cambridge: Cambridge University Press, 1976.

Note

1 Philip K. Hitti, *History of Syria, Including Lebanon and Palestine*, 2nd edn, London and New York: Routledge, 1957, p. 438.

ABU HANIFA (c.699–767)

Abu Hanifa was the founder of one of the four major **Sunni** Islamic legal schools. He was a theologian and religious lawyer. The law school he founded, the Hanafi, today has the largest following among the Muslim community. A Persian, Abu Hanifa was one of the great jurists of Islam and pioneered the science of jurisprudence (*fiqh*) that a number of individuals believed was in need of reform due to its lack of systematisation and disagreements over details from one region to the next.

The eighth-century Islamic world was vast but still in its infancy in terms of ideological and legal unity. While the death of the Prophet **Muhammad** in 632 meant that there would be no more divine revelation, it was still incumbent upon all Muslims to attempt to follow the correct path, the *shari'a*, that God had laid down for them in the Muslim holy book, the *Qur'an*. Muslims also looked to the life and teachings of Muhammad, his *sunna*, for guidance. Consequently, it was extremely important to determine what exactly the Qur'an dictates and the things that Muhammad said and did. During the period of the first four 'Rightly-Guided' (*Rashidun*) Caliphs, decisions and new concerns were dealt with as they arose. They are considered 'rightly-guided' because it is believed they truly followed in the footsteps of the Prophet Muhammad. The difficulties became more pronounced with the hegemony of the **Umayyad** dynasty (661–750, see **Mu'awiya**) and led to the need for a more systematic legal framework, including the establishment of judges (*qadi*) who relied upon the prevailing customs of the particular province, together with the Qur'an and the personal judgement of the particular judge. This, however, was hardly satisfactory as – aside from the fact that many judges were not as learned in the nascent Islamic scholarship as they should be – the result was a body of laws that differed from one region to another. The argument ran that if all Muslims were subject to God's law, then there should not be any difference in law between one Muslim and another, regardless of where they might reside.

By the eighth century, then, a number of Islamic scholars had emerged who attempted to standardise the law, notably Abu Hanifa, **Malik** ibn Anas, Muhammad **al-Shafi'i**, and Ahmad **ibn Hanbal**, who came to be regarded as the founders or leaders of the Hanafi, Maliki, Shafi'i and Hanbali law schools respectively. During the early years of the subsequent rule of the *Abbasids* (750–1258), these patterns of legalistic inquiry were elaborated upon and developed into a legal code which could be applied across the Islamic Empire. The coming of the Abbasids was accompanied by the creation of a centralised state which was bureaucratically ruled, increasing the need for standardisation and regulation. In addition, the claim to Abbasid legitimacy rested upon a religious justification; that they were more faithful Muslims than their Umayyad predecessors. It was essential, therefore, that what was agreed upon should be in the light of the teachings of Islam. In theory, at least, the judge was to be more independent of the whims of the government, as well as being more learned in Islamic teachings.

Abu Hanifa al-Nu'man ibn Thabit was born around the year 699. His grandfather Zuta is said to have been brought as a slave from Kabul (in east-central Afghanistan and now its capital city) to Kufa (in present-day Iraq), and was subsequently set free by a member of the Arabian tribe of Taym Allah ibn Tha'laba. He and his descendants thus became clients (*mawla*) of this tribe, and Abu Hanifa is sometimes referred to as 'al-Taymi' after the tribal name. He lived in Kufa and worked as a manufacturer and merchant of a kind of silk material called *khazz*. He also studied religious law and was generally recognised as the foremost authority of *shari'a* in Kufa. He gathered a large number of disciples to whom he taught religious law, but he never attained the position of judge. Abu Hanifa came to prominence as a teacher, and was not actually involved in the making of Islamic juridical law. The memorisation of the Qur'an and the **sunna** (collective Traditions of the Prophet), and the collection, elaboration and transmission of this knowledge became Abu Hanifa's major activity. The Hanafi legal school, while named after Abu Hanifa, was founded by his main pupils, Abu Yusuf and al-Shaybani.

Abu Hanifa's teachings were elaborated and developed by his disciples and, together with his contemporary, Malik, who was based in Medina, these two could rightly be described as the pioneers in the field of Islamic law. Abu Hanifa did not compose any works on religious law himself. Rather, he discussed his ideas with his disciples who then wrote these down. Some of the resulting works have become the main sources of Abu Hanifa's doctrine. Muslim scholars wrote the Muslim equivalent of creeds (in Arabic, *'aqida*, which means 'to bind' or 'to contract') although they never developed into universally uttered summaries of doctrine in the same way as the Christian Nicene Creed. One Muslim creed, known as *The Greater Understanding (Fiqh Akbar)* was composed for the community, according to tradition, by Abu Hanifa and it is likely that it does at least date back to Abu Hanifa's own circle of disciples, if not from him personally. The views and methodology endorsed by Abu Hanifa can best be described as rationalist. His school was often called '**Murji'ite**' (from Arabic *irja*, meaning 'postponement' or 'deferment') because they encouraged faith over works: serious sins are offset by faith and punishment for them is not considered to be everlasting.

Consequently, Murji'ites 'withheld' judgement on supposed sinners in this world and, rather, adopted a quietist approach. The Murji'ites appear to have emerged as a reaction to the **Kharijite** (from *kharaja*, 'going out'). This group, often extremist in nature, were a meticulously Qur'anically based movement who were strongly egalitarian and puritanical. In their doctrine major sins forfeit salvation making the sinner a *de facto* apostate which is punishable by death. They had no qualms in punishing sinners in this life. Abu Hanifa, in common with some others who earned the title *Murji'i*, believed that all Muslims should be given the benefit of the doubt in matters of personal faith. What mattered essentially was the inner conscience of the believer, and that should be judged by God alone.

The Hanafi law school, like that of the Maliki, generally encouraged judges to exercise personal reflection and independent reasoning when reaching decisions: an important principle known in Islamic law as **ijtihad**. The proviso was that the judges should be sufficiently qualified to engage in such independent reasoning of course, otherwise it would be wiser to imitate (a term known as **taqlid**) previous decisions by those more qualified. What became of increasing concern – particularly after the time of the influential legal scholar al-Shafi'i – was the greater emphasis on *taqlid*, even by well-qualified legal scholars, which resulted in the eventual stagnation of Islamic law. Hence Abu Hanifa's title of 'rationalist' in his willingness to engage in reason to determine legal decisions in the spirit of the Qur'an. However, in order to ensure that the decisions arrived at through *ijtihad* were in the spirit of the Qur'an, and not merely the independent whim of that particular individual, reasoning was carefully circumscribed by *usul al-fiqh* (the principles of jurisprudence). Qur'anic revelations which were deemed definitive (*qat'i*), were not open to interpretation. However, many verses are unclear as to whether they are commands or just recommendations, or the exact scope of an injunction is unclear. These speculative verses (*zanni*) are open to *ijtihad*. This independent reasoning, however, is not a matter of opinion but is to be understood not only within the context of the Qur'an as a whole, but also from the sources of the Prophet's own words and deeds, referred to as the **sunna**, for Muhammad was effectively Islam's greatest interpreter of the Qur'an as well as its reciter.

Aside from the sources, the Hanafi school developed a methodology in which the underlying principles and divine injunctions can be derived, as well as determining the relative importance of these. This consisted, among other things, of *qiyas* (analogical reasoning) and *istihsan* (juristic preference). The latter especially proved controversial among many legal scholars, especially the influential al-Shafi'i who placed much greater emphasis on the authority of the leaders of the first Muslim community (the **Companions** of the Prophet) and their immediate followers (the **Successors**). However, *istihsan* has played an important role in the adaptation of Islamic law to the changing requirements of society. *Istihsan* allows for greater flexibility and development of law and helps to bridge the gap between law and social reality. The concern is that judges, exercising the rather ambiguous term 'juristic preference', can over-rely on *istihsan* to resolve problems rather than struggle to determine what the myriad injunctions of the Qur'an and *sunna* may have to say on the matter. Jurists such as al-Shafi'i, as well as legal schools of Shi'a Islam, reject *istihsan* completely for this reason.

Even more ambiguous was Abu Hanifa's support for the methodology of *ra'y*, which can be interpreted as 'subjective opinion'. These decisions are based on the personal judgement of the jurist and only indirectly on the Qur'an or the *Sunna*. It was Abu Hanifa's use of his 'sound opinion' in reaching a legal decision that allowed his disciples to add their own reasoning to these opinions, which sometimes led to opinions which differed from those of their teacher. Inevitably, members of the Hanifite law school were not always clear as to which principle overrides which: is analogical reasoning superior to 'juristic preference', and what status does 'subjective opinion' have in relation to these? While Abu Hanafa initiated a stricter and more methodological approach to legal decisions, its very openness and flexibility could also be to its detriment, hence the reaction against it by al-Shafi'i, among others.

Abu Hanifa died in prison in Baghdad in 767, where he was buried, and where, centuries later in 1066, a dome was built over his tomb. Some believe that he was called to Baghdad by the Abbasid Caliph al-Mansur, and that he was subsequently imprisoned for refusing to accept the appointment of *qadi*. Others have said that he was imprisoned because of his support for a Zaydi (a moderate Shi'a group influenced by rationalism) revolt. Among his descendants, his son Hammad and grandson Ismail distinguished themselves in religious law. Many of his followers gained positions of prestige in the Abbasid courts, which is perhaps a reflection of the fact that the Hanafi law school was sufficiently flexible to still allow for the needs of the caliphs, rather than the caliphs being tied by Islamic law. Abu Yusuf, who wrote a treatise on the law of land tax, became the first supreme judge in Islam under the Caliph Harun al-Rashid, and gained official sanction for what became known as the Hanafi school of law. The Hanafi school today remains the most liberal of the four established Sunni law schools. Today it is dominant in Central and Western Asia (Afghanistan to Turkey), Lower Egypt (Cairo and the Delta) and the Indian subcontinent.

Major works

The authorship of the works attributed to Abu Hanifa is dubious. None are available in English at present.

Further reading

There are many excellent works on Islamic law. Patricia Crone's is perhaps the most controversial, while some studies, such as the Schacht, are somewhat 'Orientalist' but still have their uses.

Coulson, Noel J., *A History of Islamic Law*, Edinburgh: Edinburgh University Press, 1964.
Crone, P., *Roman, Provincial and Islamic Law*, Cambridge: Cambridge University Press, 1987.
Schacht, Joseph, *An Introduction to Islamic Law*, Oxford: Clarendon Press, 1964.

MALIK IBN ANAS (c.709–795)

Abu Abd Allah Malik ibn Anas was the founder of one of the four major Sunni Islamic legal schools (*madhhab*). He was one of the great jurists of Islam and, together with **Abu Hanifa**, pioneered the science of jurisprudence (*fiqh*). He was one of the first to codify existing Islamic legal and religious practices and gave his name to the Maliki school of law.

An important element of Islamic culture is *shari'a*, which although usually translated as 'law' is much more than that, for it is the expression of the will of God as manifested in the holy book, the Qur'an, and in the guidance provided by the Prophet **Muhammad**. The law, as the expression of the will of God and his guidance, is essential for Muslim identity as well as providing a blueprint for the good Muslim society. With the death of Muhammad, the decisions regarding what kind of life Muslims should lead was left to some extent in the hands of the new leaders, the so-called 'Rightly-Guided' (*Rashidun*) Caliphs, of whom there were four (**Abu Bakr, Umar,** Uthman, and **Ali**). On the death of the fourth Caliph, power fell into the hands of the **Umayyad** dynasty (661–750) and, during this period, Islamic law developed to some extent with a system of judges (**qadi**), although much power still rested with the Caliphs in enacting law as and when required. With the overthrow of the Umayyad by the **Abbasid** dynasty, the quest for legitimacy resulted in an increase in the systematisation of Islamic law, the theory being that the will of God should be the same for all Muslims, regardless of where they might reside. Before this time, the law in one Islamic territory could be very different from the law in another.

Consequently, the concern arose over what the will of God actually was, how the Qur'an was to be interpreted and to what extent, what the Prophet Muhammad said and did and how reliable these sources were, and what other sources should be referred to should there be no definitive decisions within either the **Qur'an** (the holy book of Islam) or Muhammad's **sunna** (deeds and sayings). It was essential that the sources were scrutinised as much as possible using whatever tools of analysis were available to the scholars. It began with careful exegetical analysis of Qur'anic text with the apex of this trend achieved in the monumental work of Muhammad b. Jarir **al-Tabari** (d. 923). While the Qur'an developed into some kind of systematic exegesis, the collection of Muhammad's sayings and deeds into a reliable body was another matter. Malik's main concern, as with many other **ulama** (religious scholars) of the time was in determining what it was that Muhammad actually did say before memories faded altogether, and during this period there were many scholars roaming Islamic lands seeking out people who either had known Muhammad personally, or knew someone who had, and so on. The inevitable problem is in determining the reliability of these accounts, not only from the point of view of memory, but also whether the sources had ulterior motives in providing false accounts. By the end of the first Islamic century there existed a pool of **hadith** (a 'report' of what the Prophet said) transmitters residing in important regional centres of the Islamic world. Malik, residing in Medina, had the obvious advantage of having access to sources much closer to Muhammad in the sense that Medina had been the Prophet's main residence during his formative years and home of the first Islamic city-state.

The transmission of Muhammad's *hadith* probably consisted of both oral and written accounts from its very beginning, although the written form took longer to be established as there was some opposition from some quarters to the idea that there could be any written source other than the Qur'an. A single tradition is called a *hadith*, literally a story, anecdote or narrative of an event, although the same

31

term is used to apply to the entire collection of tradition literature. Each single *hadith* is supposed to have two elements: the actual content of the *hadith* (*matn*), and the list of its chain of transmitters (*isnad*) going back to the original source which, ideally, should be the Prophet himself and, if not, to the **Companions** (those who lived at the same time as Muhammad) or to the **Successors** (the next generation after Muhammad's death). One example, traced back to a Companion of the Prophet, taken from *The Trodden Path* will illustrate this:

> Malik informed us that al-Zuhri reported from Sa'id b. al-Musayyab to the effect that: Nufay'a, a slave of Umm Salamah, had as a wife a free woman against whom he uttered a double-divorce formula. The husband sought a legal opinion on the matter from Uthman b. 'Affan, who said that the wife had thus become forbidden to him.[1]

Here we have the list of transmitters (*isnad*) of a famous *hadith* collector himself, al-Zuhri (d. 742), and a reputable expert in legal matters al-Musayyab (d. 713). The actual content (*matn*) describes how a slave, Nufay'a, had appealed to the Caliph Uthman (one of the Rightly-guided Caliphs and, therefore a Companion of the Prophet) in the hope that he had not irrevocably dissolved his marriage, bearing in mind that the normal procedure for divorce was to utter 'I divorce you' *three* times. However, the Caliph declared that, as Nufay'a was a slave, twice was in fact sufficient. Here is a good example of the use of analogy to come to legal decisions for it is based on a Qur'anic verse detailing that slave-girls (and thus slaves also) should receive half the punishment due to free women who commit fornication. This halving of the judgement (half of three being understood as two, the nearest whole number) was thus applied to the three declarations of divorce that made a divorce irrevocable in the case of free men and women. In this case, the complication involved the status of a slave man married to a free woman and Uthman determined that his judgement is 'half' that of a free man.

The development of *shari'a* and its methods was due to a number of religious scholars and lawyers, of which four have particular note in Sunni Islam: **Abu Hanifa**, al-Malik, Ahmad **Ibn Hanbal** and **al-Shafi'i**. Together the four schools named after them constitute the **Sunni** understanding of God's will. An important biography of these figures was written by Ibn Khallikan (d. 1282) in which he records factual information as well as interesting anecdotes about them. In the case of Malik, he provides a brief account of his appearance as a tall, well-attired, man of a ruddy complexion with a balding forehead, a moustache and grey hair. He was born, lived and died in the holy city of Medina in what is now Saudi Arabia. Little is known about his early life, including the precise date of his birth, which ranges from 709 to 716 according to which authority you refer to. He died in 795 after a short illness. Many of the stories surrounding his early life tell us more about the story writers than the source of these biographies, being a maze of legends beginning with a tale that Malik spent three years in his mother's womb! One authority describes Malik as extremely handsome while another tells the story of how Malik wanted to become a singer but was advised to change career as he was too ugly.

He had a number of teachers, although, again, the figure of up to nine hundred mentors that has been suggested seems rather far-fetched. More believable accounts state that his father and grandfather had, like Malik himself, been collectors of the sayings and deeds of the Prophet Muhammad, or *hadith*, before him. He knew Abu Hanifa, the founder of the Hanafi school of law, when he had studied in Medina, and Malik also was the teacher of the great **al-Shafi'i**, founder of the influential Shafi'i school of law. It is said that Malik remained independent of the governing authorities, which was not always an easy thing to achieve during those times. It is reported that when the mighty Abbasid Caliph Harun al-Rashid visited Medina to pay his respects to the tomb of the Prophet, he met Malik and asked him to come to his residence to teach his two sons. Malik replied, 'Oh, Caliph, science is of a dignified nature, and instead of going to any person, requires that all should come to it.'[2] The Caliph, instead of throwing Malik in prison, apologised and sent his sons to Malik's class where they sat among commoners to receive instructions.

He was strongly devoted to the traditions of the Prophet and would only transmit them when in a state of ritual purity (after having performed his ablutions). His fame results in the production of one work, *The Trodden Path* (*Kitab al-Muwatta*). Although other works have been attributed to him, their authenticity is dubious. However, *The Trodden Path* in itself is a remarkable work, being the first systematic attempt to produce a compendium of Islamic law. It contains around two thousand *hadiths*. Malik himself did not produce a definitive text of his work, however, and for some time it existed in a number of recensions, only four of which are still extant in full.

Malik's main intention in compiling *The Trodden Path* was to codify legal and religious practice that already existed in Medina during his time. The basis of this was how it was actually practised ('amal) as well as consensus of opinion by the local people (known as *ijma*). He also often refers to the Qur'an and the Prophet's *sunna*. In terms of preference, however, the emphasis, with the exception of the Qur'an, is more on the consensus of the local people (by 'local people' this refers to the learned elite) than on the Prophet's *sunna* where conflicts arise. In the case where no decisions can be determined on a particular issue Malik feels free to exercise independent judgement (*ra'y*). The work is arranged in chapters according to subject matter and includes sections on Times of Prayer, Purity, the Qur'an, Burials, *Zakat* (alms tax), Fasting, the *Hajj* (pilgrimage to Mecca), Inheritance, Marriage, Divorce and Blood Money. In its transmission it is less precise than subsequent writers, but nonetheless its importance lies in providing a model to follow and to improve upon.

Both Malik's work as well as the man himself have enjoyed a great deal of respect and admiration among Muslims. **Al-Shafi'i**, for example, has stated that after the Qur'an there is no book on Earth sounder than the book of Malik. His name is often referred to in the great *hadith* collections of al-Bukhari and al-Muslim. The founding of the Maliki school of law is more due to his pupils than to Malik himself. In the centuries that followed, the school acquired influence and authority mainly in the Muslim West (including Spain, during the Islamic period), and the school also has many followers in Upper Egypt. Towards the end of his life Malik withdrew into a life of spiritual reflection and died in 795 CE at the advanced age of 85.

Major work

The Trodden Path has been translated into English by Bewley, although other translations are also available.

Al-Muwatta of Imam Malik ibn Anas: The First Foundation of Islamic Law, trans. A. Abdurrahman Bewley, London: Bookwork, 2001.

Further reading

There are many excellent works on Islamic law.

Coulson, Noel J., *A History of Islamic Law*, Edinburgh: Edinburgh University Press, 1964.
Crone, P., *Roman, Provincial and Islamic Law*, Cambridge: Cambridge University Press, 1987.
Schacht, Joseph, *An Introduction to Islamic Law*, Oxford: Clarendon Press, 1964.

Notes

1   *The Muwatta of Malik, the Recension of al-Shaybani*, ed. 'Abd al-Wahhab 'Abd al-Latif, Cairo: Al-Maktabat al-'Ilmiyyah, 1979, *hadith* no. 555, p. 186.
2   Thomas P. Hughes, *A Dictionary of Islam*, London: W.H. Allen, 1935, p. 312.

RABI'A OF BASRA (*c.*717–801)

Rabi'a al-Adawiyya al-Qaysiyya, or 'Rabi'a of Basra' as she is more commonly known, is remembered in Islamic folklore as a great mystic who emphasised the less speculative and more devotional form of **Sufi** (the mystical branch of Islam) worship. While undoubtedly an historical figure, much of what is said of her belongs to the realms of legend, yet it is the legend that informs us of an important aspect of Sufi belief; of the love of God and a life of asceticism and piety.

There is very little factual information on the life of Rabi'a as there are no biographies written of her in or near her own time. In terms of the most complete early biography we must refer to the *Tadhkirat al-Awliya* (*Memoirs of the Saints*) by the Persian poet Farid al-Din 'Attar, who was born around 1120, and thus writing some three hundred years after her death. In this biography, it is difficult to disentangle myth from fact, however. No doubt 'Attar had access to sources that have now been lost and he was at great pains to refer to what earlier sources were available to him. However, in his attempt to provide as much information as possible, he no doubt allowed himself poetic licence to colour the facts with myth. By the time of 'Attar, there were many legends attached to Rabi'a, and 'Attar would have seen no reason why he should not include them. Other earlier sources are available which, if nothing else, give credence to her existence and status.

Rabi'a was probably born in around 717 in Basra, in Iraq, and spent most of her life there. 'Attar states that she was born to a poor home and was the fourth daughter, hence her name Rab'ia ('the fourth'). Her parents died when she was a child, and she was left an orphan, being forced into slavery. Again, some sources suggest she was not a slave at all and, in fact, was from a wealthy family. However, according to the modern biographer Margaret Smith, there is strong evidence to suggest she was indeed a slave. The fact that Rabi'a has no patronymic and is referred to by the name of her tribe is indicative of slave status. 'Attar provides us with an account of how she journeyed towards spiritual awakening, accompanied by manumission from her master. The story goes that one day she slipped on the road and fell to the ground, and said, 'Oh Lord, I am a stranger and without mother or father, an orphan and a slave and I have fallen into bondage and my wrist is injured, [yet] I am not grieved by this, only [I desire] to satisfy Thee. I would fain know if Thou art satisfied [with me] or not.' In reply, a voice said. 'Be not sorrowful for on the day of Resurrection thy rank shall be such that those who are nearest to God in Heaven shall envy thee.'[1]

Subsequent to this, Rabi'a pursued a life of fasting during the day while carrying out the arduous work of her master. 'Attar recounts how she was freed from her enslaver when, one night, her master looked out of his window and saw Rabi'a praying. He saw a light above her head which was suspended without any chain and it illuminated the whole of the house. This is symbolic of holiness, the *sakina*, derived from the Hebrew *Shekina* and synonymous with the halo of Christian saints. Witnessing this, her master set her free and Rabi'a journeyed into the desert. What happened next is, again, recorded in mixed accounts although it seems that in time she built herself a place of retreat and lived a life from then on of solitary devotion to God.

Apparently Rabi'a received many offers of marriage but chose a life of celibacy in keeping with her monastic lifestyle. One offer of betrothal came from 'Abd al-Wahid b. Zayd (d. 793) who was himself a well-known ascetic, theologian and preacher who had founded one of the earliest-known monastic communities near Basra. Another was from Muhammad b. Sulayman al-Hashimi, the Abbasid Amir of Basra who offered her a fortune for a dowry. Most famously are the accounts linking her to Sufi mystic Hasan of Basra, although he died seventy years before she did! Hasan was known as the 'weeping Sufi' (those who constantly weep or *al-bakka'un*) for he had a great fear of the Day of Judgement and was steeped in sadness for the state of the world. One account says that he once had his head out of the window and was weeping. His tears fell onto Rabi'a below and she thought it was raining! While it is highly unlikely, given the chronology, that these two met, it no doubt symbolises the form of Sufism that both of these mystics adhered to: tending towards the less speculative and more devotional element, as well as, in both cases, a rejection of worldly goods or status.

In terms of more likely associates, one of these was the ascetic Rabah al-Qays of Basra who, like Rabi'a, advocated a life of chastity, repentance and acts of piety. He also emphasised the importance of the saint (*wali*) over that of the Prophet and, in fact, Rabi'a would often criticise another close colleague of hers, Sufyan al-Thawri, for being too devoted to the Prophetic traditions (**hadith**) for, she believed, this distracted him from worship of God. Again, another dubious association but nonetheless informative in terms of understanding her own beliefs, was with the great Egyptian Sufi Dhu al-Nun al-Misri. He was a major exponent of gnosis (*ma'rifa*), an esoteric movement which flourished in the first and second century especially. Gnosis (from the Greek 'revealed knowledge') believed that humanity possesses a 'divine element' that can be reawakened. He elaborated the Sufi conception of unification (**tawhid**) with God through love. It seems that most of her associates were men with only occasional reference to women who visited her, aside from that of her own two female servants.

There are many stories of Rabi'a asceticism (*zuhd*) and poverty (*faqr*), her lack of concern for bodily desires or for help from others when particularly in need. Her form of devotion is characterised by a love of God that left little room for other earthly concerns. A number of miracles (*karamat*, literally 'favours from God') are attributed to her that help throw light upon her character. Many of these stories have been retold by 'Attar in particular. One tells of when two religious leaders stopped off at Rabi'a's home in hope of some food. Rabi'a produced two loaves of bread but before the religious leaders could eat them, a beggar came in and she gave the loaves to him. However, then a slave-girl arrived to give Rabi'a eighteen loaves from the slave-girl's mistress. Rabi'a, after counting them, refused to take them. The slave-girl had taken two loaves for herself but, out of guilt, she replaced them and came back with twenty loaves. These Rabi'a accepted and then fed the sheikhs with them. Rabi'a said to the religious leaders:

> When you came in I knew you were hungry and I said, 'How can I set two loaves before two honourable persons?' When the beggar came in, I gave them to him and I prayed to God Almighty, 'O, my Lord, Thou hast said that Thou wilt give ten for one, and I am sure of this. Now I have given two loves for the sake of pleasing Thee in order that Thou mayest give me back ten for each of them.' When the eighteen loaves came, I knew that either there was a deficiency due to misappropriation or that they were not meant for me.[2]

In the time of Rabi'a, Sufism was still in its infancy, and although she was not a systematic mystic, her teachings have been inspirational to many Sufi scholars who did develop Sufism into a set of doctrines. She placed great emphasis on the concept of repentance (*tawba*) as the first stage in the path towards God. Like Hasan of Basra, she wept freely in sorrow for her sins. For her, repentance is a 'gift from God' and so cannot be sought. However, she believed that sincere penitence would nonetheless result in forgiveness. She taught that sin was the cause of separation between the soul and God, hence the need for sorrow at such a separation. The outward signs of grief, through weeping, are in remorse for sins one has committed, as well as for acts that one has omitted to do. It was not the punishment for sin that caused Rabi'a's sorrow, but the severing it caused in a loving relationship with God.

Another stage on the path towards God is that of patience (*sabr*) and Rabi'a did not seem to lack this virtue. She accepted all as the will of God, even when she was a slave and had to suffer the various adversities presented to her. She regarded patience as an essential part of faith for if she were to will something that God did not will, then she would be guilty of unbelief. Complementary to patience is gratitude (*shukr*). All things, blessings as well as misfortunes, are gifts from God and so one should praise and give thanks to God. We must also be thankful for our misfortunes because they could always be worse than they are. Rabi'a prayers were full of thanksgiving, as this one story indicates:

> It is related that at one time she saw someone who had a bandage bound about his head. She said, 'Why is this bandage bound [around your head]?' He said, 'My head is paining me.' Rabi'a asked him how old he was. 'Thirty years old', he replied. She asked him, 'Were you in pain and trouble for the greater part of your life?' 'No', he answered. Then she said, 'For thirty years [God] has kept your body fit and you have never bound upon it the bandage of gratitude, but one night of pain in your head and you bind it with the bandage of complaint.'[3]

Rabi'a was quick to admonish, as this story illustrates. She did not suffer fools or hypocrites lightly and could hold her own among a company of male religious experts. Rabi'a was one of the first mystics to emphasise the doctrine of love. In response to the question, 'What is love?' she is recorded as quoting the Qur'an:

> Love has come from Eternity and passes into Eternity and none has been found in seventy thousand worlds who drinks one

drop of it until at last he is absorbed in God, and from that comes the saying 'He loves them [his saints] and they love Him.'

(Qur'an 5:59)[4]

She lived to the age of nearly 90 and, if her teachings were anything to go by, one suspects she looked forward to death as the union with God which would submerge any fears she may have for her sins. Rabi'a was no great intellect, and it is debatable whether she really contributed anything either original or doctrinal to the body of Sufi knowledge. Nonetheless, her contribution lies in the inspiration she has been to many, most especially women who see Rabi'a as an archetype for spiritual freedom when social freedom may not be so readily obtained.

Major works

There are no 'collections' of Rabi'a's work as such, but writings attributed to her can be found in the Further reading section.

Further reading

Attar, Farid al-Din, *Muslim Saints and Mystics: Episodes from the Tadhkirat Al-Auliya* (Memorial of the Saints), trans. A.J. Arberry, New York: Arkana, 1990.
El-Sakkakini, Widad, *First Among Sufis: Life and Thought of Rabia Al Ada-wiyya, the Woman Saint of Basra*, ed. Daphne Vanrenen, trans. Nabil Safwat, London: Octagon Press, 1989.
Smith, Margaret, *Rabi'a, The Life and Works of Rabi'a and Other Women Mystics in Islam*, Oxford: Oneworld, 1994.

Notes

1 Attar (1990).
2 Ibid.
3 Ibid.
4 Ibid.

MUHAMMAD AL-SHAFI'I (768–820)

Al-Shafi'i was a jurist, theologian, teacher, poet and essayist who established the foundations of Islamic jurisprudence (*fiqh*). Without doubt the single greatest Islamic legal scholar, his supreme contribution was to put Islamic law on a more solid and scientific footing, especially in his strict approach to the authentication of the sayings (*hadith*) of the Prophet **Muhammad** as a source for law. More than any other figure of his time he restored the unity to an Islamic community that was seemingly on the verge of breaking up.

Muhammad Idris ibn al-Shafi'i was born in Gaza, southern Palestine in 768 and his father died soon after. His widowed mother took the young al-Shafi'i to Mecca to attend a good mosque school and, as was the practice at the time, he also spent some time living among the bedouin, learning skills of horsemanship and archery as well as the distinct social and moral ethic they possessed. He spent ten years with a tribe. Of especial importance during this period was the development of his command of a pure Arabic, unsullied by urban life. He enjoyed Arab poetry and also developed the skill of memorising large amounts, not uncommon among such an oral society.

A turning point in his life came when he read the well-known work by the jurist **Malik**, *The Trodden Path* (*al-Muwatta*), which contains the traditions of the Prophet Muhammad as well as the legal decisions of the early jurists of Medina. He proceeded to memorise the whole work and, still not satisfied, he then spent eighteen months learning from al-Malik himself before the latter died. By this time al-Shafi'i was 28 years old and yet to make a career for himself. However, he soon met the governor of Yemen while on a pilgrimage and the latter offered him a job in the royal court. Although the details are obscure, it seems that al-Shafi'i got involved in some kind of rebellion with some other Yemenis and, as a result, was hauled up in chains in Baghdad before the Caliph Harun al-Rashid on charges of treason. One by one, the Yemenis were beheaded but, when it came to al-Shafi'i, it seems that he suitably impressed the Caliph with his learning and was freed, although it may also be due to having influential friends for, although from a poor family, it was a noble one from the Quraysh tribe: the tribe of the Prophet Muhammad.

Al-Shafi'i took full advantage of this enforced visit to Baghdad. Having studied the tenets of al-Malik, the founder of the legal school, the Malikis, he now spent time among the disciples of the late **Abu Hanifa**, founder of the legal school, the Hanafites. He spent two years in Baghdad before returning to Mecca with his camel loaded with books. He spent the next nine years teaching, preaching and writing but he missed the intellectual life of Baghdad and returned there, and it was not long before he had his own circle of followers who would seek his guidance on legal, religious and social affairs. One of his admirers was the great jurist **Ibn Hanbal**, who later broke off from what had become the al-Shafi'i school of law to found his own, the Hanbali school. While in Baghdad, al-Shafi'i wrote *al-Risalah* (*The Epistle*), which is regarded as the first scientific treatment of Islamic law, and this helped to spread his scholarly reputation.

In 815, for reasons unclear, al-Shafi'i chose to move to Cairo, although at that time it was not yet the intellectual and cultural centre that it was to become. Al-Shafi's reputation had gone before him and he was welcomed there, being considered by some to be the next 'renewer' (*mujtahid*) of Islam. The title 'Renewer of Islam' is a designation based on the popular *hadith* (saying of the Prophet Muhammad) that at the beginning of each century a great man will come to restore and revitalise the Muslim community, to renew (*tajdid*) Islam and return Muslims to the straight path. 815 in the Muslim calendar was 199 (the number of years after the Prophet Muhammad moved from Mecca to Medina) and so al-Shafi'i was seen as the renewer for the third Muslim century that was about to begin. Interestingly another follower of the al-Shafi'i school, **al-Ghazali**, was to be designated the renewer for the sixth Muslim century. Al-Shafi'i would lecture daily at the mosque on such topics as the Qur'an, the *hadith*, grammar and poetry. He taught and wrote for five years before his death at the age of 52, apparently due to haemorrhoid bleeding.

Al-Shafi'i laid the foundations of the science of jurisprudence (*fiqh*). This new Islamic science is unique in that it is entirely Islamic for al-Shafi'i developed it without recourse to, for example, Aristotelian logic or dialectic. The aim of *fiqh* was to regulate all man's relations to God, to establish the right way to live according to the Islamic sources. *Fiqh*, then, is much more than law, it is a way of life. It gives regulations on religious duties such as prayer, fasting, almsgiving and pilgrimage. It also details criminal law and civil law. Every act that man performs is divided into what it permitted (*halal*) and what is forbidden (*haram*) with several gradations in between.

In terms of what Islamic sources to rely upon as the basis of *fiqh*, the first point of call is, of course, the Qur'an. In theory, at least, the Qur'an is meant to be comprehensive and so all other laws should at some point derive from revelation. However, the Qur'an is not explicit in terms of providing many rules and regulations and so the next point of call is the holy book's greatest interpreter, the Prophet Muhammad. For al-Shafi'i, the Prophet is essentially the Qur'an 'made flesh' and so his practice (*sunna*) should act as a model of correct behaviour for it is sanctioned by revelation. At this point al-Shafi'i diverged from the views of the Maliki legal school (and indeed his old mentor) which included the *sunna* not only of

Muhammad but of his **Companions** and his **Successors** as equally authoritative. Al-Shafi'i limited the *hadith* to the *sunna* of the Prophet only, but also raised the status of Muhammad to one that was virtually equal to that of the Qur'an. From this developed the notion of the Prophet's infallibility. Given the status of Muhammad's *sunna*, al-Shafi'i recognised the need to be sure that the *sunna* is correct. In other words, that the Prophet's sayings are true and not spurious.

In al-Shafi'i's time, there were many thousands of *hadith* and what al-Shafi'i did was develop a science of authentication. For example, the chain of authorities that transmitted a saying of Muhammad must not be broken and those transmitters themselves should be proven to be reliable sources. As a result, many *hadith*, including a number in Malik's *The Trodden Path,* were rejected. The importance of the *sunna* lies in its ability to explain and illustrate points in the Qur'an, but they cannot contradict or abrogate verses in the Qur'an. Theologians, on the other hand, often preferred to reject *hadith* altogether and rely on the Qur'an alone, but making use of the skills of dialectic (**kalam**) to determine its meaning, Al-Shafi'i did not have so much faith in the skills of the theologians, however. Once a *sunna* of the Prophet has been fully authenticated, its authority has equal footing with the commands of the Qur'an. The insistence that *hadith* cannot contradict the Qur'an raised a number of problems. For example, the Qur'an punishes the thief with the cutting off of his hand (5:42), but an authentic *hadith* states that Muhammad said the penalty can be waived if the theft was of an inconsequential amount.

Consequently, there was the need for a third source of law: 'consensus' (*ijma,* literally 'agreement'). This source was widely used before al-Shafi'i but the problem with it was, the consensus of whom? Was it just of the local community, or the whole Islamic community? Should it be even more limited than that? If only the local community, this meant that law in say, Baghdad, could differ in many aspects from law in Mecca (as, in fact, was the case). Al-Shafi'i, although not always clear himself on the view he adopted, seemed to veer towards defining the 'community' as that of the learned jurists in Islam as a whole as he obviously disapproved of laws differing from one region to another. However, as a result, when a practice could not be found either in the Qur'an or in the *hadith,* the people would look to the rulings of learned jurists which would often sanction pre-Islamic practices which are not cited in the Qur'an or in *hadith.* However, the advantage of *ijma* was that it could, in principle anyway, allow the law to be flexible and keep up with change.

The final source, or 'root', of law was the use of analogy (*qiyas*, literally measurement). *Qiyas* involves the personal opinion of someone (especially that of a learned Muslim scholar who knows his Qur'an and *hadith* well) based upon making an analogy between a case in the Qur'an or *sunna* and a newly arisen case. For example, in the case of theft, what the punishment was for, say, theft of a camel as stated in the Qur'an or *sunna* may be comparable to the theft of another valuable item that is not referred to specifically in the sources but is equivalent in value. Again, this was in common usage before al-Shafi'i, especially among the Hanafi school of law, whereas the conservative Hanbali law school could determine little support for it in the Qur'an and therefore saw it as an un-Islamic innovation. Al-Shafi'i, for his part, was not that enthusiastic about it either, but acknowledged its need only as a last resort, i.e. if no instruction can be established from either the Qur'an, the *sunna* or *ijma*. Consequently the use of reason, or *ijtihad*, became virtually redundant and, from then on, jurists looked to the corpus of past judgments for their decision-making. Many modern scholars today have argued that in the modern world, where change is rapid, the only way Islam can respond is by re-introducing *ijtihad* and placing more emphasis on the reasoning skills of the scholar than in the past decisions of the scholars of the Middle Ages and earlier.

With this establishment of the science of *fiqh*, al-Shafi'i succeeded in providing a comprehensive and coherent legal system. The Shafi'i school became the fourth legal school (known as **madhhab**) after the Hanafi, Maliki, and Hanbali. None of them differ to any considerable degree and, as a result of al-Shafi'i, the other schools adapted their views on their own sources, particularly their reliance on spurious *hadith*. Today the Shafi'i *madhhab* is prominent in the Malaysian-Indonesian archipelago, southern Arabia, East Africa, and lower Egypt.

Major works

There are a number of translations but the Khadduri is probably the best.

Islamic Jurisprudence: Risala, trans. M. Khadduri, Baltimore, MD: Johns Hopkins University Press, 1961,

Further reading

Coulson, Noel J., *A History of Islamic Law*, Edinburgh: Edinburgh University Press, 1964.

Crone, P., *Roman, Provincial and Islamic Law*, Cambridge: Cambridge University Press, 1987.

Schacht, Joseph, *An Introduction to Islamic Law*, Oxford: Clarendon Press, 1964.

AHMAD IBN HANBAL (780–855)

Ahmad ibn Hanbal was the founder of one of the four main schools of law, the Hanbali legal school (*madhhab*). He was a famous jurist and theologian and was known as the Imam of Baghdad. Most of his works are actually Traditions (*hadith*) of the saying of the Prophet **Muhammad**, his major work being of some 30,000 *hadith*. Ibn Hanbal's school is generally considered the most orthodox and traditional of the legal schools and ibn Hanbal himself defended his traditional approach against rationalist tendencies that existed during the time of the **Abbasid** Caliphate.

Abu AbdAllah Ahmad ibn Muhammad ibn Hanbal ibn Hilal al-Shaybani was born in Baghdad in Iraq in 780. He was from a noble Arab clan, the Banu Sahyban. The clan had played an important part in the Muslim conquests of Iraq and Khurasan during the first century of Islam. His father had served in the army and died just before the birth of his son. Ibn Hanbal was brought up by his mother who played an important role in his education. Because of the nobility of his family, ibn Hanbal was fortunate enough to inherit a small family estate that allowed him to live independently. From what little is known, he married twice and had one son by each of his wives. Both his sons went on to play an important part in the development of the Hanbali school.

Ibn Hanbal developed an enthusiasm in the religious sciences from an early age. In Baghdad, which at the time was the seat of Islamic learning, he studied lexigraphy, jurisprudence and the Prophetic Traditions (*hadith*). He attended the lectures of the famous legal scholar **Abu Hanifa** who, at the time, was Chief Justice of Baghdad. From 795 ibn Hanbal spent four years in the study of *hadith,* and visited the great centres of learning in Iraq at the time, such as Kufa and Basra, as well as the Hijaz and Yemen. It is said he made the pilgrimage to Mecca at least five times in his life and on one of these pilgrimages he met the founder of the Shafi'i law school, Muhammad ibn Idris **al-Shafi'i**, attending his lectures. Al-Shafi'i himself, on a visit to Baghdad in 804, made a point of spending time in the company of ibn Hanbal. Undoubtedly al-Shafi'i had a great deal of admiration and respect for ibn Hanbal, despite certain doctrinal differences.

From around the age of 40, ibn Hanbal himself developed his own following by giving lectures in the Baghdad mosque. These proved to be very popular.

However, in 832, when ibn Hanbal was in his early fifties, the Abbasid Caliph **al-Ma'mun** (reigned 813–833) appointed Ahmad ibn Abi Dawud as the new Chief Justice of Baghdad. The significance of this lies in the fact that Abi Dawud was a sympathiser of the *Mu'tazilite* ('rationalist') school of theology and it is generally considered that he encouraged the Caliph to enforce Mu'tazilite doctrine. One of their doctrines was the concept of Allah's unity (*tawhid*) and challenged the popular idea that God could be seen by the faithful in the afterlife. It was an attack on anthropomorphic interpretations of the attributes of God such as the view that He had hands, sat upon a throne, and so on. Many of these views of God could be found in the *hadith* and so it was also an attack upon those who appealed to the *hadith*. Among such 'Traditionists' must be counted ibn Hanbal. The Mu'tazilites also believed that the Qur'an was 'created' in time, rather than being pre-existent and eternal for, if it were the latter, it would mean another eternal body that exists alongside God which would qualify his unity and Oneness. Essentially what the Mu'tazilites were trying to counter were any possibilities of polytheism or non-Muslim accretions such as the Christian belief in the trinity or Magian dualism. The Chief Justice, with the support of the Caliph, attempted to force judges to accept Mu'tazilite teachings and there followed what was essentially an inquisition, known as the *mihna* ('trial') in which people were imprisoned if they refused to submit.

It seems that most of the religious scholars yielded to the pressure of the *mihna* with the exception of ibn Hanbal and a young scholar known as Muhammad ibn Nuh. Both were chained and sent before the Caliph. However, the Caliph died before the two reached Tartus where he was camped and they were sent back to Baghdad. Ibn Nuh died on the way back while ibn Hanbal was put in prison where he spent the next two years. Al-Mam'un's successor, al-Mu'tasim, who reigned from 833 until 842, was also a Mu'tazilite. Ibn Hanbal refused to budge from his position and so was freed, although his activities were severely restricted until the next Caliph, al-Mutawakkil finally ended the *mihna* and orthodox theology was once more in place. As a result of the *mihna*, ibn Hanbal's fame had spread and he was treated with due deference by the new Caliph.

Ibn Hanbal, though a renowned scholar and theologian, was mostly famous for his collections of the Traditions and his emphasis upon the Qur'an and the *hadith* as the primary sources of legal knowledge. Consequently, Hanbali juristic doctrine has a strong traditionalist and conservative character. His most famous work is *al-Musnad*, which is a collection of around 28,000 traditions which were classified and collected by him and his son AbdAllah. It is one of the earliest *hadith* collections and it is classified according to the transmitters of the *hadith*, starting with the first generation of Muslims. He also wrote *Kitab al-'ilal wa ma'rifat al-rijal (Book on the Inadequacies and Merits of Men)*, which provides important biographical material as well as a critical examination of the *hadith* transmitters on the basis that a *hadith* is only as good as the person who transmits it. This book was again compiled by Ibn Hanbal's son AbdAllah but was apparently not as widely circulated as *al-Musnad*. Other works attributed to Ibn Hanbal include *Kitab al-salat wa ma yalzamu feeha (A Book on Prayer and its Requirements)*, which is said to be a response to his own observations of a group of men in prayer whom he believed were doing it incorrectly. While he was in prison, he wrote a treatise attacking Mu'tazilite theology called *Al-radd 'ala al-zanadiqa wa'l-Jahmiyya (Response to the Heretics and Jahmiyya)*.

Ibn Hanbal himself was not overly fond of the religious science of **kalam** (theology) as he felt that it engaged in unnecessary speculation and should, on the whole, be avoided. Inevitably, however, he was compelled to defend himself against the teachings of the Mu'tazilites during the *mihna* and he adopted what one would expect on such issues: a Traditionist approach which states that one should look to the primary sources of the Qu'ran and the *hadith* and accept what is written without interpretation or further discussion. Consequently as the Qur'an refers to God's 'hands' then God has hands, not 'metaphorical hands'. However, he does not subscribe to the view that God has human form. Rather, to put things simplistically, the hands of God are not like human hands, but they are 'God-like' hands. He also believed it was not within the power of humans to pass judgement on who is a good Muslim and who not. If someone commits a grave sin, such as explicitly renouncing his faith, then it is nonetheless up to God to punish or forgive and not for man to pass judgement. Consequently, he believed in destiny and that the faithful will indeed see God on the Day of Judgement, although he refrained from speculating what this vision might actually entail. He also believed the Qur'an is the uncreated word of God.

As regards his jurisprudence, as already stated, the primary sources for guidance rest with the Qur'an and the *hadith*. Even a *hadith* that is known to be weak (as in, the sources cannot be relied upon) nonetheless takes precedence over the analogical reasoning of any jurist. The judge can only use his own reasoning if nothing at all is to be found in the Qur'an or Traditions. The result, certainly in the case of Ibn Hanbal, was a reluctance to pass judgement on any issue if it was not contained in the Qur'an or Traditions, such was his distrust of human reasoning.

The Hanbali law school currently dominates Saudi Arabia and the Gulf States, and has a limited following in Syria and Iraq. Among the most prominent adherents of Hanbali doctrine were Taqi al-Din ibn **Ibn Taymiyya** (d. 1328) and, more recently, Muhammad ibn Abd **al-Wahhab** (d. 1792) whose alliance with Ibn Saud, ancestor of the founders of Saudi Arabia, resulted in the Hanbali school becoming the official doctrine in that country.

Major works

There is still very little available in English. However, the following gives a taste of ibn Hanbal's views.

Chapters on Marriage and Divorce: Responses of Ibn Hanbal and Ibn Rahwayh, ed. Susan A. Spectorsky, Austin, TX: University of Texas Press, 1993.

Further reading

Coulson, Noel J., *A History of Islamic Law*, Edinburgh: Edinburgh University Press, 1964.
Crone, P., *Roman, Provincial and Islamic Law*, Cambridge: Cambridge University Press, 1987.
Schacht, Joseph, *An Introduction to Islamic Law*, Oxford: Clarendon Press, 1964.

AL-MA'MUN (786–833)

While history does not remember al-Ma'mun as either the greatest of statesmen or for his military conquests, his importance in terms of his patronage of Islamic learning is especially important. As the seventh *Abbasid* Caliph, he fathered a great intellectual movement in his capital Baghdad, resulting in the translation of Greek and Syriac works that opened doors to knowledge lost in the Western world at the time.

In the year 786, Harun al-Rashid was installed as the fifth Caliph of the powerful Abbasid dynasty. At this time the dynasty was at its zenith in terms of power, and the reign of al-Rashid was to initiate a great cultural renaissance. Harun al-Rashid was a patron of the arts, thus literary criticism, philosophy, poetry, mathematics, astronomy and medicine flourished in Baghdad as well as other cities across the empire such as Kufah, Basra and Harran. However, in sharp contrast to the reign of the Rightly-Guided Caliphs (the **Rashidun**), Harun al-Rashid ensured peace by being an absolute monarch. He distanced himself from his subjects, and courtiers would have to kiss the ground when they came before him. He had his executioner standing behind his throne to remind people that the Caliph had the power of life and death. Government was largely left in the hands of the vizier (prime minister) while the role of the Caliph was, according to the title he gave himself, to be the 'Shadow of God on earth': to lead the faithful in Friday prayer, and lead his army into battle when necessary. Harun al-Rashid is famous largely because of the association of his sumptuous and celebrated court with the *Arabian Nights*. So far as history is concerned, however, and not fiction, the greater man was his son al-Ma'mun.

In the same year that Harun al-Rashid acceded to the throne, his two sons were born. The first son was Abu-l-'Abbas 'Abd Allah, or 'al-Ma'mun' ('the trusted one') and the second by six months was al-Amin ('the trustworthy'). Although al-Ma'mun was the elder by six months it was at the age of 5, al-Amin who, was designated the successor to Harun al-Rashid. The reason for this is that al-Amin was the son of Zubaydah, who in turn was the granddaughter of the second Abbasid Caliph al-Mansur. Al-Ma'mun, however, could not claim such a pure lineage, for his mother was a Persian slave girl called Marajil.

However, as the two brothers grew older, Harun realised that al-Ma'mun was intellectually and morally the better and began to have doubts over his designation of al-Amin as his successor. Zubaydah continued to insist on her son as the next Caliph, causing Harun to suggest the two be given a test by asking each of them what they would do if they were Caliph. Whereas the impulsive al-Amin said he would give his father gifts and land in return for the caliphate, al-Ma'mun said that it was not his place to even consider the caliphate but to serve his father and lay down his own life for him if need be. In 799, then, Harun designated al-Ma'mun as his second successor, although one suspects he would have preferred him to be the first. Harun drew up two documents: one, for al-Amin to sign, indicating that he would forfeit the caliphate if he were ever to contest al-Ma'mun's right to be Harun's successor; the second, for al-Ma'mun to sign, requiring him to pledge loyalty to his brother. The two documents were signed, witnessed, and placed within the *ka'ba* itself when Harun made a pilgrimage there in 802. At around the same time al-Ma'mun was appointed governor over Khurasan which required him to leave Baghdad while his brother stayed behind.

With the death of Harun in 809, the rivalry between the two brothers was to come to the fore, despite Harun's efforts to avoid it. The two brothers represent a conflict of world-views. On the one hand, al-Ma'mun was intelligent, cultured, pious and ambitious, while al-Amin was frivolous, self-indulgent and more concerned with the courtly delights of wine and women. Also, al-Amin, because of his lineage, represented Arabian **Sunni** Islam, whereas al-Ma'mun represented Persian **Shi'a** Islam. It is not too much of an exaggeration to make the generalisation that Arab Islam tends more towards the traditional, conservative and orthodox, whereas Persian Islam, with its own pre-Islamic culture rich in philosophy, religion and art, tends towards the more innovative and unorthodox.

It was not long before the two faced a showdown. At first, al-Ma'mun paid homage to the new Caliph in Baghdad, but from his powerful province in Khurasan, al-Ma'mun was already preparing his own army and spies. In 810, al-Amin ordered that his infant son Musa should be mentioned next to him in the Friday prayers. This was an affront to al-Ma'mun as it suggested that al-Amin's son would be the successor. Al-Ma'mun stated that this was in contravention of their father's will, to which al-Amin responded by ordering the will to be taken from the *ka'ba* and burnt. Al-Amin then sent an army of 40,000 against his brother but his general was over-confident and incompetent so that al-Ma'mun's small force of some 4,000 troops led by independent Khurasanian warlords easily defeated Al-Amin's troops. And, in 812, al-Ma'mun laid siege to Baghdad. When, the next year, al-Amin attempted to flee from the city, he was captured and killed.

But al-Ma'mun was not able to assume the mantle of Caliph for another six years. He did not have the support of everyone, least of all Arab Muslims. Al-Ma'mun first of all had to quell rebellions in the Western half of the empire, while in the eastern half al-Ma'mun felt it diplomatic to ally himself to the Shi'a by declaring that the Imam and descendant of the fourth Caliph **Ali**, by the name of Ali ibn Musa al-Rida, would be his successor to the caliphate. Al-Ma'mun went so far as to order the replacement of the black flags and uniforms with that of green (the former being the colour of the Abassids, the latter of the Shi'a), thus enraging Sunni Arabs further. As it turns out, al-Rida did not outlive al-Ma'mun and died in 817. He was buried next to the grave of Harun al-Rashid in a village outside Tus. This became a venerated shrine (*mashhad*) and gave its name to the city which grew out of it, Masshad. Al-Ma'mun was finally able to march into Baghdad in 819 and take up the official position of Caliph, although he was to put down rebellions throughout the rest of his reign.

Al-Ma'mun continued and built upon the renaissance initiated by his father. Not only was Baghdad an intellectual centre but, because of its situation close to the Euphrates and not far from the Persian Gulf, it also became an important commercial and industrial centre, but it is in the contribution to Islamic thought that is of most concern here. One important process that was given extra impetus by al-Ma'mun was the translation of foreign works which would thus open the Islamic world to new knowledge. Especially significant was the increased Hellenization: the adoption of Greek language and ideas. The Syrian translator al-Hallaj ibn-Matar produced an Arabic version of the Alexandrian scientist Ptolemy's *Almagest* which revealed theories of astronomy and geography. Al-Hallaj also translated Euclid's *Elements* which provided the basis of the science of geometry. Another notable translator was the physician Yuhanna ibn-Masawayh (known to the Western world as Mesue) who translated medical and philosophical works. Al-Ma'mun also built an academy in Baghdad called the House of Wisdom (*Bayt al-Hikmah*) which included an observatory and an extensive library.

From a theological perspective, al-Ma'mun, after the death of the Shi'a Imam al-Rida, leant towards the doctrine of the rationalist **Mu'tazilites**. This group did not choose their popular name and preferred to be called 'the people of justice and unity' (*ahl al-'adl wa'l-tawhid*) and it was their concern with unity (**tawhid**) of God, as well as the importance of reason working alongside revelation, that motivated them. Their main topics of concern can be briefly outlined:

1 *God and his attributes.* The Qur'an contains many passages that make reference to God's nature and attributes, for example that he has hands (3:73; 26:71), eyes (11:37) and a face (2:115). Also the language used talks of God speaking, hearing and seeing. The Mu'tazilites believed that such language should be seen as metaphorical. For example, his 'hands' are really a reference to God's 'grace'. The reason for this is that they believed it challenged the concept of God's unity (*tawhid*): God, being One, cannot have 'attributes' or parts. Further, they did not want God to seem too human-like as they were concerned that Islam would suffer the

fate of Christianity with its doctrine of the Trinity which, for the Mu'tazilites, smacked of polytheism and anthropomorphism.

2 *The creation of the Qur'an.* Was the Qur'an created at a point in time (i.e. when Muhammad actually received the revelations) or had it existed eternally? The Mu'tazilites rejected the view that it had existed eternally because, again, this challenges *tawhid*: nothing can exist alongside God, for only God is eternal. Also, they were again concerned with the Christian overtones of divine *logos* (word).

3 *Free will and responsibility.* For the Mu'tazilites, humans, if they are to be punished or rewarded, must therefore be responsible for their actions. While God always wills what is good for his creation, humans possess free will and may choose to do evil, in which case the responsibility lies with them. God, they argued, was bound by necessity to punish evil, and so could not do otherwise. God's acts are not just good because He wills them; rather, God wills only things that are just and good. Reason, for its part, is able to determine what this universal, natural good and bad are.

In 827, al-Ma'mun went so far as to declare the Mu'tazilite creed the state religion, in particular the concept of the creation of the Qur'an, issuing a proclamation that all judges must sign up to this doctrine or be relieved of their office. In fact, he initiated something of an inquisition (*mihna*, meaning 'trial') which was the first of its kind in Islamic history. It was during this time that the founder of the legal school, the Hanbalis, **Ibn Hanbal** insisted upon the uncreated nature of the Qur'an and this caused al-Ma'mun to place him in prison for two years, but to no avail. The Mu'tazilite doctrine was continued under the next Caliph, al-Mu'tasim (833–842) but was then abolished and fell into decline. It could not be said to be al-Ma'mun's greatest moment.

While his father was more concerned with culture and the arts, al-Ma'mun brought to the Islamic world science and philosophy, which only enhanced the power and prestige of the Muslims even more. During his reign, Baghdad became the intellectual centre of the world and this resulted in the development of Islam as more that just traditional and imitative, but rather as innovative and creative.

Further reading

All the books below provide a good study of Islamic history not only during the time of al-Ma'mun, but before and after. The LeStrange and Shaban are particularly useful for this specific period.

Hodgson, Marshall, *The Venture of Islam: Conscience and History in a World Civilization*, vol. 1 of *The Classical Age of Islam*, Chicago: University of Chicago Press, 1977.

Hourani, Albert, *A History of the Arab Peoples*, London: Faber and Faber Ltd., 2002.

Lapidus, Ira M., *A History of Islamic Societies*, Cambridge: Cambridge University Press, 2002.

LeStrange, George, *Baghdad during the Abbasid Caliphate*, Whitefish, MT: Kessinger Publishing, 2004.

Shaban, M.A., *Abbasid Revolution*, Cambridge: Cambridge University Press, 1979.

YAQUB IBN ISHAQ AL-KINDI ('ALKINDUS') (*c.* 801–873)

Al-Kindi is known to Muslims as 'the Arab Philosopher' (*Faylasuf al-'Arab*) and by the Western world as 'Alkindus'. In fact, al-Kindi was the first Muslim to bear the title 'philosopher' and was the only one of pure Arab blood, of note anyway. He wrote hundreds of works in such fields as astronomy, astrology, psychology, medicine and music, but it is his reputation as Islam's first great philosopher that has stood the test of time. He is a major contributor to the introduction of Greek philosophy to the Muslim world, although he was not afraid to contradict the great Greek thinkers if he believed it conflicted with Islamic teachings. Despite that, many of his philosophical views were highly contentious and treated with suspicion by orthodox Muslims.

Al-Kindi was born in about 801 (the precise date is unknown) at Kufah in southern Iraq. Kufah at the time was a great cultural centre and capital of the **Abbasid** caliphate which reigned at this time. He came from an influential family, indicated by the fact that both his grandfather and father were governors of Kufah, although al-Kindi's father died shortly after his birth. He had a noble pedigree going back to a royal Arab tribe of Kindah. He received his early education in his hometown and he later moved to Basra, a port in southern Iraq close to the Persian Gulf. The twin cities of Kufah and Basra were originally founded as Arab military camps but, by the ninth century, they had both become cities of culture. Basra, for example, was the birthplace of the great theologians Hasan al-Basri (d. 728) and **al-Ashari** (d. 935), and both cities were important centres for the science of philology.

From Basra, al-Kindi then went to Baghdad. Baghdad was built by the Abbasid Caliph al-Mansur in 762 on the Western bank of the Tigris, opposite an old Iranian village also named Baghdad. The original city was round, with three concentric walls. Within the next half century the city reached a peak of prosperity and influence under the infamous Caliph Harun al-Rashid although when al-Kindi arrived there the caliph was another great historical figure and patron of the arts, **al-Ma'mun** and the round city lay in ruins due to the recent war of secession. Al-Kindi enjoyed royal patronage, both under al-Mamun and his successor al-Mutasim, becoming a tutor and adviser in the royal court. Although he knew no Greek himself and had to rely on translations, he studied ancient Greek science and philosophy, especially that of Aristotle.

The early part of his career coincided with the ascendancy of the *Mu'tazilite* movement (a movement which sought to accord reason as much, if not more, status than revelation; see also **al-Ashari, al-Maturidi** and **al-Zamakhshari**), and he has sometimes been iden-tified as a Mu'tazilite sympathiser The Mu'tazilite movement was considered to be rationalist and favoured Greek logical techniques, although they were not the free-thinkers that some have believed, engaging in an 'inquisition' (*mihna*) that resulted in the persecution of those who did not uphold the religious doctrine of the Mu'tazilites. The legal scholar **Ahmad ibn Hanbal** was one such victim of the inquisition. However, during the reign of al-Ma'mun, it was the official school of the state and it did al-Kindi no harm to be a Mu'tazilite. This may well have resulted in his downfall as the Mu'tazilite doctrine fell out of favour in the mid-ninth century. His extensive library was for a short period confiscated and removed to Basra, and al-Kindi spent his old age in seclusion as he had made a number of enemies in the courts, partly because of his own intellectual arrogance, and, apparently because he had a reputation for miserliness that alienated many and is regarded in Arab circles as a particular vice. The date and cause of his death are not certain, but it was around 873.

As al-Kindi was from a wealthy and aristocratic background, so he was able to employ a large number of mostly Christian translators to engage in the task of translating ancient Greek works into Arabic, translations that proved to be an important contribution to Islamic knowledge. He appears to have been particularly interested in the ideas and works of Aristotle and Plato, and he himself was responsible for the composition of an impressive number of works. Some researchers have credited him with over three hundred works in such diverse fields as philosophy, psychology, medicine, mathematics, music, astron-omy, geography, logic, politics and astrology. Unlike some of his successors, he held astrology to be a genuine science, but refused to write on alchemy, which he considered a form of deception. He also wrote a number of commentaries on Aristotle. Unfortunately, the majority of his works are now lost, most as a result of the Mongol invasions that sacked Baghdad in 1258. Only around forty of his works have survived and so it is difficult to evaluate the importance of his overall work, which is not helped by the fact that his work was soon superseded and consequently he is rarely referred to by later authors.

In the medical field, he devised a sophisticated system for calculating the effectiveness of drugs, and combined his mathematical and medical interests by attempting to devise a rule for estimating the likely course of a disease. Al-Kindi's main contribution was in shifting the intellectual focus from theology to philosophy. His best-known work is *Fi al-falsafa al-ula* (*Treatise on the First Philosophy*), and in his Introduction he states the following:

> The noblest in quality and highest in rank of all human activities is philosophy. Philosophy is defined as knowledge of things as they are in reality, insofar as man's ability determines. The philosopher's aim in his theoretical studies is to ascertain the truth, in his practical knowledge to conduct himself in accordance with their truth.[1]

Al-Kindi's view that truth that is gained from philosophy is universal and supreme proved to be one of the most contentious issues in the Islamic intellectual world and resulted in philosophers being treated with suspicion, if not downright hostility, by orthodox Muslims, especially the theologians. One particular bone of contention was that, unlike the Muslim sciences of theology (*kalam*) and law (*shari'a*), philosophy was perceived as a foreign import and, therefore, was not 'Islamic'. This contradicted the view held by many of the orthodox that Islam is self-sustaining: all knowledge about every aspect of life can be found within revelation as contained in the Qur'an. Pre-empting this criticism, al-Kindi writes in the same work:

> We should never be ashamed to approve truth and acquire it no matter what its source might be, even if it might have come from foreign peoples and alien nations far removed from us. To him who seeks truth no other object is higher in value. Neither should truth be underrated, nor its exponent belittled. For indeed truth abases none and ennobles all.[2]

Al-Kindi argued that the truth attained through the science of theology is not incompatible with that attained through philosophy and argued that theologians should make use of the tool of philosophical logic in their argumentation rather than rely on literalism. The truths of the prophet are, likewise, in accordance with the truths of the philosopher, although al-Kindi is keen to point out that the prophet is greater than the philosopher because prophetic knowledge is spontaneous and infallible whereas the philosopher must struggle through the application of logic and demonstration and is liable to error. However, provided the philosopher is sufficiently skilled, the truth he acquires is equal to that of the prophet. Such remarks are dangerous territory for it begs the question why there should be any need for revelation or prophethood if a philosopher can acquire all knowledge that there is to acquire.

Al-Kindi's purpose in writing *First Philosophy* was to establish the proof of God's divinity. Unlike his successors **Ibn Rushd** and **Ibn Sina**, who adopted the Aristotelian view, al-Kindi accepted the orthodox doctrine that God created the universe *ex nihilo* ('out of nothing') and therefore, matter being finite, it requires an infinite being to bring it into existence. This infinite, al-Kindi argued, is God. God is both creator and sustainer, the Prime Cause. Despite his fondness for Greek learning, where the Greek tradition disagrees with traditional Islamic interpretations, al-Kindi does not hesitate to reject the Greek tradition entirely. The most obvious, and important, example of this is in his discussion of the origin of the world, which Aristotle had posited to be eternal. Al-Kindi, on the other hand, argues that the world was created by God *ex nihilo*. For him, all matter and time are finite; only God, the Eternal, is infinite and unchanging. On the soul, al-Kindi stated that it is simply an entity emanating from God in the same way the rays emanate from the sun. Therefore, it does not have material substance but is spiritual and divine in origin. With the death of the body, the soul returns to the Divine light and shares in the supernatural.

In addition to his more speculative and philosophical work, al-Kindi's interest in ethical and practical philosophy is apparent from a number of titles, among them *Fi al-hila li-daf al-ahzan* (*On the Art of Avoiding Sorrows*), though the attribution of this work to al-Kindi has been challenged. He here appears to have drawn on the tradition of the Stoics. The foundation of Stoic ethics is the principle that good lies not in the external world, but in the state of the soul itself, in the wisdom and restraint by which a person is delivered from the passions and desires that trouble the ordinary life. The four cardinal virtues of the Stoic philosophy are wisdom, courage, justice, and temperance, a classification derived from the teachings of Plato. Like the Stoics, al-Kindi advised his readers to concentrate on the life of the spirit rather than that of the body, and warned against the excessive development of attachments to worldly goods.

Although al-Kindi served as a court physician, he does not seem to have practised this discipline to any great extent, preferring to write medical works rather than practise medicine. Of thirty-six medical essays by him that have survived, little is original. His contribution rests more in his style and presentation than in his originality and it is to his credit that he was the first Arab writer to provide a systematic and comprehensive classification of the sciences. He also wrote fourteen works on mathematics, although most have not survived, and forty-four works on astronomy which early on were translated into Latin in the West and spread the name of Alkindus in Europe. Another important contribution to his reputation in Europe at least was his work on optics in which he argued that light takes no time to travel and vision is achieved through rays sent from the eyes to the object. While not always correct, his writing introduced into Europe the science of optics which influenced the work of the English philosopher-scientist Roger Bacon (d. 1294) among others. Al-Kindi was also a music theorist. While borrowing heavily from Neo-Pythagorian, as well as Neo-Platonic, theories of music, he did add a theoretical fifth string to the lute and therefore reached the double octave without resorting to the shift.

Many of his works were translated into Latin and Hebrew and he was widely read by the scholars of Muslim Spain in particular. Although his work was in general soon overtaken by that of later Islamic philosophers such as **al-Farabi** (born a year before al-Kindi's death) and Ibn Sina, his approach influenced the later *Ikhwan al-Safa* (a brotherhood responsible for composing an encyclopaedia), and Latin translations of his works had a major impact on later generations of European philosophers and scientists.

Major works

There is not yet much available in English, although his *Treatise on First Philosophy* is translated well by Ivry and there are certain medical texts for those so inclined.

Medical Formulary, trans. M. Levy, Madison, WI: University of Wisconsin Press, 1966.
Al-Kindi's Metaphysics: A Translation of the Treatise on First Philosophy, trans. A.L. Ivry, Albany, NY: State University of New York Press, 1974.

Further reading

The Atiyeh is still the best account of Al-Kindi's philosophy. Aside from that, there are various works in English on, for example, his optics and weather forecasting!

Atiyeh, G., *Al-Kindi: Philosopher of the Arabs*, Oxford: Oxford University Press, 1968.
Lindberg, David C., *Theories of Vision from Al-Kindi to Kepler*, Chicago: University of Chicago Press, 1976.

Notes

1 Muhammad 'Abd al-Hadi abu-Ridah, *Rasa'il al-Kindi al-Falsafiyah,* vol. 1, Cairo, 1950, p. 97.
2 Ibid, vol. 1, p. 103.

ABU AL-HASAN AL-ASHARI (837–935)

Al'Ashari was a great theologian who countered the rationalist tendencies of the **Mu'tazilite** school of thought while avoiding the approach of strict literal Traditionism that was characteristic of the Hanbalite school (see **Ibn Hanbal**). Like the legal scholar **al-Shafi'i** in the religious science of jurisprudence, al-Ashari developed a synthesis of opposing views in theology which emerged as the Asharite school, a powerful and influential school that has held sway among **Sunni** theologians.

Abu al-Hasan Ali ibn Ismail al-Ash'ari was born in the city of Basra in Iraq in 837. It is said that he was descended from Abu Musa al-Ash'ari from the Asha'ira clan of Yemen who was governor in Iraq during the time of the Prophet's **Successors**. Belonging to such a noble family, Al-Ash'ari had a small private income that meant he could be independent. Basra at that time was an important Muslim intellectual centre and, after initially studying law there, he devoted his time to theology under the prominent Mu'tazilite theologian Abu 'Ali al-Juba'i (d. 915). It was said that al-Ash'ari proved to be a brilliant student and spent most of his youth and early adulthood as a keen disciple of Mu'tazilite doctrine. However, around 912, he broke away from this rationalist school. The reasons given for this split are various. It is said that prior to this, he had spent two weeks in solitude during which he examined his own convictions and felt that they were not compatible with Mu'tazilite rationalism. Other reports claimed that al-Ash'ari abandoned the Mu'tazilites when the Prophet appeared to him three times in dreams and instructed him to defend the Islamic Tradition (the **sunna**) assuring him that he would receive divine inspiration and aid in this undertaking. Whatever the reason, al-Ashari used the Mu'tazilites' own weapon, theological dialectic (**kalam**), to refute their teachings.

Al-Ashari went on to defend the non-rational elements of belief which, he argued, transcended human categories and experience. It seems that he had grown to dislike the excessive rationalism embodied by the Mu'tazilites because, he believed, it had turned God into a dry abstraction and life into a meaningless series of causalities. An example of al-Ashari's view that human reason is limited is provided by the famous question he asked of his teacher al-Juba'i:

> Let us imagine a child and a grown-up person in Heaven who both died in the True Faith. The grown-up one, however, has a higher place in heaven than the child. The child shall ask God: 'Why did you give that man a higher place?' 'He has done many good works,' God shall reply. Then the child shall say, 'Why did you let me die so soon that I was prevented from doing good?' God will answer, 'I knew that you would grow up into a sinner; therefore, it was better that you should die a child.' Thereupon a cry shall rise from those condemned to the depths of Hell, 'Why, O Lord! did You not let us die before we became sinners?'[1]

Mu'tazilite rationalism had no answer to the call of those condemned to Hell, and so al-Ashari chose a different path by making public repentance and repudiation in the mosque of Basra for his errors. Following this break, he started to frequent the learning circles of the Sunni jurists and gradually came under the influence of three eminent Traditionist scholars, namely AbdAllah ibn Kallab (d. 854), al-Harith ibn Asad al-Mahisibi (d. 857), and Abu al-Abbas al-Qalanissi (d. 868–869). In jurisprudence, al-Ash'ari was a follower of the Shafi'i school of law (see **al-Shafi'i**), although he had great respect and admiration for **Ibn Hanbal**. In fact, al-Ashari considered himself a Hanbali, but Hanbalis themselves adopt a literal interpretation of the Traditions (Qur'an and **hadith**) and have little regard for theology.

Many works have been attributed to al-Ashari, varying between fifty and over a hundred. However, only a handful of his works are in existence today, the most famous being *Al-ibana 'an usul al-diyana* (*The Elucidation of the Fundamentals of Religion*), *Maqalat al-islamiyyin wa ikhtilaf al-musallin* (*Discourse of the Adherents of Islam and Disagreements of the Pious), Kitab al-luma' fil radd 'ala ahl al-zaigh wal bida (Highlights of the Polemics against Deviators and Innovators)* and (a short (*Treatise on Theological Argument*) (*Risala istihsan al-khawd fi 'ilm al-kalam*)). All these works bear the name of al-Ashari although there is much debate among Asharite scholarship as to whether they actually were all written by him. For example, the *Fundamentals* adopts a strict Traditionist approach whereas the *Polemics* is more sympathetic towards rationalism. However, it could well be that these need to be seen in the context of al-Ashari's own intellectual development for it is not altogether clear which were written when he was a Mu'tazilite, or when he was a Hanbalite, or when he went on to synthesise the two doctrines.

When he broke with the Mu'tazila, al-Ash'ari declared the following to summarise his new stand:

> The position we take and the religious views we profess are: to hold fast to the book of our Lord and the Sunnah of the Prophet and to what has been related on the authority of the companions and the followers of the Imams of the Hadith. Moreover we profess what Abu AbdAllah Ahmad ibn Muhammad ibn Hanbal taught ... and we contradict all who contradict his teachings.[2]

While this, and similar statements, may suggest a strict adherence to Hanbali literalism, as already stated, if this was the case, it was not permanent as he came to develop a distinctly Asharite approach by combining the best of rationalism and Traditionism. He argued that the sole reliance on Scripture (*al-nass*) is the attitude of the lazy or the ignorant, whereas reliance on reason alone (*al-'aql*) is dangerous. The best approach, he believed, was to combine reason with revelation. The Qur'an can be justified by reason up to a certain point, and beyond that it simply must be accepted as revealed truth. Certain aspects of doctrine, therefore, were 'off limits' to rational speculation and one must simply accept 'without asking how' (*bila kayfa*). Such a suspension of judgement was a consequence of man's limits to knowledge in comparison to that of God's. The will of God being so beyond human comprehension His acts may well seem arbitrary to the extent that if God so wished to send the pious to hell and the sinners to heaven then we must accept this as, simply, God's will and not attempt to interpret it within a human understanding of what constitutes coherency and logic. The Mu'tazilites argued that it was possible for human rationality to predict the final destinies of people based upon the actions they do in this world because the Qur'an clearly states what is good and what is bad and if God does not fulfil his promises and carry out his threats, then He would be a liar!

For the Mu'tazilites, humans, if they are to be punished or rewarded, must therefore be responsible for their actions. While God always wills what is good for his creation, humans possess free will and may choose to do evil, in which case the responsibility lies with them. God, they argued, was bound by necessity to punish evil, and so could not do otherwise. God's acts are not just good because He wills them; rather, God wills only things that are just and good. Reason, for its part, is able to determine what this universal, natural good and bad is. However, the concern for both Hanbalites and Asharites here is that this is placing a limitation upon God's omnipotence by stating that He has a specific nature that He is bound by. Everything is possible for God. We cannot impose a rational purpose on God as this shows a lack of faith in his essential justice, mercy and compassion. He has the power to will belief and unbelief, obedience and disobedience. Also, if reason can determine what morals one should abide by, then what is the point of revelation? Al-Ashari, however, did not go down the road of extreme determinism, realising that the consequences of determinism result in moral laxity. Al-Ashari developed a curious, and not entirely satisfactory, view on free will and responsibility known as 'acquisition' (kasb) which is an attempt to preserve human responsibility and God's omnipotence. He states it in this way:

> Allah did not compel any of His creatures to be infidels or unfaithful. And He did not create them either as faithful or infidels, but He created them as individuals, and faith and unbelief are the acts of men. Allah knoweth the man who turneth to belief as an infidel in the state of his unbelief; and if he turneth to belief afterwards, Allah knoweth him as faithful, in the state of his belief; and He loveth him, without change in His knowledge or His quality. All the acts of man – his moving as well as his resting – are truly his own acquisition [kasb], but Allah creates them and they are caused by His will, His knowledge, His decision, and His decree.[3]

For example, al-Ashari argued that we are conscious of certain involuntary motions in our body like when we shiver when it is cold or have a temperature when we are ill. We are conscious that these involuntary actions are distinct from such voluntary actions as 'coming and going' which we seem to be able to do quite freely. These latter acts, he argued, are a power within us created by God, hence they are 'acquired'. And so, while they originate with God, they are nonetheless voluntary acts on the part of the individual. This attempt at reconciliation between omnipotence and determinism has caused much debate and was considered largely unsatisfactory, as al-Ashari himself admits that both the involuntary and acquired acts are acts of God who, in his omniscience, must know what man will do. Given this, it is very hard to see how He created man as neither faithful nor infidel. Attempts to later modify al-Ashari's views met with little success too, including one suggestion that the agent's choice or intention must precede the 'acquired' act created by God.

Al-Ashari also believed that God is the creator of both good and evil acts, which is a position the Mu'tazilites denied as God, being all-good, could not possibly create evil acts. However, again, al-Ashari's primary concern is to maintain God's omnipotence, and so it is not possible to assert that God 'cannot' do anything. Evil is not created by God for Himself, and so He can still be all-good, rather it is created for His creation. Man cannot know what good is unless evil also exists as its counterpart (as opposed to evil being merely the absence of good). God does not command evil, but He does create it.

One final important issue on which the Asharites and Mu'tazilites disagreed was that of God's unity (**tawhid**). Both agreed that nothing can be compared with God and that he is one, single and eternal. From this point, the Mu'tazilites argued that the descriptions of His attributes that are contained in the Qur'an – for example when it refers to God's hands, eyes, face, and so on – must be understood allegorically or metaphorically. For example, by reference to God's 'hands' this should be interpreted as God's grace. The Hanbalites, being literalists, argued that if the Qur'an talks of God's hands, then it is God's hands and that is the end of it. Al-Ashari stated that if the Qur'an states that God created with His two hands (as it does in 38:75), then that is sufficient proof that He did so. Linguistically, he argued, it does not make sense to say God had created 'with My grace'. However, the attributes are not to be understood in a crude anthropomorphic way either, but rather the descriptions just have to be accepted, employing the formula referred to earlier, 'without asking how' (*bila kayfa*).

The further development of Asharite doctrine was a consequence of the achievements of a number of prominent Muslim scholars such as the judge Muhammad ibn al-Tayeb al-Baqillani (d. 1012/13?), Abd al-Malik ibn AbdAllah al-Juwayni, known as Imam al-Haramayn

(Imam of the Two Sanctuaries; d. 1046), the famous Abu Hamid **al-Ghazali** and the philosopher Fakhr al-Din al-Razi (d. 1209). The former two contributed greatly to the scholastic transformation of the Asharite school, while the latter two developed it in a philosophical manner.

Major works

Aside from the annotated translations by McCarthy, al-Ashari's works are not readily available in English.

The Theology of al-Ash'ari: Being Annotated Translations of Two Arabic Texts with Appendices, trans. R. McCarthy, Beirut, 1953.

Further reading

The Corbin and Watt are both good on Islamic philosophy generally.

Corbin, H., *History of Islamic Philosophy*, trans. L. Sherrard and P. Sherrard, London: Kegan Paul, 1993.

Makdisi, G., 'Ash'ari and the Ash'arites in Islamic Religious History', *Studia Islamica* 17–18 (1963).

Watt, W.M., *Islamic Philosophy and Theology: An Extended Survey*, 2nd edn, Edinburgh: Edinburgh University Press, 1985.

Notes

1 There are many versions of this story. This is the one recounted by Fazlur Rahman in *Islam*, 2nd edn (Chicago: University of Chicago Press), 1979, p. 91.

2 Quoted in I. Goldziher, *Introduction to Islamic Theology and Law*, pp. 104–105.

3 Quote taken from A.J. Wensinck, *The Muslim Creed: Its Genesis and Historical Development* (London: Frank Cass, 1965), p. 191.

MUHAMMAD AL-TABARI (839–923)

Muhammad ibn Jarir al-Tabari was a prolific writer on the subjects of theology, literature, and history. He is best known for his commentary on the *Qur'an* as well as a universal history of the world from creation until his own time. Both became definitive reference works in their fields and are regarded as one of the great contributions to the formation of classical Arabic-Islamic culture.

Abu Ja'far Muhammad ibn Jarir ibn Yazid ibn Kathir ibn Ghalib al-Tabari was born in 839 in Amul, which is the capital city of Tabriz (hence al-Tabari), now East Azerbaijan. His father, Jarir ibn Yazid, was very supportive in providing his son with a sound education in the religious sciences and al-Tabari was able to be financially independent by inheriting some property upon his father's death. It meant that he could afford the luxury of refusing any gifts or stipends offered particularly from those in government, as well as rejecting any offers to take up a position in the court himself. Therefore, he was not only able to maintain financial independence but was free from government pressure to toe the party line. Most biographers state that he never married and, in fact, remained celibate throughout his life. He died in Baghdad in 923.

It was common practice for young scholars to travel around the Islamic world to the great intellectual centres in search of knowledgeable teachers. Because of the support from his father, al-Tabari was encouraged to do this. It is said that he had memorised the whole of the Qur'an when he was 7, led the prayers when he was 8, and started studying the Prophetic Traditions (**hadith**) when he was 9. From the age of 12 he began his trips in the quest for knowledge, taking him first to Rey (the site of present-day Tehran; Rey was destroyed by the Mongols in 1221) where he stayed for five years. Here he was taught by Abu AbdAllah Ibn Humayd al-Razi (d. 862), a Traditionist (authority on *hadith*) who was a contemporary of the great legal scholar Ahmad **Ibn Hanbal**.

Al-Tabari then went to Baghdad, the most important cultural and intellectual centre of the Islamic world at the time. He hoped to be taught by the great scholar Ibn Hanbal himself but arrived there shortly after the death of the latter in 855. However, he continued his studies in Baghdad for another year, setting off once more for southern Iraq where he studied in Kufah and Basra. He returned to Baghdad in 858 and stayed for eight years this time. He studied jurisprudence and Qur'anic studies and found employment as tutor to the son of the **Abbasid** Vizier Ibn Khaqan. After this, he visited Egypt, Syria, Palestine and Beirut. He made a point of familiarising himself with the teachings of all the legal schools (**madhhab**). While on these travels al-Tabari took the opportunity to record the history and interpretation of the Qur'an according to the reputable scholars he met. He began writing works on Qur'anic exegesis (**tafsir**) and Islamic history and he became a prestigious scholar in his own right being respected especially for his knowledge of Qur'anic exegesis and jurisprudence. His *Jami' al-bayan 'an ta'wil ay al-Qur'an* (*Full Exposition of Qur'anic Commentary*) brought together, for the first time, a huge body of exegetic Tradition which prompted one scholar, Abu

Hamid al-Isfara'ini, to remark famously, 'If a person has to go to China to obtain a copy of Muhammad ibn Jarir [al-Tabari]'s *Tafsir*, it will not have been too much effort.'

His *Tafsir* was dictated to his students over a seven-year period (finishing it in around 903) and, in modern editions, constitutes thirty volumes. The approach he adopted was to list different Traditions in relation to one specific verse of the Qur'an. This could amount to up to twenty different Traditions each possibly providing varying opinions on the interpretation of a Qur'anic phrase or even a single word. Importantly, al-Tabari endeavoured as much as possible to only include Traditions that he believed to have been authentically transmitted over time from its original source. In parts of the *Tafsir*, al-Tabari merely records the difference of opinion and leaves it at that, whereas at other times he engages critically in the assessment of the varying Traditions in an attempt either to establish some kind of synthesis or to defend one opinion over another. While al-Tabari also discussed variant readings of the Qur'an or of the grammar of the text he avoided engaging in speculative allegorical or metaphorical exegesis, unlike the rationalist **Mu'tazilite** school (see **al-Zamakhshari** who produced a Tafsir with a Mutazalite interpretation after al-Tabari).

Al-Tabari himself was suitably impressed with his *Tafsir*, and so was prompted to say:

> It is a book containing all that people need [concerning the interpretation of the Qur'an]. It is so comprehensive that with it there is no need to have recourse to other books. We shall relate in it arguments wherein agreement was achieved and where disagreement persisted. We shall present the reasons for every school of thought or opinion and elucidate what we consider to be the right view with utmost brevity.[1]

Indeed, scholars did rely heavily on this work, as well as another definitive reference work in the field of history, his *Mukhtasar tarikh al-rusul wa'l-muluk wa'l-khulufa* (*History of Prophets and Kings*). It is a history of the entire world, beginning with Adam at Creation and ending in the year 915. Such an ambitious project does not, in fact, cover a history of the *entire* world, of course, but history from an Islamic perspective tracing the biblical (and, hence, also Qur'anic) people and prophets, the history of ancient Iran, especially during the period of the Sassanids (the Persian Empire) and the rise of Islam with the Prophet Muhammad, the four Rightly-Guided Caliphs (**Rashidun**), the **Umayyad** dynasty (661–750) and then the reign of the Abbasids from 750 until the year 915 when the book was completed. Like the *Tafsir* he had written before, his *History* again stuck to a Traditionist approach, recounting historical events that he had recorded during his travels, while avoiding adopting the viewpoint of doctrinal schools such as the Mu'tazilite or *Shi'a*, although it may be argued that the Traditionist view is a school of its own. In describing his method, al-Tabari said the following:

> The reader should know that with respect to all I have mentioned and made it a condition to set down in this book of ours, I rely upon traditions and reports which I have transmitted and which I attribute to their transmitters. I rely only very exceptionally upon what is learned through rational arguments and produced by internal thought processes. For no knowledge of the history of men of the past and of recent men and events is attainable by those who were not able to observe them and did not live in their time, except through information and transmission.[2]

Al-Tabari was not unusual for his time in being a polymath. Aside from his expertise in Qur'anic exegesis and historical studies, he was also considerably learned in jurisprudence. As already mentioned, he studied the teachings of the four major law schools and is generally considered to be sympathetic to the Shafi'i (see **al-Shafi'i**) law school, and so he is not as Traditionist as the Hanbali. In fact, he even went so far as to found his own law school, known as the Jaririyya school, but – like so many law schools – this was not to survive the test of time and, besides, differed little from the Shafi'i so as to make it virtually surplus to requirements.

After all of his travels, al-Tabari remained in Baghdad for the rest of his life, but he would make a point of visiting his home town as often as possible. However, his last recorded visit there was in 903 when, apparently, he had to flee Tabriz due to threats to his life from the growing Shi'a influence in the region: al-Tabari was very outspoken in his anti-Shi'a views. Aside from the Shi'a, he also attacked the views of the Mu'tazilites. However, this did not make al-Tabari a Traditionist either, for the Hanbali were also hostile towards him and, ironically, accused him of having Shi'a sympathies. This is curious for, although he was not strictly a Traditionist, it could hardly be said that he was hostile towards them as his writings adopt a Traditionist approach in all but name. The sticking point seems to be that al-Tabari, for whatever reason, did not recognise Ibn Hanbal as a jurist and, in actual fact, al-Tabari probably has a point, for the law school named after him, the Hanbali, adopted Hanbal as its eponym and only then did it develop as a law school. Hanbal himself is regarded more as a collector of Traditions than a law-maker. Such a seemingly minor detail must be seen within the context of the time and place in which al-Tabari was living, for if he had lived just a few years longer his *History* could have been rounded off with the effective end of the Abbasid Caliph. However, when al-Tabari died in 923, there were many demonstrations against him by Hanbali loyalists and subsequently he was denied a proper burial.

Major works

The State University of New York Press have made a gallant and rewarding effort to translate al-Tabari's *History*. Highly recommended if you have a few days to spare to read them.

The Commentary on the Qur'an: Being an Abridged Translation of Jami' al-bayan 'an ta'wil ay al-Qur'an, Introduction and notes by J. Cooper, Oxford: Oxford University Press, 1987.

The History of al-Tabari, English trans., 39 vols, cd. E. Yar-Shater, New York: State University of New York Press, 1989–1998.

Further reading

Ayoub, M., *The Qur'an and its Interpreters*, vol. 1, Albany, NY: State University of New York Press, 1984.

Notes

1 Ayoub, *The Qur'an and its Interpreters*, p. 4.
2 *History*, vol. 1, p. 170.

ABU NASR AL-FARABI ('AVENNASAR') (*c.* 870–950)

Known in the West by his Latinised name 'al-Farabius' or 'Avennasar', al-Farabi was one of the most prominent of Muslim philosophers. He was also a **Sufi** (Muslim mystic) and something of a musician. His major contribution to Islamic thought was to illustrate how Greek philosophy could answer and support the many critical questions being raised by Muslims at the time. He was the first truly systematic philosopher of Islam.

Al-Farabi's full name was Abu Nasr Muhammad ibn Muhammad ibn Tarkhan ibn Awzalagh (or Uzlugh), although he was known as 'al-Farabi' as he was likely born in the town of Farab in Turkestan. His father was said to have been a military officer in the Persian army, though of Turkish extraction. There is little information about the life of al-Farabi and what there is cannot be entirely relied upon. He was born around 870 and, although the details of his early education are unclear, he seems to have spent his early years learning Arabic as well as Persian and Turkish and to have studied jurisprudence, the tradition (*hadith*) of the Prophet **Muhammad**, and interpretation of the Qur'an. He then, at the age of 40, travelled to Baghdad where he lived for twenty years. At that time, Baghdad was the intellectual and cultural centre of the Islamic world and there he was taught logic by Nestorian Christian scholars and introduced to the thought of ancient Greek philosophers, especially Aristotle. By al-Farabi's time, most of Plato, Aristotle and their late Greek commentators had been translated, partly by Eastern Christians via Syriac. From the eighth to the eleventh centuries, the period when issues of political authority were widely discussed, interest in Greek philosophy was at its height. During his time in Baghdad al-Farabi wrote such works as *Ihsa al-'ulum* (*Survey of the Branches of Knowledge*), and *Tahsil al sa'ada* (*The Achievement of Happiness*).

It seems al-Farabi became a teacher himself and although he stayed outside of the patronage of the royal court for much of his life, he did, in 942, travel from Baghdad to Syria, travelling to Aleppo to join the royal court of Saif al-Dawla of the Hamdanid dynasty to be court musician. This court was *Shi'a* and al-Farabi himself was a Shi'a Muslim. His major works, particularly in the field of political philosophy, were written during this time. He died in Damascus in 950, said to have been killed by robbers while travelling. Over one hundred works have been credited to him, but this is likely exaggerated and only a small number have survived.

He also wrote a great deal on logic and philosophy of language which includes commentaries on Aristotle's works in logic, but he goes beyond a mere summary and explication by developing his own personal interpretations of Aristotelian logic. A concern of his was to mark out precisely the relationship between philosophical logic and the grammar of ordinary language. This issue was particularly pertinent as Arab scholars were struggling with understanding Greek philosophical logic in the context of translations into Arabic. Al-Farabi argued that logic was not a foreign import as such but a kind of universal grammar that provides the ground rules for reasoning in whatever language one adopts, whereas grammar is particular to the language of a specific culture. In this way, grammar and logic are distinct sciences, one universal and one particular. Al-Farabi recognised that an understanding of logic was dependent upon how it is interpreted through the medium of one's chosen language. Al-Farabi followed in the footsteps of Aristotle's logic, arguing that logic helps distinguish truth from error and, as a guide, also indicates where to begin one's thought processes and how to reach final conclusions. Following Plato, al-Farabi holds that all true philosophers are charged with the task of communicating their philosophy to others and so the arts of rhetoric, poetics and dialectic, though not universal in the way logic is, are nonetheless essential elements of philosophy for they are the means by which the philosopher communicates with the vast majority of the people.

Al-Farabi's writings on logic provided him with a reputation among Muslim philosophers of the Middle Ages which, in the words of the philosopher of history **Ibn Khaldun**, justified giving the title to al-Farabi as the 'second teacher', second only to Aristotle himself. However, al-Farabi himself gave great importance to the field of political philosophy, and here it is the influence of Plato that shows through. Plato's concept of the perfect state ruled over by the Philosopher-Kings also, al-Farabi believed, fits in well with the *Shi'a* world-view with its emphasis on the authority of the Imam. The tenth century has been referred to as the Shi'a century as it was then in its ascendancy. Baghdad itself, the seat of the Caliph – the ruler of the *Sunni* Muslims – was being gradually taken over by a new Shi'a military dynasty, the Buyids, and during al-Farabi's lifetime the Twelfth Imam transferred from lesser occultation (*ghayba*) to greater occultation in 941, raising serious questions regarding religious and political authority.

Al-Farabi believed that the Prophets, including Muhammad, were first and foremost philosophers, for it was true philosophers – as opposed to those with faith – who have access to 'revelation' in the sense of knowledge of God. 'God', for al-Farabi, was equivalent to the Active Intellect, not unlike Plato's conception of the Form of the Good that is 'accessed' through reason. This view of God as 'Active Intellect' is derived from a Neo-platonic conception of God. Neo-platonism was founded by the Egyptian Plotinus (d. 270) and his disciples. It is best described as a brand of Greek philosophy that brings together the thought of Platonic, Aristotelian, Pythagorean and Stoic teachings and then recasts them with an Eastern religious and mystical world-view. The first encounter with Western philosophy for Arab Muslims was not the direct works of Plato or Aristotle, but rather Neo-platonism, which resulted from the capture of Alexandria in 641. Alexandria had become the cultural centre of the ancient world with its extensive libraries and universities. It was not surprising that when the Arabs first started to translate these ancient texts, there was some confusion over what the difference was between Plato, Aristotle and Neo-platonism, and authorship was also sometimes incorrect.

It is a very Neo-platonic conception of a God that is a Perfect Being who, being superabundantly good, 'emanates' this goodness in the same way the sun gives off rays. The result of this emanation is levels of creation, but these are not caused by God, rather they are a natural 'by-product'. Briefly put, the world of human beings rests fairly low in this hierarchical process of emanation but, nonetheless, the human soul is the seat of the Active Intellect and, therefore, even human beings have a 'spark' of the divine within them. The soul ultimately rests with the Active Intellect but is bound by the material body. Al-Farabi equates happiness with the soul's rejoining with the intelligible world but, to achieve this, al-Farabi did not believe in seclusion and asceticism, but that man was a 'political animal' who can only gain fulfilment through interaction with others. Hence personal fulfilment is only possible through societal fulfilment and this in itself is only possible if society is governed by those who have already attained such a state of well-being.

Following on from Aristotle, al-Farabi believed that political science was the master science, for its ultimate aim is true happiness. It therefore has a moral aspect as it is concerned with how we should live and what kind of society promotes well-being and fulfilment. In his best-known work, *al-Madina al-Fadila (On the Principles of the Views of the Inhabitants of the Virtuous City)*, written in 942–943, al-Farabi argues that political knowledge, that is the knowledge needed to produce the ideal state, can only be achieved through political science. Like Aristotle, al-Farabi equates the craft of politics with other crafts or skills in which a person can improve by learning the rights and wrongs of that craft. For example, a good doctor is one who is well practised in his craft and has learned the necessary knowledge. In the same way a good politician is one who is practised in his craft and has learned the 'knowledge' required to run the state. The problem, of course, is whether the knowledge required to run a good state really equates with the knowledge required to cure a sick person. This was a criticism levelled against both Plato and Aristotle, but al-Farabi, not unlike most Muslim philosophers of the time, uncritically accepted that the teachings of both Plato and Aristotle were right.

Again, like Plato, who believed that philosophy was only open to an elite and, therefore, the Philosopher-Kings would be a select few who would rule, al-Farabi made a clear distinction between those few who were capable of philosophy and the majority who needed religion. Al-Farabi, like Plato and the Shi'ite theologians, based leadership on knowledge (knowledge being understood as that which is infallible). Given that there is such a thing as 'truth', al-Farabi argued, and the best method of attaining this truth is through philosophy, then the philosophers are the best qualified to rule because they *know* how to rule (what is best for the people). This elitist view argues that the 'common people' do not have the mental capacity to understand the inner meaning of revelation and, therefore, God's true commands, for they can only understand the Qur'an at a literal level, rather than its symbolic, metaphorical meaning. The elite, being expert not only in the tools of philosophy, but also in their knowledge of the Islamic sciences of jurisprudence (*shari'a*), theology (*kalam*), and mysticism, are closer to a knowledge of God and, to some extent, 'partake' in God's will. This is a peculiarly Shi'a concept of authority in which the Imams, while not being prophets in the sense of bringing forth new revelations, are nonetheless guided by God, giving them immense power. But without the perfect ruler there can be no perfect city. Al-Farabi makes close reference to Plato's *Republic* in outlining the system of education required of those who are to rule, being taught the skills of persuasion and demonstrative knowledge, although al-Farabi does not engage in as much practical detail as Plato does. While the virtuous city, like Plato's Republic, is a moral and theoretical model, it is obvious that al-Farabi had in mind as his ideal state the Shi'a state ruled by the Imams although, for Plato, the ruler was essentially 'reason' rather than any particular culture or belief system. However, al-Farabi saw no contradiction here for religion, when understood correctly, equates with reason.

Al-Farabi's writings on logic and philosophy of language, particularly the importance of grammar in our understanding of our world, would not be out of place in the field of modern Anglo-American analytic philosophy and, more recently, this aspect of al-Farabi's philosophy (his works are still being translated into English) is being recognised as impressive. The reason for the high esteem he has among Islamic, Jewish and, to a lesser extent, Christian philosophers, is that what emerges from all his philosophy was his intent to communicate in a coherent and lucid fashion the many seemingly divergent beliefs. While the extent to which Platonic philosophy can really be blended with Shi'a Islam is debatable, the links he makes are not only intellectually fascinating, but have had practical implications in, for example, **al-Khomeini's** efforts to produce such a 'virtuous state' in Iran in the late twentieth century. Many Muslim philosophers have expressed their debt to al-Farabi, including **Ibn Sina** and **Ibn Rushd**.

Major works

Due to al-Farabi's popularity in the Western world there are many excellent English translations of his works.

On the Perfect State: (Mabadi Ara Ahl Al-Madinat Al-Fadilah), trans. R. Walzer, Chicago: Kazi Publications, 1997.
Al-Farabi's Philosophical Lexicon: English Translation, vol. 2, trans. and ed. Ilai Alon, Cambridge: E.J.W. Gibb Memorial Trust, 2002.

Further reading

There is considerable scholarship in this area. Below are some particularly insightful works.

Fakhry, Majid, *Al-Farabi, Founder of Islamic Neoplatonism: His Life, Works and Influence*, Oxford: Oneworld, 2002.
Galston, Miriam, *Politics and Excellence: Political Philosophy of Alfarabi*, Princeton, NJ: Princeton University Press, 1990.
Netton, I., *Al-Farabi and His School*, London: Routledge, 1992.

UBAYDALLAH 'AL-MAHDI' (c. 873–934)

Ubaydallah al-Mahdi is an enigmatic figure who was believed to be the '**Mahdi**' ('guided one') by his followers. A **Shi'a** Muslim, he was presented as the **Imam** who had come to lead the Muslim people to a new era of purity and peace. Together with the wily al-Shi'i, they conquered lands from Egypt in the West to the Sind province of India in the east in what became known as the Fatimid dynasty which existed from 969 until 1171.

Little is known of the mysterious figure who called himself Ubaydallah ('little slave of God') al-Mahdi (the Guided One). What is known is that he was born in Salamiyah in Syria in around 873. He claimed descent from the seventh Shi'a Imam, Ismail, which also goes back even further to **Ali**, the fourth Rightly-Guided Caliph, and his wife (as well as the Prophet **Muhammad**'s daughter) Fatima, although most **Sunni** authors think his genealogy is a fabrication, and that al-Mahdi was an impostor. Consequently, *Sunni* sources often insist on referring to him as Ubaydallah to emphasise this family dynasty. In fact, some have gone so far as to state that Ubaydallah is from Jewish parentage, although it was not uncommon for such accusations to be made of any obscure historical figure considered to be contentious.

To appreciate the importance of al-Mahdi, some background material is necessary in terms of, first, who the **Ismailis** were in the context of Shi'a Islam and, second, what were the historical conditions of the time in the region in question. We can then go on to look at al-Mahdi's life and the subsequent Fatimid doctrine that emerged.

A branch of the Ismailis are still in existence today as a wealthy merchant community led by the multi-millionaire, the Aga Khan. However, they were originally a revolutionary movement that engaged in assassinations and coups. At their peak, during the Fatimid dynasty (969–1171), they ruled an area from Egypt in the West to the Sind province of India in the East. The Ismailis are a Shi'a group, as distinct from the majority of Muslims who are *Sunni*. With the death of the fourth Rightly-Guided Caliph, Ali, in 661, the caliphate fell into the hands of the Umayyad dynasty (see **Mu'awiya**). However, their rule was disputed by those, called at this time 'Alids', who argued that the caliphate should go to Ali's direct descendants. During the reign of the Umayyad Caliph Yazid (r. 680–683), Ali's son Husayn led a revolt but he and his troops were massacred by the Umayyad army at Karbala in 680. The memory of this event and Husayn's 'martyrdom' are the essential paradigm for all Shi'a groups. The 'partisans' (*shia*) of Ali believed that the Umayyad had usurped the rightful heir and so they rejected the caliphate as a legitimate source of Islamic authority. In fact, the Shi'a believe that Ali should have succeeded Muhammad and thus not only do they reject Caliphs subsequent to Ali, but also the notion of the previous three 'Rightly-Guided' Caliphs (see **Abu Bakr**, and **Umar**).

This is the fundamental difference between Sunni and Shi'a; for the former we have the doctrine of the caliphate, for the latter the doctrine of the imamate. Whereas Caliphs are selected or elected, the Imam is a divinely-inspired, infallible, sinless, religious and political leader who must be a direct descendant of Ali who was the first Imam. Consequently, although Imams are not prophets, they are the next best thing and they possess incredible religious authority. However, the Shi'a disagree among themselves over succession, resulting in three major divisions: (1) the Zaydi; (2) the Imami (or Ithna Ashari); and (3) the Ismaili. Briefly, the Zaydi claimed that the grandson of Husayn, Zayd ibn Ali, was the fifth Imam, however, the majority Shi'a recognised Muhammad al-Baqir and his son Jafar al-Sadiq as rightful heirs. The Zaydis were the first Shi'a to gain political independence when they founded a dynasty in Tabaristan on the Caspian Sea in 864. Another Zaydi state was established in Yemen in 893 and existed until as recently as 1963.

In the eighth century, a dispute occurred over who the sixth imam, Jafar al-Sadiq, designated as his heir. The majority, which became known as the Imamis, accepted his younger son Musa al-Kazim as the seventh Imam, while a minority believed it to be his older son, Ismail. The Imams are also known as the 'Twelvers' because their line of Imams continued until the twelfth imam who 'disappeared' (*ghayba*, or state of occultation) in 874 and will return one day as the Mahdi (guided one or 'expected one'). The Ismailis, on the other hand, are called the 'Seveners' because they trace their lineage via the seventh imam whom they regard as Ismail. To complicate things even further, there are divisions also among the Ismailis themselves: some believe that the Imamate effectively came to an end with the death of Ismail, others – like the Imamis – believe he has disappeared also but will return as the Mahdi, and yet another group accepted Ismail's son, Muhammad, as the Imam and so the line continued.

First reports of al-Mahdi occur in 902 when he left Salamiyah with his wife, and his son al-Qasim, and headed through Palestine towards Egypt. With him was also his small number of disciples for he was already the leader of a small sect in Syria. The reason for his journey to Egypt was because he had received a message from an Ismaili missionary by the name of Abu 'Abd Allah Husayn, who was also known as al-Shi'i ('the Shi'ite') and it is really due to the latter's remarkable political and military skills that the Fatimid dynasty came into being. However, al-Shi'i also realised that a successful state must have strong legitimacy, hence the need for al-Mahdi. As is the case with all Shi'a groups, it must be remembered that they believe that their Imam is the rightful ruler of *all* Muslims. He is the direct descendant not only of Ali, but of the Prophet Muhammad himself. Al-Shi'i presented Ubaydallah as 'the Mahdi', the true Imam who had come to save the people and establish a pure Muslim community on earth. By all accounts, al-Shi'i, originally a Twelver Shi'a, proved to be a charming, charismatic and convincing character and took on the John the Baptist role of heralding the Mahdi with amazing vigour and propagandist skill. Seemingly single-handed, al-Shi'i set out to convert North Africa to Ismailism.

The Africa to which al-Shi'i preached was a veritable mess of mini states of various forms of Sunni, Shi'a and other religions. Lacking unity, it was also, on the whole, unstable and economically impoverished. Al-Shi'i, in around 895, went first to the Ketama Berbers in North Africa. They were Shi'a Muslims on the whole, but also had a strong Gnostic tradition, so that much of al-Shi'i's teaching would have had a familiar ring to it. The Ketama, a group of whom al-Shi'i had initially met while in Mecca, occupied an area in what is today north-east Algeria. Al-Shi'i circulated a *hadith* (a saying of the Prophet Muhammad) which said that 'the sun shall rise in the West' and he also came up with another that would have had particular appeal to the Ketama, which read, 'the Mahdi shall appear in a land far away from his to be supported by a people of righteousness, a people with a name derived from *kitman* ['secrecy'].' They were told that this Mahdi could perform miracles, including raising the dead, and he was currently on his way. To prepare for his coming, the Ketama must, said al-Shi'i, take up arms and engage in military missionary activity to convert the people in preparation for his coming.

Al-Mahdi, in fact, had entered Egypt disguised as a merchant, but the Abbasid dynasty had their spies. He had to keep travelling but was eventually caught and thrown into prison in Morocco in 905. However, al-Shi'i had somehow managed to muster, so it is said, some 200,000 men, and tribes soon succumbed to his message, either through gentle or less gentle persuasion. In 909, al-Shi'i and his Ismaili army were at the gates of the mightiest fortress on the whole continent, the still surviving incredible walled city of al-Qayrawan in northern Tunisia. It was the capital of the Sunni Aghlabid dynasty and its king, Ziyadat-Allah III, fled the city and with him went the end of his dynasty. Al-Shi'i easily took the city and installed himself in the royal palace and spent the next three months enjoying the life of a king. It was quite possible that al-Shi'i had second thoughts about freeing al-Mahdi at all, but the failure of his messianic promises would no doubt cause his followers to grow restless and perceive al-Shi'i as a usurper. So al-Shi'i headed off with his army to Morocco, to the city of Sijilmasah where Ubaydallah was in prison. The city fell and al-Mahdi, together with his son, was released. There followed forty days of celebration.

They returned to al-Qayrawan and al-Mahdi now lived in the royal palace together with his family. His son was made heir apparent and there now existed a new force in Africa to rival the declining power of Sunni Islam. Al-Shi'i was put in charge of military operations. In some respects, al-Qayrawan was handicapped by the title

'Mahdi' because of the huge expectations laid upon him, and so he did not engage in any further missionary activity but rather employed a process of conciliation and consolidation, making use of the administrative system that was already there (consisting largely of Sunni Muslims) and not insisting upon conversion. Perhaps deliberately, Ubaydallah made as little use of his Mahdi label as possible, but this also meant that some started to question whether he was the Mahdi at all, and some would ask for 'signs', for the miracles he was able to perform. Al-Mahdi suspected al-Shi'i, who had fallen out of the limelight, of being the initiator of such rumours and, for all his trouble, al-Mahdi. had al-Shi'i executed. This did not suppress the doubts over Ubaydallah's leadership, however. The Ketama especially, who had a strong affiliation with al-Shi'i, rebelled, while other tribes presented their own mahdis.

Feeling insecure, al-Mahdi, in 912, built a new fortress and capital called al-Madiyya, 16 miles south-east of al-Qayrawan, a virtually impregnable fortress with high walls, metal doors and deep moats. A common tactic to suppress internal rebellions is to go to war externally and so al-Mahdi turned his armies upon the last **Abbasid** Sunni stronghold of Egypt. His first attempt at its conquest was in 914, but reinforcements were sent from Baghdad so that Ubaydallah was forced to retreat. Two years later a second attempt was made and there followed a four-year war during which what parts of Egypt Ubaydallah had managed to occupy were taken back by the Abbasids. The Mahdi never succeeded in taking Egypt, but it was to fall to the Ismailis fifty years later.

Aged 61, Ubaydallah died in al-Madiyya. Undoubtedly much of his success is due to al-Shi'i, but al-Mahdi was to reign for twenty-five years and, despite insurrections in his early days, he was able in time to father the Fatimid dynasty that was well ordered and prosperous, as well as uniting what was a warring, tribal, fractious people. In 969 Egypt was conquered by his great-grandson al-Mu'izz and Cairo became the new capital, and, under his son al-'Aziz (r. 965–996), the Fatimid Empire reached its zenith. The Fatimid dynasty was a strong centralised monarchy which ruled across North Africa, Egypt, Sicily, Syria, Persia, Western Arabia, and Sind province in India. It was officially a Shi'a empire, although the majority of its people remained Sunni. It was an immense cultural and commercial success, and the well-known religious centre, the Al-Azhar in Cairo, acted as the university for religious scholars. The Fatimids even managed to briefly occupy Baghdad but they never succeeded in ruling over the whole of the Muslim world. The end of the Fatimid dynasty came abruptly when, in 1171, the great **Salah al-Din** conquered Egypt and restored it to the Sunni rule of the Saljuk.

Further reading

Aside from any history of Islam (see, for example, the entry on **Mu'awiya** for general books) available, the two below will provide a more focused account. The first is a translation of a first-hand account, the 'Kitab al-Munazarat' (The Book of Discussions) by Ibn al-Haytham who reports on the thoughts and activities of al-Shi'i.

Ibn al-Haytham, *The Advent of the Fatimids: A Contemporary Shi'i Witness*, ed. and trans. Wilfred Madelung and Paul Walker, London: I.B. Tauris, 2001.

Lewis, Bernard, *Origins of Isma'ilism: A Study of the Historical Background of the Fatimid Caliphate*, London: Ams Pr Publishing, 1986.

ABU AL-HASAN ALI AL-MAWARDI (972–1058)

Al-Mawardi was a great jurist, sociologist and an expert in political science. He was a jurist in the school of Islamic jurisprudence (*fiqh*) and his book *On the Ordinances of Government* is held in high regard to this day. It has long been recognised as a classic in its field, much discussed by Arab authors and orientalists, as well as being quoted in courses on Islamic law and government. He wrote on many subjects, including Qur'anic interpretation, religion, government, public and constitutional law, language and ethics.

Abu al-Hasan Ali Al-Mawardi was born in Basra, Iraq, in 972. The son of a rose-water merchant, he was educated first in Basrah where, after completion of his basic education, he learned Islamic jurisprudence from the jurist Abu al-Wahid al-Simari. He then went to Baghdad for advanced studies under Sheikh Abd al-Hamid and Abdallah al-Baqi. He proved himself to be skilled in jurisprudence, as well as philosophy, political science and literature. He was appointed as a judge (*qadi*) and gradually was promoted to the highly prestigious position of Chief Judge at Baghdad. The **Abbasid** Caliph al-Qaim bi-amr Allah appointed him as his itinerant ambassador and sent him to a number of countries as the head of special missions. In this capacity he played a key role in establishing harmonious relations between the declining Abbasid Caliphate and the rising powers of **Shi'a** Buyids and Saljuk Turks. He was still in Baghdad when it was taken over by Buyids. Al-Mawardi died in 1058.

In the light of the political turmoil of the time with various dynasties fighting over rule of the Muslim people, the perennial topic of who has the right to rule – a topic that had been of concern since the first Muslim century on the death of the Prophet **Muhammad** – was particularly pertinent. Aside from the question of who should rule, the issue was also of the limits of power and the duty of the Muslim to be obedient towards the ruler. Whereas Shi'a Islam centred authority in such charismatic and infallible figures as *Imams* who could make new laws, *Sunni* Islam had gradually moved to the belief that the Caliph was head of the Muslim community (*umma*) but was by no means an interpreter of the faith, hence the need for clear Islamic law (*shari'a*) as well as a counsel of religious scholars, the *ulama*, to defend the faith against unIslamic practices. In theory, then, the Caliph could only act within the bounds of *shari'a*, of God's law. The possibility existed that a Caliph could be unrighteous, in which case it was the right and the duty of Muslims to overthrow that ruler. This argument had been used by the Abbasid dynasty to overthrow in 749 the **Umayyad** caliphate which, they argued, had abandoned their Islamic principles. The Abbasids, for their part, were constantly at pains to legitimise their own rule, although the same accusation could easily be levelled against them in most cases.

It was not until the tenth century that the fullest formulation of the theory of the caliphate was developed. The Abbasid dynasty was, at this time, only too aware of the threat to their legitimacy posed by rising powers. The creation of the Shi'a Fatimid Caliph in Cairo, together with the existence of the Umayyad caliphate now residing in Andalusia, raised the question of not only who was the legitimate Caliph, but whether there could exist more than one Caliph at a time. In addition, within Baghdad itself, a military dynasty called the Buyids had effectively seized power, keeping the Caliph as a symbol of unity, despite the fact that the Buyids were Shi'a sympathisers. Further, another force was on the horizon: the Saljuk Turks, who had succeeded in conquering Baghdad during al-Mawardi's lifetime.

It was in this context that the most famous theoretical elucidation and justification of the caliphate was written by the Shafi'ite scholar (one of the four classical legal schools: see **al-Shafi'i**) al-Mawardi. His main political work, *On the Principles of Power* (also often translated as *On the Ordinances of Government*, *Kitab al-Ahkam al-Sultaniyya*) was written between 1045 and 1058 which was the same time the Saljuk Turks came to power in Baghdad. In this treatise he expresses his preference for a strong caliphate and one that is based on revelation. Hence his concept of the Caliph is not unlike that of the Christian Pope, although also able to exercise political as well as religious authority. Here al-Mawardi was criticising the view of philosophers that reason alone was sufficient for an understanding of how to rule a state. For al-Mawardi, reason – being a human construct – has its limitations whereas revelation is God's word and, logically, knowledge of what God requires of man is greater than what reason requires. Islamic leadership cannot be deduced from reason. Like the Christian thinker, St Thomas Aquinas, al-Mawardi saw a direct link between the divinely-revealed order and political order.

In defining the relationship between the Caliph and his political minister, the vizier (or prime minister), al-Mawardi recognises the political reality of the times in which the vizier – whether he bears the title of Sultan, Amir, or another – would frequently possess far more power than the Caliph. While al-Mawardi notes that in some cases the position of vizier is conferred by the Caliph to perform specific political – and even certain religious – duties, the possibility that a vizier may come to power by force should be permissible provided the vizier acknowledges the Caliph as the leader of the Muslims, even in a nominal sense, and also rules according to Islamic law. However, it is not made clear who is to decide whether the vizier is acting justly or not, and there is no indication as to whether this is an option open to the Caliph, or even if the Caliph has the option to refuse to recognise the authority of a conquering vizier.

Al-Mawardi hoped that the power of any vizier could be checked by the establishment of what he called the Redress of Grievances court consisting of judges appointed by the caliphate. While *shari'a* was one way of checking the power of a vizier, al-Mawardi was aware that *shari'a* could not always provide the answers to changing circumstances. The Redress of Grievances court, however, did not operate by *shari'a*, but actually had much wider and more unfettered powers than that. However, while in principle the court may provide an additional check, in practice, it was unlikely to do so for it raised the issue of how 'Islamic' any such court would be if it is not within the confines of *shari'a*. Also it is unlikely that any powerful vizier would willingly allow a Caliph *carte blanche* to appoint his own court to pronounce whether the vizier was behaving himself. In reality, what happened – especially in the case of the Ottoman Empire – was that the vizier merely gave himself more of the Caliph's functions until the title of 'Sultan-Caliph' was held by one and the same person.

Here al-Mawardi was reacting against a trend towards a separation between secular power and religious power by recombining them into the authority of the Sultan-Caliph. This ruler acts as the fulcrum of the socio-political system by managing the Muslim populace as well as providing religious dispensation. The Sultan-Caliph, therefore, has authority over every aspect of people's lives, as he states in his *Principles of Power*:

> God ... ordained for the People (*umma*) a Leader (*caliph*) through whom He provided for the Deputyship of the Prophet and through whom He protected the Religious Association; and he entrusted government (*al-siyasa*) to him, so that the management of affairs should proceed (on the basis of) right religion ... The Leadership became the principle upon which the bases of the Religious Association were established, by which the well-being of the People was regulated, and affairs of common interest were made stable, and form which particular Public Functions emanated.[1]

Like so many other Muslim scholars, he was a polymath who wrote voluminously. Another significant work of his was *Kitab Adab al-dunya was 'l-din* (*On the Conduct of Religion in the World*) where he provides an insightful summary of the social and political order, or 'worldly order' (*salah al-dunya*). He outlines six sources of world order. First of all is the need for an established religion which keeps man's passions in check. Second, he stresses the need for a powerful ruler (sultan) because religion on its own is not sufficient to prevent people from committing evil acts. Third is the need for justice towards equals, subordinates and superiors. Fourth, law and order, and fifth, economic prosperity. Finally, he points out that people require hope and progress. Politics, economics, religion and law are thus all interdependent and are required for solidarity.

Al-Mawardi has been considered as one of the most famous thinkers in political science in the Middle Ages. His original work influenced the development of this science, together with the science of sociology, which was further developed later on by **Ibn Khaldun**. Al-Mawardi's *Principles of Power*, in particular, became widely accepted as an authoritative account of Sunni doctrine on the power of the ruler and, in fact, helped legitimise political authority, especially under the Ottoman Empire.

Major works

The Ordinances of Government: Al-Ahkam As-Sultaniyyah W'at Wilayat Al Dinniyya, trans. Wafaa Wahba, Reading: Garnet Publishing, 2000.

Further reading

While there is no one single work on al-Mawardi and his thought, there are a number of good books on Islamic political thought during this particular period that make reference to al-Mawardi.

Arnold, Thomas W., *The Caliphate*, Oxford: Clarendon Press, 1924.

Gibb, H.A.R., *Studies on the Civilisation of Islam*, Princeton, NJ: Princeton University Press, 1962.

Lambton, Ann K.S., *State and Government in Medieval Islam: An Introduction to the Study of Islamic Political Thought: The Jurists*, Oxford: Oxford University Press, 1981.

Note

1 Quoted in Lambton (1981), p. 85.

ABU ALI IBN SINA ('AVIRENNA') (980–1037)

Better known as Avicenna in the West, Ibn Sina's contribution to philosophy and medicine was immense. To this day, in Iran especially, his philosophy continues to be influential, while his research in medicine remained standard teaching until the seventeenth century. Due to Ibn Sina, much of the classical learning of Greece was pre-served during the European Dark Ages when such knowledge would otherwise have been lost. He was an outstanding philosopher and physician and in the West he was given the title 'Prince of Physi-cians'. He influenced Christian scholarship by bringing the Greek philosopher Aristotle's *Metaphysics* to their attention, and he had a significant influence on the thought of the great Jewish thinker Moses Maimonides (d. 1204).

Ibn Sina was born in the small village of Afshanah near Bukhara in Western Uzbekistan. His father was a commander in the nearby citadel. Bukhara, at the time, was a leading centre of Islamic learning under the Arabs and the Persian Samanid dynasty, and Ibn Sina's family moved to this city when he was just a young boy. His father became initiated into the **Ismaili** tradition and he introduced his son to it as well. Ibn Sina was a precocious child, having memorised the Qur'an by the age of 10 and as a child was already familiar with many of the great works of Arabic literature. If we are to believe Ibn Sina's autobiography, he says that by the age of 14 he knew more than his teachers and, by the age of 18, he had mastered a number of the sciences, including medicine which he claimed he had found easy.

Apparently, at this young age, he had already begun practising his medical knowledge on trusting individuals. One such patient was a Samanid prince whom Ibn Sina succeeded in curing. As a reward, the prince allowed Ibn Sina ready access to his considerable royal library so that Ibn Sina could pursue his own independent studies in law, medicine and metaphysics. It seems that he had something of a photographic memory for he had devoured the whole collection of works within eighteen months. In the course of these years he gained a thorough grasp of Aristotle's *Metaphysics* with the aid of a commentary by **al-Farabi** and he wrote his own book on philosophy when he was 21. Ibn Sina's autobiography, a rare genre in itself at the time, was communicated to a close friend of his when he was 32 years old and offers an interesting insight into the mind of a young genius. As this example of his method of study illustrates:

> Whenever a perplexing problem confronted me or a middle term in a syllogism escaped me, I would repair to the mosque, there to pray and implore the All-Creator until the hidden was revealed and the difficult eased. Returning home I would at night set a lamp before me and engage in reading and writing. Whenever sleep or fatigue came near overcoming me, I would resort to wine and drink until my strength was fully recovered. Thereupon back to reading I would go. In case slumber did overtake me, I would go on in my sleep considering what I was considering before. In fact, many a problem was thus solved. Thus I continued until I had mastered the totality of sciences. My comprehension of them then [at age 18] attained the limits of human possibility. All that I learned during that period is precisely what I know now.[1]

Such over-confidence in his own abilities, however, was compromised when confronted with Aristotle's *Metaphysics*, a work which Ibn Sina had to read some forty times still without being able to understand it. It was not until he came across al-Farabi's commentary on it that he began to make sense of the work. It signalled a turning point in his studies, devoting more of his energies to philosophy, especially the branch known as Neo-platonism.

In terms of earning a living, he was enlisted into royal service, becoming a minister in the Samanid government. However, whereas the Samanids were relatively enlightened and cultured, their power was on the wane and, in 999, Bukhara was conquered by a Turkish dynasty known as the Ghaznawids. This dynasty was far more orthodox and ruthless, with little respect for learning. Having lost his royal patronage, and his father having died, Ibn Sina fled and led largely an insecure existence, often having to pack his bags and move to the next city and another royal court and even spending some time in prison. His precarious existence often depended on his abilities to cure the various rulers of a selection of maladies. He earned his living as a court physician by day, and then at night he wrote the great works that made such a valuable contribution to the corpus of knowledge. Such a prolific output is even more outstanding when it is remembered that, for the most part, he had to rely upon his own memory as a source of reference. However, what he produced was not merely a copy of what he had memorised, for his intellect lies in synthesising the works of classical Greek philosophy especially, with the realities of the world he lived in at the time. He spent the last fourteen years of his life in the not always secure position as physician in the Buyid court in Hamadan in Western Iran. The Buyid dynasty were **Shi'a** Persians who claimed descent from the pre-Islamic kings of Persia and for many years had ruled Baghdad with the caliphs as little more than symbolic puppets of their regime. During this time, Ibn Sina achieved the rank of vizier, a ministerial position of considerable power, although, again, this position was not always secure, spending occasions in prison. It was only his abilities as a physician that would save him. He died in 1037 at the age of 57 following an illness contracted three years earlier while on campaign with the ruler.

The fact that Ibn Sina did not always seem to get on with people indicates a man of intellectual arrogance, who was also the subject of jealousy among the conspiring courts for the favouritism he was given. In addition, he was often suspected of heresy, which was not an uncommon accusation levelled at those influenced by the liberal-minded Isamili sect. He was something of a recluse who sought solace in wine and women.

Unfortunately, not all of Ibn Sina's works have survived the various conflicts and some important works were lost while Ibn Sina was still alive. In the amount of writings he equals that of **al-Kindi** and more modern biographies catalogue over 270 works attributed to him, of which some two hundred have survived. Three encyclopaedic works stand out, two in philosophy entitled *al-Shifa* (*Healing*) and *al-Isharat w-al-Tanbihat* (*Directives and Remarks*), and one in medicine, *Qanun* (*Canon*). *Healing* is the longest work he wrote and, in fact, is probably the longest book of its kind written by one man, consisting of four major books on logic, physics, mathematics and metaphysics. His

Canon records the accumulated contemporary learning on this topic and his own discoveries and experiences. Of immense range, for almost seven hundred years it remained the single most famous and influential book on medicine. His *Directives and Remarks* is his most personal work, in which he depicts the stages of enlightenment for the mystic.

By speculating on philosophical matters, Ibn Sina inevitably roused the suspicion of orthodox Muslims who regarded the subject as potentially harmful to the faith and prone to heresy due to the fact that it drew on non-Islamic sources, notably translations of the Greek greats Plato and Aristotle. Of particular interest to Ibn Sina, as it was to Aristotle, was the nature of being (ontology). For Ibn Sina, God was pure being, necessary and self-subsistent. He is the creator of the universe and, therefore, transcends it. Whereas Aristotle refers to an abstract God as a Prime Mover, the God of Ibn Sina is more the Semitic God that not only Islam, but Judaism and Christianity, could closely relate to. An example of Ibn Sina's reasoning is particularly enlightening:

> Every series arranged in the order of causes and effects – whe-ther finite or infinite – if it includes only what is caused, clearly needs an external cause linked to it at one end of the series. It is equally clear that if the series does not include anything uncaused, this is the end of the series, its limit. Every series therefore ends at the Being, which is necessary by itself.[2]

This passage is most remarkable in that, although it does borrow heavily from Aristotle (and let us rightly acknowledge the importance of the Greek philosophers here), it also mirrors what has become known as the cosmological argument for the existence of God, especially the 'Five Ways' presented by the Christian scholastic St Thomas Aquinas over two hundred years later.

Ibn Sina was influenced by Plato in his view of the dual nature of man, as both body and soul. Man's soul is a substance in itself, inde-pendent of the body and surviving after the death of the material substance. The soul, then, is immaterial, incorruptible, and immortal. Unlike Plato, however, Ibn Sina rejects the notion of reincarnation, that the soul enters another body, although – against accepted Muslim orthodoxy – Ibn Sina also rejected the belief in bodily resurrection.

The role of the prophet was less clear in Greek philosophy, where prophethood was not an institutionalised doctrine. Ibn Sina, however, argued for its necessity and, in line with the belief of the philosopher al-Kindi, he held that a prophet represents the highest, most perfect state of man. A prophet is endowed with superior intelligence, a vivid imagination, and the ability to lead. He is the receptor of knowledge in a sudden intuitive manner, rather than through the normal learning process. The function of a prophet is to communicate revelation, but, importantly, he is also its interpreter for a people who can only understand God's knowledge through the use of symbols, parables and metaphors. On the thorny issue of free will versus determinism, Ibn Sina adopted the free will approach in line with the view that man is responsible for his own actions. God, for His part, maintains overall control of major forces, but leaves the details to mankind. Again, this led to condemnation by many orthodox who argued that free will undermined God's power and knowledge.

Ibn Sina is better known, certainly in the Muslim world, as a physician rather than a philosopher. There are over forty medical works to his name and, in his *Canon* especially, we have a wonderful synthesis of medical knowledge from the Greek as well as Indo–Persian and Syro–Arabic canons, aside from his own experience and experimentation. It remained an authoritative work in the East until at least the twelfth century, while in Europe this work was the standard medical text until the seventeenth. What is most remarkable about this work is its holistic approach to health, recognising, for example, the influence of climate and diet on a person's physical condition. Consequently, it is not uncommon to hear Ibn Sina still referenced in modern health guides.

With Ibn Sina, the series of eastern Muslim philosophers, generated some two hundred years earlier under the patronage of **al-Ma'mun**, comes to an end. Arab intellectual activity was now focused on theological and legal fields, culminating in that other great system-atiser **al-Ghazali**. Al-Ghazali wrote the celebrated *Tahafut al-Falasifa* (*Incoherence of the Philosophers*), in which he accused philosophers of committing heresy in their works. Al-Ghazali was particularly critical of Ibn Sina on three particular issues. First, Ibn Sina's view that only the soul survives after death, whereas al-Ghazali would point to Qur'anic references that state *bodily* resurrection. Second, Ibn Sina, by stating that God let mankind have free will, raised the problem for al-Ghazali who, again, by referring to the Qur'an, points out that God is concerned with every single detail of the world (that is, not just 'universals', but also 'particulars'), even the activities of an ant. Third, Ibn Sina had held that the universe is eternal and not created 'out of nothing' (*ex nihilo*) whereas al-Ghazali argued that no Muslim has ever supported such a view.

Whereas philosophy declined in the East, it began to emerge from the Dark Ages in the West, and one philosopher by the name of **Ibn Khaldun**, from North Africa, acknowledged the influence of Ibn Sina. More generally, Ibn Sina's contribution rests in tackling the problem of relating Greek philosophy to monotheistic beliefs. While some may argue that the two systems are incompatible, Ibn Sina made an influential attempt to marry the two, acknowledging the Islamic decree to seek knowledge everywhere: it would be a foolish man who did not seek to understand and make use of the wisdom of the Greeks, even if this did lead to intellectual conflicts with religion. St Thomas Aquinas (d. 1274) has already been mentioned as someone influenced by Ibn Sina, but also the English philosopher and scientist Roger Bacon (d. 1294) considered Ibn Sina to be the greatest philosopher after Aristotle. And, while it is debatable as to the extent to which Ibn Sina was a practising *Sufi* (a Muslim mystic), the last three chapters of his *Directives* are devoted to thirty-two titles on Sufism and he emphasises the importance of prayer and contemplation of God with the vision of God as the ultimate goal. Hence, Ibn Sina helped to open the doors to the philosophy of Illumination (*hikmat alishraq*) inaugurated by his follower **Suhrawardi** (d. 1191).

Major works

Because of his importance in the West, a number of his works are available in English, especially his medical texts. The first two are expensive works, the first of them currently retailing at £145.

The Propositional Logic: A Translation from Al-Shifa': Al-Qiyas, with Introduction, Commentary and Glossary by Nabil Shehaby (Synthese Historical Library), Berlin: Kluwer Academic Publishers, 1973.
Canon of Medicine, Chicago: Abjad Book Designers and Builders, 1999.
The Metaphysics of the Healing, trans. Michael E. Marmura, Utah: FARMS, 2004.

Further reading

There are many good books on Ibn Sina to choose from. The following are all by recognised scholars and are particularly illuminating.

Afnan, S.M., *Avicenna: His Life and Works*, Westport, CT: Greenwood Press, 1980.
Goodman, L.E., *Avicennna*, London: Routledge, 1992.
Rahman, F., *Avicenna's Psychology*, New York: Hyperion, 1981.

Notes

1 *Al-Qifti, Ta'rikh al-Hukama*, ed. by Julius Lippert (Leipzig, 1903), p. 415.
2 *Directives and Remarks*, ed. by Salayman Dunya, parts 3–4 (Cairo, 1958), p. 455.

ABU HAMID MUHAMMAD AL-GHAZALI
(1058–1111)

The theologian, jurist, philosopher, and mystic al-Ghazali is universally known as the 'proof of Islam' (*hujja al-islam*) and the great 'renewer' (**mujtahid**) of the faith. Much of this is due to his attempt to synthesise the three main strands of Islamic rationality: theoretical and philosophical enquiry, juridical legislation and mystical practice. His importance to Islamic thought lies in his skills in redirecting and reinvigorating Sunni religious thought in the aftermath of the **Shi'a** intellectual dominance of the previous century. His life and writings have been subject to more study in the Western world than probably any other Muslim, with the exception, of course, of the Prophet **Muhammad**.

The world of Islam in which al-Ghazali was born was one of political and religious turbulence. The Islamic world was broken up between the **Umayyad** dynasty ruling in Spain, the Shi'a Fatimid dynasty in North Africa and beyond, and then there was the aging and ailing **Abbasid** dynasty which reigned from Baghdad but no longer ruled. Baghdad, only three years before al-Ghazali was born, had been conquered by Saljuk Turks and, previous to that, the nominally Shi'a dynasty of the Buyids had ruled in Baghdad for over a century. The Abbasid Caliphs, who were **Sunnis**, were kept as the symbolic and unifying head of the Muslim world, but were essentially prisoners in their own palaces. The tenth century, therefore, has been called the Shi'a century. Although Islamdom no longer functioned as a single political unit, it was by no means in decline. In fact, rather than one capital in Baghdad, there were now several great cultural centres such as Cairo under the Fatimids, and Cordoba under the Umayyads. The eleventh century, under the Saljuk Turks, was to witness the re-emergence of Sunni Islam as a force, and it was in this historical and intellectual context that al-Ghazali inherited and operated.

Al-Ghazali was born in 1058 in the Iranian city of Tus, in the province of Khurasan. This small town is now in ruins, destroyed in the fourteenth century, but in al-Ghazali's time it was a thriving place. His father and his grandfather before him were wool-spinners (Arabic '*ghazzal*') and he belonged to an unlearned but devout family. His brother, Ahmad Ghazali, went on to become a famous **Sufi** (Muslim mystic) preacher and scholar, and Abu Hamid al-Ghazali himself received Sufi instruction in his hometown by a family friend who was a Sufi. As a teenager, al-Ghazali made a point of travelling to be instructed by other learned figures; in particular, he was attracted to the respected theologian al-Juwayni who resided in Nishapur, 30 miles south-west of Tus. This *imam* (religious teacher) agreed to be al-Ghazali's teacher. Al-Juwayni held a chair at the newly founded Nizamiyya school which had been established by the celebrated Nizam al-Mulk, vizier to the Saljuk Sultan Malikshah. This vizier made a point of establishing many new schools in an effort to renew Sunni Islam, and these institutions provided free tuition, board and lodging. Here he spent eight years, from 1077–1085, studying the teachings of the Ash'ari (see **al-Ash'ari**) doctrines of *kalam* (theology) as well as philosophy, logic and the natural sciences. While studying, he taught part-time as al-Juwayni's assistant, which, it seems, led to the latter feeling jealous about al-Ghazali's greater intelligence and popularity as a teacher.

In 1085, al-Ghazali went to Baghdad and joined the court of Nizam al-Mulk, who, though a vizier, was effectively a monarch in all but name, and at the height of his power. Realising the importance of having the religious authorities on your side, Nizam lavished his patronage on religious leaders, built grand Sufi lodges and established theological colleges, all of which were named after him. Al-Ghazali became a close friend of the vizier and was appointed to teach Shafi'i jurisprudence (see **al-Shafi'i**, founder of one of the four main Sunni schools of law) at the Nizamiyya school in Baghdad. The popular new teacher rapidly acquired a large student following and, in 1091, was appointed professor of theology at the college. Al-Ghazali was considered as living an exemplary Muslim life, yet the man in his thirties was riddled by doubts at the time of his greatest success:

> I considered the circumstances of my life, and realised that I was caught in a veritable thicket of attachments. I also considered my activities, of which the best was my teaching and lecturing, and realised that in them I was dealing in sciences that were unimportant and contributed nothing to the attainment of eternal life. After that I examined my motive in my work of teaching, and realised that it was not a pure desire for the things of God, but that the impulse moving me ... was the desire for an influential position and public recognition.[1]

Every morning he longed to leave Baghdad and the trappings of his career, but he found he could not tear himself away from the luxuries of his life:

For nearly six months beginning with Rajab 488 [July, 1095], I was continuously tossed about between the attractions of worldly desires and the impulses towards eternal life. In that month the matter ceased to be one of choice and became one of compulsion. God caused my tongue to dry up so that I was prevented from lecturing.[2]

This points to a mental and emotional crisis for al-Ghazali and essentially made the decision for him to leave his teaching position, for he physically could not teach any longer, even if he tried. He then took up the life of a wandering Sufi for the next ten years. He went to Syria and Palestine, and made a pilgrimage to the two holiest cities of Mecca and Medina. He led the life of an ascetic, wearing coarse and shabby clothing and sleeping in the mosque. Through abstinence, self-discipline, prayer and meditation he found the peace of mind that his material success had not given him. In 1106, he was persuaded by the new Seljuq vizier Fakhr al-Mulk to return to teaching at the Nizamiyya Madrasa (religious school) in Nishapur. He remained there for little more than two years, retiring in 1109 to his home town of Tus where he died two years later in 1111.

Al-Ghazali was a prolific writer, with over four hundred titles to his name. Some of these are no doubt of dubious authorship and a number are short essays. However, he seems to have covered virtually every discipline of learning known at the time, including poetry and music. His best-known, and largest, work is *Ihya' 'Ulum al-Din* (*The Revival of the Religious Sciences*). Written after his return from his ten-year sojourn, this work presents the relationship between the inner and outer life, between that of being a good Muslim in daily life (that is, following Islamic law or **shari'a**) and of pursuing spiritual needs (Sufism). In his view, the essence of the human being is the soul (*nafs*) which in its original state – that is, before being attached to the body – is a pure, angelic and eternal substance. Through reason, the soul has the potential to know the essence of things and knowledge of God, but to achieve this potential it must attach itself to a body, for the body is the vehicle that carries the soul on its journey to God. However, while the soul is pure in its original state, the body is a corrupting influence as it succumbs to anger, desire and evil. Consequently, the soul, though still possessing its divine elements, also has 'animal' elements. Therefore, to perfect the soul, the person must subordinate the animal qualities and pursue the virtues of temperance, courage, wisdom and justice. This can be achieved through Sufi practices which shut the gate to worldly desires. However, al-Ghazali points out that it is still important to engage in outer acts (*zahir*), especially the rituals associated with Islam such as pilgrimage, prayer, ablutions, alms, fasting, reading the Qur'an, following the *shari'a*, and so on. The inner activities of abstinence, meditation, and so on that are engaged in by the mystic, inform the outer activities of all Muslims. The mystical insight gives the believer a greater understanding into the more ritual aspects, rather than simply conducting the rituals without meaning. In this journey of the soul we can see al-Ghazali's own personal quest.

The *Revival* soon became a great classic of Muslim literature, comparable to the Christian theologian Thomas Aquinas' *Summa Theologica* in respect of the believer's response and love of it. Scholars have compared its greatness as second only to the Qur'an. Much of its attraction lies in the beauty of the writing, for al-Ghazali was not only a good teacher, he was also a first-rate writer. His style is lucid, and he uses anecdotes and parables to illustrate his teaching. For example, he compares the self-deluded man to a gardener who is content with pulling out the weeds yet leaving the network of roots underground intact.

In the same way his *Revival* is compared to *Summa Theologica*, his *al-Munqidh min al-Dalal* (*Deliverance from Error*), is comparable to St Augustine's *Confessions* in that it presents us with a fascinating autobiographical sketch which was a rare form of literature in the Arab world at the time. An early work, *Maqasid al-Falasifah* (*The Aim of Philosophers*) is a study of the work of Muslim philosophers, notably that of **al-Farabi** (d. 950) and **Ibn-Sina** (d. 1037), but his critique of these individuals in particular is reserved for his celebrated work, *Tahafut al-Falasifa* (*The Incoherence of Philosophers*) written just before he left his teaching post to go into retreat. There had for some time been a recognised tension between philosophy (*falsafa*), with its emphasis on truth through reason, and theology (*kalam*) which points to revelation as the primary source of truth. Al-Ghazali set out to demonstrate that reason does not in all cases lead to the ultimate truth and that a transcendent God cannot be known by rational insight, although he would employ Aristotelian logic to demonstrate his own arguments. He acknowledged the importance of philosophy for the study of nature and mathematics, but he argued that revelation was the most important source in religious matters. Likewise, he acknowledged that theology has its limitations: it was useful as an intellectual tool to defend religious truth, but in itself was not able to confirm God's existence. For that al-Ghazali praised religious experience, specifically that gained through mystical techniques employed by the Sufis.

While al-Ghazali was certainly very critical about philosophy, he left his most vitriolic attack for that of the **Ismailis**. This group were essentially Shi'a to the extent that they could trace their origins to the first Shi'a Imam, **Ali**, but claim that his line ended with Ismail, son of the sixth Imam, Jafar as-Sadiq. It was a charismatic and esoteric movement that, in 983, had conquered Egypt and set up a dynasty, the Fatimids (see **al-Mahdi**), that was to last for nearly two hundred years. Al-Ghazali obviously did not approve of the Gnostic tendencies, but he no doubt had personal reasons for his dislike of them. The Ismailis often attempted to de-stabilise the Sunni regime in Baghdad through assassinations of their enemies (the term 'assassin' derives from the Arabic '*hashish*', as the assassins would be given hashish to make them braver), including al-Ghazali's two friends, the vizier Nizam al-Mulk and his son. In fact, a more cynical interpretation of the reasons for al-Ghazali's ten-year retreat was that he was more concerned for his own material life than his spiritual faculty. He wrote half a dozen critiques of the sect, focusing on contradiction in their teachings.

Al-Ghazali was trained in both theology and law, and he criticised both. He followed the theological school established by al-Ashari, while in law he followed al-Shafi'i. His criticism of both theology and law as being too stagnant and lacking spiritual values undoubtedly had a lasting effect and helped both to revive. Perhaps al-Ghazali's greatest influence, however, is with Sufism, although some scholars have argued that his brother did far more in this cause. Nonetheless, it must be remembered that his first ever teacher, in Tus, was a Sufi and he did spend his mature years as a Sufi himself in which he could not help but be impressed by their conduct compared with the wealthy and materialistic citizens of the court. He believed that mysticism is the prime motivation for our lives, for without it all religious practice and belief are meaningless. Some misunderstood his writings on Sufism as being against orthodoxy and, in some places, his books were burned but, more recently, he has been accused of watering down true Sufism to make it more amenable to the orthodox Sunni community. On the whole, however, he did more to help the spread of new Sufi orders – regardless of how true to the 'essence' of mysticism they may have been – than hinder it.

Certainly, his impact on non-Muslims was mostly a result of his mystical writings. Less than half a century after al-Ghazali's death, a Jewish convert to Christianity in Toledo had his works translated into Latin, and the Jewish philosopher Maimonides (d. 1204) of Cordoba often referred to his work *The Aim of the Philosophers*. Al-Ghazali's mystical writings on such topics as the soul and on emanation led to debate among Jewish scholars. In Western Christianity, St Thomas Aquinas studied the writings of 'Algazel' as he was known in the West and the great poet Dante (d. 1321) frequently quotes al-Ghazali and even had the generosity to confine him to limbo in his poem rather than the inferno where one might expect non-Christians to reside. In the end, al-Ghazali has achieved an integration and religious synthesis that have earned him a place as a great Muslim scholar.

Major works

So many of al-Ghazali's works are now available in English it would not be possible to list them all. The Islamic Texts Society is doing a grand job of translating his *Revival of the Religious Sciences* as a series of books which I would certainly recommend.

Revival of the Religious Sciences, trans. various, London: Islamic Texts Society, 1989–.
The Confession of Al-Ghazali, trans. Claud Field, New Delhi: Kitab Bhavan, 1992.
Al-Ghazali's Deliverance from Error and Other Works, trans. R.J. McCarthy, Louisville, KT: Fons Vitae, 2001.
The Alchemy of Happiness, trans. Claud Field, London: Octagon Press, 2003.
The Incoherence of the Philosophers (Islamic Translation Series), trans. Michael E. Marmura, Utah: Brigham Young University Publications.

Further reading

Mitha, Farouk, *Al-Ghazali and the Ismailis: A Debate on Reason and Authority in Medieval Islam* (Ismaili Heritage Series), London: I.B. Tauris, 2001.
Watt, W.M., *The Faith and Practice of al-Ghazali*, Oxford: Oneworld, 2000.
Zayd, Abdur Rahman Abu, *Al-Ghazali on Divine Predicates and Their Properties*, New Delhi: Kitab Bhavan, 1994.

Notes

1 Quoted in Watt (2000), pp. 21, 56–76.
2 Ibid.

MAHMUD IBN UMAR AL-ZAMAKHSHARI (1075–1144)

Al-Zamakhshari was a theologian, Qur'an commentator, lexico-grapher and grammarian. He was the most important figure in

Qur'an studies and grammar in the twelfth century and he produced the greatest Qur'an commentary after **al-Tabari**'s. His commentary on the Qur'an, which was admired for its precise grammar and style, was popular everywhere. He also sought out the philosophical implications of his commentary, providing it with a *Mu'tazilite* (rationalist) interpretation. He produced a grammar of Arabic that became the standard work and he also published works in lexicography and other related subjects, a collection of proverbs, some *hadith* studies, and even some poetry.

Abu al-Qasim Mahmud ibn Umar al-Zamakhshari was born in 1075 in Khwarizm, now known as Khiva, in Uzbekistan and spent much of his life there, although he also studied in Bukhara in Western Uzbekistan and Baghdad in Iraq. He travelled to Mecca twice, on both occasions residing there for two to three years. He was able to travel to many of the important intellectual centres of the Islamic world at the time and be tutored by many eminent scholars. It was one such scholar, Abu Mudar al-Isfahani, who introduced al-Zamakhshari to the Mu'tazilite theological school. His first language was Persian but he rejected the use of this for scholarly purposes, preferring Arabic. Al-Zamakhshari was sufficiently ambitious to attempt to secure high government office under the vizier Nizam al-Mulk, but this was not successful and, after a serious illness in 1118–1119, he decided to devote the rest of his career to teaching and writing. He spent the remainder of his life in his hometown and died there in 1144.

While al-Zamakhshari wrote on a variety of subjects – not an unusual practice among Muslim scholars of the period – it was his monumental commentary on the Qur'an, *al-Kashshaf 'an haqa'iq ghawamid al-tanzil* (*The Unveiler of the Truths of Revelation*), which cemented his reputation. In the Introduction to this work, al-Zamakhshari states that the original motivation for its writing was the request by a Mu'tazilite scholar in Mecca who felt that there was a need for a Qur'an commentary that reflected the Mutazilite theological stance. Apparently, al-Zamakhshari was initially reluctant to write it, which makes it all the more remarkable that he managed to complete it in only two years.

To put this work into context, the Arabic for Qur'anic exegesis is *tafsir* ('commentary' or 'interpretation'), although the term *ta'wil* is also used but it has a connotation with allegorical interpretation. *Tafsir* can be a generic term for the entire field of Qur'an commentary or, more specifically, a study of the language, grammar, expressions and ambiguities of the plain text itself. For this latter form of interpretation there is not so much dispute, although there remains a variety of understanding of the meaning of specific words, phrases, and so on. It is the *ta'wil* level where symbolic and inner meanings are explored which has caused controversy and sectarianism, particularly between **Shi'a** and **Sunni** Muslims. The sixth Shi'a Imam, Ja'far al-Sadiq, most notably, referred to the Qur'an as having a hierarchy of different meanings, including an inner meaning (*awliya*) which is only accessible to a spiritual elite. Over time, however, there evolved a mainstream of Qur'anic interpretation which is learned by all scholars today and is referred to as *tafsir ma'thur* ('traditional commentary' or, more literally, 'commentary handed down'). The greatest exponent of that was al-Zamakhshari's predecessor, al-Tabari. Al-Tabari was not only a legal and Qur'anic scholar but also a great historian and was able to incorporate his extensive knowledge in various fields to the contextualising of the Qur'anic text. Although writing some two hundred years after the death of Prophet **Muhammad**, he was able to reproduce much of the commentary that existed up to his own time which otherwise would have been lost.

Another type of Qur'anic commentary, however, is known as *tafsir bi al-ra'y* ('interpretation based on individual reasoning'). This method and style of enquiry are more speculative and philosophical. Al-Zamakhshari, being a Mu'tazilite rationalist, falls into this camp of *tafsir*. This form of *tafsir* makes much use of rational analysis and speculation and has often been regarded with suspicion by the more orthodox who see it as too subjective, and this parallels the general antagonism shown towards Mu'tazilite rationalism as a whole demonstrated by more conservative elements (for background to this debate, see **al-Ashari**). However, the philological merits and reputation of his commentary served to ensure that al-Zamakhshari's version found acceptance among scholars of most shades of opinion. There have been 'counter-commentaries', the most renowned being that of Al-Baydawi (d. *c*.1286) which contained much of the material from *The Unveiler* but expurgated and adjusted (the Mu'tazilite elements being excised) so as not to offend the orthodox. The result is a much shorter *tafsir*, but immensely popular in Sunni Islam to the extent that it has attained a virtual 'scriptural' status of its own. However, many scholars still hold to the genius of al-Zamakhshiri's work. The orthodox and learned scholar **Ibn Khaldun** (d. 1406) considered it to be superior to all other commentaries:

> Competent orthodox scholars have ... come to disregard his [al-Zamakhshiri's] work and to warn everyone against its pitfalls.

However, they admit that he is on firm ground in everything related to language and style (*balaghah*). If the student of the work is acquainted with the orthodox dogmas and knows the arguments in their defence, he is no doubt safe from its fallacies. Therefore, he should seize the opportunity to study it, because it contains remarkable and varied linguistic information.[1]

While inevitably any attempt to illustrate al-Zamakhshiri's skills as an interpreter is coloured by the fact that it cannot be properly appreciated without a detailed knowledge of Arabic and its intricacies, it is nonetheless perhaps helpful to the reader if one example that translates well into English is provided. Below al-Zamakhshari is providing a commentary on the Qur'anic verse, 'We have not taught him [Muhammad] poetry; it is not seemly for him' (36:69):

> Some took the Messenger of God to be a poet, and indeed it is related that (the Meccan) 'Uqba ibn Abi Mu 'ait was one who did this. Thereupon it was said (by God): We have not taught him poetry; that is, while teaching him the Qur'an, we have not taught him poetry. This is to be understood in the sense that the Qur'an is neither poetry nor does it have anything to do with it, but on the contrary is far removed. Poetry contains statements that convey meaning through metre and (poetical) rhyme (*muqaffa*). Where, however, are metre and (poetical) rhyme (in the Qur'an)? And to what extent are the themes (*ma 'ani*) to which the poets devote themselves the themes of the Qur'an? How far removed, furthermore, is the structure (*nazm*) of the poet's assertions from the structure and style of the Qur'an? Thus, close investigation shows that the only relationship between the Qur'an and poetry, is that both are written in the Arabic language.[2]

This kind of interpretation requires a sophisticated understanding of technical terms, hence the fact that the translator has kept them in brackets. Al-Zamakhshari's method was to comment on each phrase of the Qur'an in sequence, bringing his range of philosophical, philological and lexicographical talents to bear. His method is incredibly rigorous which makes it even more remarkable that it was completed in such a short space of time. Such linguistic enthusiasm and knowledge is a rare thing. The subjective element is evident in his Mu'tazilite leanings and so he is keen to eliminate from his commentary any traces of any interpretations incompatible with reason, as well as any suggestions of superstition or anthropomorphism. In fact, he can be mocking or ironic regarding ideas that smack of a literal interpretation of the text, no doubt to the chagrin of a number of Traditionists. For example, scholars who upheld Tradition, such as Ibn Hanbal, argued that as the Qur'an talks of God creating the world with his hands, then this is not to be seen as metaphorical but, literally, He made the world with his hands, whereas many Mu'tazilites interpret 'hands' to mean God's grace.

By illustration of the difference between al-Zamakhshari's approach to the Qur'an and that of the orthodox al-Baydawi referred to earlier is the passage 'We never punish until We have sent a Messenger' (17:15). For the Mu'tazilites believed that we are able to determine what is right or wrong through the exercise of reason. While God always wills what is good for his creation, humans possess free will and may choose to do evil, in which case the responsibility lies with them. God, they argued, was bound by necessity to punish evil, and so could not do otherwise. God's acts are not just good because He wills them; rather, God wills only things that are just and good. Reason, for its part, is able to determine what this universal, natural good and bad is. Consequently, they believed that we are able to punish sinners even without revelation. Al-Baydawi, by contrast, denies that the knowledge of God has any connection with reason, and interprets this verse as denying the possibility of punishment before the revelation of the Divine Law, since it is only through revelation that the knowledge of God becomes obligatory on man, not through reason.

Aside from *The Unveiler*, there are some fifty works by al-Zamakhshari that are recorded, with around half of them having survived. The best known of these is his *al-Mufassal* which is a major work on Arabic grammar. The work is arranged in four sections: one section each on nouns, verbs, particles and finally phonology. Like *The Unveiler*, it quickly gained respect and admiration for its detail, breadth and conciseness and generated a number of commentaries and imitations as well as providing the framework for a more Western work of Arabic grammar by M.S. Howell.[3] Al-Zamakhshari produced a shorter version of this work entitled *The Model (al-Unmudhaj)* as well as a dictionary, *The Basis of Eloquence (Asas al-Balagha)* the aim of which was to illuminate metaphorical and extended meanings of words. His other works included a collection of old proverbs; a series of moral discourses entitled *Maqamat*; and a *Diwan*, or collection of poetry.

While it may be argued that al-Zamakhshari's contribution to Arabic grammar *per se* is limited, the most important contribution to Arabic thought lies in his incisive philological skills used to illuminate the text of the Qur'an. Consequently, despite the rationalist tendencies, great respect for him has been maintained throughout the centuries.

Major works

None of his works are yet readily available in English translation.

Further reading

There is little still available on al-Zamakhshari aside from some articles in various journals.

Ibrahim, L., 'Al-Zamakhshari: His Life and Works', *Islamic Studies* 49 (1980).
——, 'The Relation of Reason and Revelation in the Theology of al-Zamakhshari and al-Baydawi', *Islamic Culture*, April (1980).

Notes

1 Franz Rosenthal, trans., *The Muqaddimah: An Introduction to History*, vol. 2 (Princeton, NJ: Princeton University Press, 1967), p. 447.
2 From *al-Kashshaf*, trans. in Helmut Gatje, *The Qur'an and Its Exegesis*, trans. and ed. Alfred T. Welch (London: Routledge & Kegan Paul, 1976), p. 60.
3 The widely respected *Grammar of Classical Arabic* (New Delhi: Gyan Publishing House, 1996).

ABU AL-WALID MUHAMMAD IBN RUSHD ('AVERROES') (1126–1198)

Ibn Rushd is better known in the West by his Latin name Averroes. He was an Islamic philosopher, judge and physician, born in Spain, who had a major impact on Western thought by re-introducing the works of the ancient Greek philosophers Plato and Aristotle, as well as providing valuable 'commentaries' on these works which influenced such Jewish thinkers as Moses Maimonides and the great Christian theologian, St Thomas Aquinas.

Ibn Rushd was born in Cordoba, Spain, in 1126. Spain in the twelfth century was experiencing something of a cultural fluorescence, with Cordoba as its intellectual centre. Before Ibn Rushd's time, Spain had such scholars as the philosopher and musician ibn Bajjah (Avenpace) and the philosopher and physician Abu Bakr (Abubacher) ibn Tufayl. Cordoba's library could boast some 400,000 books – an astounding number at the time considering the state of most other European cities – and a university with one of the finest reputations in the world. Ibn Rushd himself attended this university as a physician and a jurist. Both his father and grandfather had served as jurists in the Maliki school (see **Malik ibn Anas**) and so it was no surprise that Ibn Rushd should also enter this profession. He served initially as a judge in his hometown, but in 1169 he was appointed judge of Seville, at that time the capital of al-Andalus. Ten years later he returned to Cordoba as judge, only to be appointed a second time to Seville in 1179 and then, subsequently, returning to Cordoba three years later as Chief Judge. Aside from his legal work, Ibn Rushd also practised medicine, succeeding Ibn Tufayl as court physician to the Almohad prince Abu Ya'qub Yusuf. This appointment provided Ibn Rushd with that rare thing for philosophers, security, as well as the opportunity to engage in his writing relatively unhindered. On the death of Abu Ya'qub in 1184, his son, al-Mansur, also warmly welcomed Ibn Rushd as judge and physician but, for reasons that have remained mysterious, he fell from favour and, at the age of 68, the scholar was exiled to the small town of Lucena, south of Cordoba, a town inhabited largely by Jews. Most of his books were burnt. Possibly the sultan was offended by some doctrinal dispute. However, he was asked to take up his post once more two years later, but Ibn Rushd fell sick after his return and he died in December 1198.

From what is known of his character, he was a generous man, who was also humble and an ascetic. Despite his obvious intelligence, he lacked the intellectual arrogance of, say, **Ibn Sina**. Because many of his books were burnt, it is not possible to determine how much he wrote. One biographer lists fifty titles by him, consisting of work in philosophy, medicine and law. His medical work, *al-Kulliyat fi al-Tibb* (*Generalities in Medicine*) is an encyclopaedia with sections on such topics as anatomy, physiology, disease, and hygiene. It was translated into Latin (*Colliget*) but was soon supplanted by Ibn Sina's *Canon*.

Ibn Rushd was better known as a philosopher rather than a physician. Ibn Tufayl recommended Ibn Rushd to the Sultan abu-Ya'qub and as Ibn Rushd himself reports this first meeting:

The first question addressed to me by the commander of the believers, after inquiring about my name, my father's name and my pedigree, was: 'What are the philosophers' views about heaven [the world], is it eternal or created?' So abashed and terrified did I feel that I began to offer excuses, even denying that I ever dealt with philosophy. I had no idea then what the sultan-caliph and ibn Tufayl had in mind for me.[1]

Ibn Rushd may have been right to be apprehensive, for taking a side on such doctrinal issues can lead to either royal patronage or banishment depending on the answer given. However, the actual task the sultan and Ibn Tufayl had in mind was the commission to attempt to make Aristotle intelligible. This would be no easy task, for Ibn Rushd did not understand Greek himself and so had to rely on Arabic translations. The problem may well have been not so much the fault of Aristotle, as with the translations. Nonetheless, Ibn Rushd succeeded in producing commentaries on Aristotle for three different levels: beginners, intermediate, and advanced. For the advanced, he dissected Aristotle's works paragraph by paragraph, providing detailed commentaries, therefore adopting the science of *tafsir* (interpretation) that was well known to Qur'anic scholars. In addition to the commentaries on Aristotle, Ibn Rushd composed a commentary, surviving only in Hebrew, on Plato's *Republic*. Ibn Rushd goes beyond merely commenting on works in the traditional sense. For example, in his commentary on the *Republic*, he draws on Plato's comments on the deterioration of the idea of the state by comparing it with states either in history or in the contemporary Islamic world. Likewise, Plato's derogatory remarks concerning the sophists (itinerant teachers who provided instruction in various branches of learning for a fee) was applied by Ibn Rushd to certain Islamic theologians.

In fact, Ibn Rushd was not shy of attacking the teachings of certain theologians, particularly the towering figure of **al-Ghazali**. The latter had accused philosophers of committing heresy in their works, and Ibn Rushd felt duty-bound to defend his profession and colleagues. Al-Ghazali wrote the celebrated *Tahafut al-Falasifa* (*Incoherence of the Philosophers*) and, in turn, Ibn Rushd wrote the rebuttal *Tahafut al-Tahafut* (*The Incoherence of the Incoherence*). These two works sit side by side as examples of sustained philosophical argument (ironically, although al-Ghazali attacked philosophers, he was skilled himself in the techniques of philosophical discourse). Al-Ghazali was particularly critical of Ibn Sina on, for example, predestination versus free will. Ibn Sina, by stating that God gave mankind free will, raised the problem for al-Ghazali who, by referring to the Qur'an, points out that God is concerned with every single detail of the world (that is, not just 'universals', but also 'particulars'), even the activities of an ant. Ibn Rushd's response to this specific issue argued that man's acts are neither fully free nor fully determined, but rather his will is conditioned by external forces working uniformly, an intermediate position that many philosophers have found to be unsatisfactory.

In another work, *Fasl al-Maqal* (*The Decisive Treatise*), Ibn Rushd made a point of arguing that philosophy and religion are compatible, and, like his *Incoherence*, this was written during his mature period (around 1180) and was translated into Hebrew and Latin. As he states:

> Philosophy is the friend and milk-sister of religion; thus injuries from people related to philosophy are the severest injuries [to religion] apart from the enmity, hatred and quarrels which such [injuries] stir up between the two, which are companions by nature and lovers by essence and instinct.[2]

For Ibn Rushd, the truth achieved through the study of philosophy does not differ from the truths of revelation as contained in the Qur'an. What may appear as difference is rather a matter of interpretation. Ibn Rushd falls into the rationalist camp in arguing that in the same way reason, through philosophy, can reach truth, so exercising reason in interpreting the Qur'anic text can do likewise. The Qur'an contains many symbols, allegories, analogies and so on that can be instructive to the less learned but, Ibn Rushd argues, those possessed of suitable intellect should determine their real meaning rather than treat them literally. He accused the theologians of literal interpretation of Qur'anic passages. Qur'anic descriptions of the afterlife, for example, with its physical rewards and punishments for the virtuous and the wicked, in his view, serve mainly as a motivating factor for the unsophisticated believer to act virtuously and avoid immorality.

While acknowledging that theology had a role to play, it should be subject to the scrutiny of philosophy to determine the intent of divine law. Al-Ghazali, however, insisted that the data of revelation were sufficient without the need of speculative reason. Ibn Rushd also presented a version of the cosmological (causal) argument for the existence of God, an argument that found support with Ibn Sina and also, later on, the Christian theologian, St Thomas Aquinas. Nothing comes into existence without a cause for its existence and, therefore, this series of causes leads to the need for a First Causer, which is God. In terms of the soul, Ibn Rushd argues that the immortality of the soul cannot be philosophically proven and if it is the case that the body is resurrected (a belief that al-Ghazzali affirmed in opposition to Ibn Sina), then it cannot be of the same form.

Despite Ibn Rushd's attempts to establish his religious credentials, he was often accused of atheism, and after his death his books were treated with suspicion and, in many cases, banned. It was perhaps only because of the empathy from Jewish and Muslim scholars that his name was kept alive in Europe at least. Besides which, disputes between philosophers and theologians died away after Ibn Rushd. While much of his writing was unoriginal, his importance rests primarily with his commentaries on Aristotle for, before Ibn Rushd, the writings of the ancient Greeks were frequently misunderstood or, indeed, writings that were not by Aristotle were attributed to him. It was these commentaries especially, which were translated into Hebrew and Latin within fifty years after his death, that made Ibn Rushd, or rather 'Averroes', a household name among scholars in Europe. In fact, the practice of 'Averroism' – studying Aristotle through Averroes' commentaries – became an important discipline in the universities. Although he often criticised Ibn Rushd, the works of Thomas Aquinas owe a great debt to his commentaries. Ironically, in the same way that the philosophers were often attacked by Islamic theologians, the writings of Ibn Rushd, and those of Aristotle, were also subjected to attack from the religious institutions. The difference being that, in the Islamic world, the orthodoxy of al-Ghazali and the literalism of the theologian won the day, while in Europe it was philosophy and rationalism that emerged the victor and, with it, the start of the Enlightenment.

Major works

Because of his popularity in the West, his major works are readily available in English. Below are just a few, but there are many more, including his commentaries on Aristotle and Plato.

Averroes' Three Short Commentaries on Aristotle's Topics, Rhetoric and Poetics, ed. and trans. C.E. Butterworth, Ithaca, NY: Cornell University Press, 1977.
Averroes' Tahafut al-tahafut ('The Incoherence of the Incoherence'), trans. S. van der Bergh, London: E.J.W. Gibb Memorial Trust, 1978.
Averroes' Middle Commentary on Aristotle's Categories and De interpretatione, trans. C.E. Butterworth, Princeton, NJ: Princeton Uniersity Press, 1983.
Averroes' Middle Commentary on Aristotle's Poetics, trans. C.E. Butterworth, Princeton, NJ: Princeton University Press, 1986.
Faith and Reason in Islam: Averroes' Exposition of Religious Arguments, trans. Ibrahim Najjar, Oxford: Oneworld, 2001.

Further reading

There are so many books on Averroes it would not be possible to list them all here.

Fakhry, M., *Averroes: His Life, Works and Influence*, Oxford: Oneworld, 2001.

Leaman, O., *Averroes and his Philosophy*, London: Routledge, 1997.

Urvoy, D., *Ibn Rushd (Averroes)*, trans. Olivia Stewart, London: Routledge, 1991.!

Notes

1 Al-Marrakushi, *Al-Mu'jib fi Talkhis Akhbar al-Maghrib*, ed. R. Dozy, 2nd edn (Leiden, 1881), pp. 174–175.

2 George F. Hourani, *Averroes: On the Harmony of Religion and Philosophy* (London: The E.J.W. Gibb Memorial Trust, 1976), (trans.).

SALAH AL-DIN ('SALADIN') (1138–1193)

Salah al-Din, better known in the West as 'Saladin', has become a figure of folklore, famous for his military encounters with King Richard 'the Lionheart' during the Third Crusade. A Muslim leader born in what is now Iraq, he pledged to his Muslim people that he would retake Jerusalem – the third holiest city for Muslims after Mecca and Medina – from the Christian Crusaders. This he succeeded in achieving. However, he is not only known for his military achievements, he is also remembered for uniting much of the Muslim world and is considered a paragon of princely virtue.

Salah al-Din Yusuf al-Ayyubi was born in 1138 in Tikrit, a fortress on the River Tigris between Mosul and Samarra in what is now Iraq. He was the son of Najm al-Din Ayyub, the Kurdish general in charge of the citadel there. He came from a military background for his uncle, Asad al-Din Shirkuh, was also a soldier. In 1139, the family moved to Baalbek (ancient Heliopolis) in Syria where his father was appointed governor and commander of the citadel.

It will help the reader to appreciate, however briefly, the political climate at the time Salah al-Din was growing up. The dynasty under which Salah al-Din and his father served were the Saljuq Atabegs of Mosul. Briefly, the Fatimid Caliphate, originally established in Tunisia in 909, had ruled over North Africa, Egypt and parts of Syria, with its capital in Cairo. But by the mid-twelfth century the empire was breaking up into mini-states ruled by military commanders on the whole, with ineffective caliphs. In the mid-eleventh century, Syria had fallen to the Saljuks and divided into two Saljuk succession regimes, one based in Aleppo and one in Damascus. Due largely to the threat of the Christian Crusaders who, between 1099 and 1109 had captured Edessa, Antioch, and Tripoli and established the Latin kingdom of Jerusalem, Syria became unified against a common enemy. In particular, it was the Saljuk Atabegs of Mosul who took the initiative. In 1128 a new governor of Mosul, Zengi (c.1127–1146) took Aleppo and, in 1144, also captured Edessa. In 1146, at the death of Zengi, his son, Nur al-Din (c.1146–1174) set out to capture Damascus which he achieved in 1154. The aim of the Saljuks, it should be stressed, was not primarily to fight the Crusaders, but rather to acquire territory, regardless of whether it was occupied by Christian or Muslim authorities. In this respect, Nur al-Din was not so concerned with re-taking Jerusalem and, in fact, made peace treaties with the Crusaders. In 1170, Nur al-Din achieved the family ambition of reuniting Syria and Mesopotamia under his household and his next target was Egypt. The Fatimid regime was in chaos and the Crusader and King of Jerusalem, Amalric, was aiming to take the country.

In 1164, when Salah al-Din was 26, a displaced vizier (prime minister) named Sharwar of the Fatimid Caliphate asked Nur al-Din for aid, promising him a third of the country's revenue. The Sultan responded by dispatching Salah al-Din's uncle, Shirkuh, at the head of a military force. Shirkuh, for his part, took along his young nephew who, apparently, went with 'great reluctance'. Why Salah al-Din should be so reluctant is a matter of some debate; while some sources say that he was more concerned with his theological studies than the horrors of war, other sources direct his concern with the delights not untypical of a prominent Kurdish family such as hunting, riding, chess, polo playing and wine. Shirkuh succeeded in his mission of returning power to Sharwar who, in return, then formed an alliance with Amalric three years later! So Nur al-Din sent Shirkuh with his nephew into Egypt a second time. It was then Salah al-Din tasted his first real battle against the Franks, and acquitted himself well. However, the battle of Egypt was a stalemate and it was not until the third venture in 1169 when Sharwar was murdered and Shirkuh took the vizierate for himself that Salah al-Din found victory. Soon after, Shirkuh died of over-eating and Salah al-Din now found himself not only to be a lieutenant of a **Sunni** Syrian king, but also the prime minister for a **Shi'a** Egyptian Caliph. He quickly built up his own army of Syrians, Kurds and loyal Egyptians and brought his family over from Damascus to command them (his father was appointed treasurer). In 1171, with the power and immense wealth of Egypt behind him, Salah al-Din took Baghdad, the seat of the symbolic **Abbasid** Caliphs. Unofficially, Salah al-Din was the new Sultan and he then proceeded to conquer other Muslim states. It is reported that from then on he gave up the various pleasures of youth and dedicated himself to his new position. The next problem was the fact that he was still technically under the command of the Sultan Nur al-Din in Damascus. A showdown would have occurred if the latter had not died in 1174. The incoming Sultan was only 11 years old and chaos ensued with the Franks taking full advantage of the disorder by encroaching on Saljuk territory. Salah al-Din took the decision to enter Damascus and marry Nur al-Din's widow. He was now the ruler of Syria.

Nearing the age of 50, Salah al-Din could claim for himself a reputation known throughout the Middle East. He had unified Muslim states that had warred against each other for generations. However, Muslim clerics especially were critical of his leadership, particularly the fact that his reputation had been acquired at the cost of many Muslim lives. In 1185, he fell very ill and believed himself to be dying. At his bedside sat Muslim holy men who would recite the Qur'an and, it is said, it was then he received a divine message to liberate Jerusalem. Salah al-Din recovered from his illness believing it was due to the intercession of God who had spared him from death so he could take back Jerusalem. Seeking atonement and to demonstrate his piety, Salah al-Din initiated a *jihad* (holy war), sending his scribes out to call for all to liberate the third holiest city of the Muslim world, for Jerusalem was also the stopping place of the Prophet **Muhammad** where he made the celebrated journey to heaven. Salah al-Din effectively used religion to inspire the Muslim people to engage in a religious crusade of their own: a powerful tool. Further, with the surrounding Muslim world now in his control, he was in a position to focus on Palestine. The European nations, for their part, however, were preoccupied in warring among themselves. Salah al-Din could not have chosen a better time to act.

The Sultan mustered 18,000 men when they marched out of Damascus in 1187. Tiberias was captured in six days and then the coast towns were taken so that Jerusalem was sealed off from reinforcements. Jerusalem itself soon fell to his siege and its population were held to ransom, a sharp contrast to when the Christian Crusaders massacred the population in 1099. Salah al-Din wanted not only to claim military superiority but also moral superiority; that the values of Islam include mercy. To Muslims, he was now known as Islam's greatest holy warrior. Salah al-Din then confided to his secretary and biographer that he next intended to divide his realm up among his aides, leave them with instructions, and head off with his army to invade Europe.

However, Europe had plans of its own. The Pope immediately ordered a decree that Jerusalem must be recaptured at all costs. Crusading was energised once more and the three most powerful kings of Western Europe took the cross: Frederick Barbarossa of Germany, Philip Augustus of France, and Richard 'the Lionheart' of England. It was Richard especially, regarded as the greatest warrior of all Europe, who boosted morale. His troops built new and powerful siege machines such as 'the cat' that could allow his men to scale walls like cats, and powerful mangonels that could hurl huge rocks. With these weapons one city after another was taken, but not Jerusalem itself. The most important to fall to the Crusaders was the key port in the eastern Mediterranean, Acre. The city had already been under siege by the Franks that Salah al-Din had freed from Jerusalem, but it was the arrival of Richard that resulted in its surrender. It was a huge blow for Salah al-Din who had enjoyed so many years of victory. As Richard had heard of Salah al-Din, so Richard's reputation had also preceded him, so both no doubt were aware of the rivalry between them and the desire to outdo each other was a strong one. Richard took three thousand prisoners in Acre and offered to exchange them for one item: the 'true cross' believed to be a relic from the cross on which Christ was crucified. Salah al-Din had acquired it in his battle with the Franks who had carried it with them in the belief it would aid them in the battle. It was of immense importance for the Crusaders and probably mattered little to Salah al-Din, but he knew of its value and so refused to return it in the hope that it would stop Richard from marching on Jerusalem. Richard decided he had little choice but to kill all the prisoners before then heading on to the next important bridgehead, the port of Jaffa. Battle took place between Salah al-Din and Richard near the city which, although he was outnumbered, was a resounding victory for Richard. Salah al-Din's army fled back to Jerusalem.

The story of the battles that took place in Palestine between the two main actors, King Richard and Salah al-Din, has become the stuff of legend. They undoubtedly had great admiration and respect for each other and even, at times, engaged in exchanging gifts. Richard knew, despite his victories, that taking, and holding, Jerusalem would be an almost impossible task and so he started making attempts at diplomacy, appealing to Salah al-Din's renowned generosity and mercy. In the negotiations, Salah al-Din's brother al'Adil became good friends with Richard, with the latter even going so far as to offer his widowed sister Joanna in marriage to al'Adil as a way of cementing a political alliance with his sister and al'Adil as joint rulers of Jerusalem.

The idea of a Christian princess marrying a Muslim prince was a remarkable one, but was also rejected by both parties. Salah al-Din, for his part, had grown old and tired and his men were war-weary, so that as Richard pressed for peace the Sultan became more tempted. In 1192, a three-year peace treaty was signed, giving Richard the coast from Tyre to Jaffa and the interior to the Sultan on the condition that Christians would be allowed to make pilgrimages to Jerusalem.

Salah al-Din returned to Damascus in honour of having retained Jerusalem as Muslim territory. He suffered an attack of malaria from which he was not to recover. He died at the age of 55. On record, only one wife is known, Nur al-Din's widow, but he left seventeen sons and one daughter. What is known of his character is that he was considerate, lacking in ostentation and, unlike his uncle, abstemious in food. He was also incredibly generous, dividing booty among his aides while leaving nothing for himself to the extent that it was said that when he died he left insufficient money for his own funeral. Instead of the many palaces his empire possessed, he preferred to reside in a military tent. Physically he has been described as fair-skinned, with square features, and sporting a neatly trimmed beard. Although he could be gentle, he could also be ruthless when need be especially against those he regarded as committing heresy, such as his order to have the Sufi illuminationist **Suhrawardi** executed. In the Western world he was greatly admired. The Italian poet Dante, in his *Inferno*, was bound to commit any non-Christian to hell but, in Salah al-Din's case, he was consigned to limbo alongside such great men as Plato and Aristotle.

Further reading

There are many works on Saladin and the Crusades. The Lane-Poole is a classic, while the Stanley is very short (only forty-eight pages) and succinct. The Maalouf provides a welcome balance to the countless Western accounts of the Crusades. The Lyons also makes use of hitherto neglected Arabic sources, including unpublished manuscript material, notably correspondence from Saladin's own court. The Tariq Ali is actually a novel of Salah al-Din's fictional memoirs.

Ali, Tariq, *The Book of Saladin: A Novel*, London: Verso, 1999.

Lane-Poole, Stanley, *Saladin and the Fall of the Kingdom of Jerusalem*, London: Greenhill Books, 2002.

Lyons, Malcolm C. and Jackson, David, *Saladin: The Politics of Holy War*, Cambridge: Cambridge University Press, 1984.

Maalouf, A., *The Crusades through Arab Eyes*, trans. J. Rothschild, London: Saqi Books, 2001.

Stanley, Diane, *Saladin: Noble Prince of Islam*, London: HarperCollins, 2002.

YAHYA SUHRAWARDI (1154–1191)

Shihab al-Din Yahya ibn Habash ibn Amirak Abu'l-Futuh Suhrawardi is well known in the Islamic philosophical and mystical tradition as the 'Master of Illumination' (in Arabic, *Shaykh al-Ishrāq*), being the acknowledged founder of the Illuminationist (*Ishrāqī*) or 'Oriental' school of philosophy. Suhrawardi established the ideas, language and methodology of the Illuminationist school which then went on to have a major impact on Islamic philosophy, mysticism and, indeed, politics. By certain orthodox elements he was considered heretical in his writings, which led to his execution at the age of 37. Suhrawardi was prolific in his writings, covering many aspects of philosophy in his attempt at a synthesis of Zoroastrian, Platonic and Islamic ideas. Many of his works, of which much has survived, are written in a symbolic and poetic form that readers have often found appealing, adopting a writing style which encourages the reader to engage in philosophical matters in a more experiential manner. He also wrote a number of prayers and invocations in a sophisticated literary style.

While the circumstances surrounding Suhrawardi's execution remain unclear, there is nonetheless a good deal of material available to construct a picture of his life. The name 'Suhrawardi' is actually a reference to his place of birth, the town of Suhraward which is in north-western Iran, near Azerbaijan. He is also known as Suhrawardi Maqtūl ('the executed') to distinguish him from two other celebrated mystics who were also from Suhraward, and lived at the same time but managed to avoid the wrath of the authorities. Shihab al-Din 'Umar b. 'Abd Allah al-Suhrawardi (1144–1234) was the founder of the **Sufi** (the name given to Muslim mystics) Suhrawardiya order which still has many followers today. Abu Najb Suhrawardi (d. 1168) was an acknowledged authority of **hadith** (the sayings of the Prophet Muhammad).

In his youth, Suhrawardi travelled in a quest for knowledge, studying under various religious and mystical scholars of the time. The Saljuk dynasty – deriving from nomadic Turkish tribesmen – ruled over Anatolia, Persia, Iraq, and Syria at this time, and it was these lands that Suhrawardi chose to visit. In Maraghah (in Azerbaijan), he studied under Majd al-Dīn al-Jīlī, who also taught the philosopher and theologian Fakhr al-Dīn al-Rāzi. He then travelled to Isfahan, in West central Iran, and then on to south-west Anatolia where he enjoyed the patronage of several Saljuk princes and rulers. In the year 1183, he moved to Aleppo in Syria where he completed his major work *Hikmat al-Ishrāq* (*Philosophy of Illumination*) in 1186. According to his follower and biographer, Shams al-Dīn Muhammad Shahrazūrī, Suhrawardi was particularly attracted to the Sufis and adopted Sufi attire: a simple woollen cloak called a *khirqa*. He performed ascetic practices such as solitary retreat, meditation and strict fasting and is portrayed as a quiet individual, of moderate stature and bearded. It was not long after his arrival in Aleppo that he became the tutor of the city's governor, Prince al-Malik al-Zāhir Ghāzī (also known as Malik Zāhir Shāh) and, by all accounts, the two got on famously.

The Prince was the son of the Saljuk Sultan Ayyubid **Salah al-Din**, better known in the West as 'Saladin', the great opponent of England's King Richard the Lionheart in the battles of the Crusades. Suhrawardi's popularity with the young Prince and the resulting increase in the philosopher's prestige and power in the court would have met with the usual jealousy among the courtly entourage. No doubt Suhrawardi's philosophical views, and his apparent willingness to express and support them in debate, would have upset many of the conservative **ulama** (the religious scholars) as well. Letters were written to Salah al-Din calling for the philosopher's execution on the basis of heresy and corrupting the young mind of Salah al-Din's son and, in turn, Salah al-Din – no doubt distracted by the Crusades at the time – wrote back on more than one occasion demanding that the Prince al-Zahir execute Suhrawardi. Perhaps aware that his own privileged position was at stake, al-Zahir did so, although the form of execution remains obscure.

It is by no means an easy task to grasp the finer details of illuminationist philosophy, as it cannot be considered one of the most accessible schools of thought. Further, it is very difficult to grasp the intricacies of illuminationist thought without placing Suhrawardi within the context of the influence of his philosophical predecessors and schools, most significantly that of **Ibn Sina** (better known in the West as Avicenna) and the philosophy he famously adumbrated, Neoplatonism. While Suhrawardi used the term 'illuminationist' to refer to a variety of ideas in his philosophical system, he also wished to distinguish the illuminationists from the Neoplatonists, or 'peripatetics' (Ar. *mashshā'ī*) as he preferred to call them. Suhrawardi, together with his followers, clearly aimed to establish a philosophy that was different from the peripatetic school which was made popular in the Islamic philosophical and mystical tradition by Ibn Sina. Whether the subtleties of each school do point to clear differences is difficult to determine, especially as Ibn Sina himself seemed dissatisfied with the tenets of peripatetism and argued that his readers should look to his own 'illuminationist' views in his works. Interestingly, Suhrawardi goes out of his way to argue that Ibn Sina cannot lay claim to being an 'illuminationist' himself.

The illuminationist school covers many different fields within philosophy itself, but it has probably had the greatest impact upon epistemology (theory of knowledge). The questions of what knowledge is, how one can acquire it, and how it is recognised have been a perennial occupation for philosophers, and Suhrawardi taps into this ancient tradition of tackling such questions for his own philosophy. In this respect, the illuminationist tradition is not Suhrawardi's 'own' philosophy, but he would rather see it as the 'true' philosophy of the ancients. In fact, Suhrawardi is fond of making reference to many ancient, especially Greek and Persian, thinkers as his predecessors in the 'Oriental' tradition. The peripatetic, or Neoplatonist, school – founded by the Egyptian Plotinus (205–270) – propounded a view of creation known as emanation. This is essentially a ripple effect in which the One, or 'the Good', emanates its goodness in a hierarchy: proceeding from the One is the Active Intellect (or *logos*), followed by the World Soul. Neoplatonism was attractive to many Christians partly because of this 'triad' of One–Mind–Soul cosmology. What is interesting is that the world of matter, that is the world mankind occupies, is at the bottom of the process of emanation and consequently is as far removed from the One as it is possible to be. In terms of addressing such questions as 'how or what can we know?' if the One is synonymous with Truth (and, therefore 'knowledge' in this sense), then mankind seems a long way from it. However, Plotinus believed that Man is both body and soul. That is, the body is tied to matter and all its negatives such as plurality, evil and so on, but he also has a soul which is a 'spark' of the One's 'light'. In fact, the analogy of light is not an uncommon one; the One represented by the Sun which gives illumination and life to all things, but also is the source of all that we see. The problem that has preoccupied many philosophers is whether what we see before our eyes is in any way a true reflection of what is real. Darkness, in this sense, represents ignorance and evil, whereas light represents truth and goodness. The Sun, of course, can also give light to illusion and we can be deceived by what we see or think we see. It will come as no surprise that Suhrawardi's preferred term for the One is 'Light of Lights'.

Suhrawardi often writes of his belief in angels. Each individual soul has a guardian angel, for the soul pre-existed in the angelic world. Upon entering the material body, the soul is divided into two: one part remaining in heaven while the other is trapped within the prison of the body, yearning to unite once more with its other half. The angels live in the world of the 'Orient', the immaterial world of pure light, while the world of matter is the Occident, a world far removed from the One. It is therefore the task of man to purify his soul as much as possible if it is to return to the angelic realm.

The peripatetic view of knowledge is that it is 'acquired' (al-'ilm al-husuli) whereas the illuminationist view is that it is far more intuitive, that is knowledge 'by presence' (al-'ilm al-huduri al-ishraqi). Suhrawardi wishes to emphasise the importance of subjective experience, whether these be dreams, visions, 'flashes' of illumination, out-of-body experiences, and so on, as valuable in themselves and, indeed, correlating with objective reality. Suhrawardi argued that the form of knowledge 'by presence' is higher than the peripatetic 'acquired' because the former consists of the most fundamental kind of knowledge, that of self-awareness. In answer to the question, 'How can you be sure your personal experience is true, objective knowledge?', the Illuminationist can respond with 'The self intuitively *knows*!'

Suhrawardi describes the path that must be taken by the philosopher to realise this self-awareness. This involves 'abandoning the world' through a series of practices not uncommon for ascetics such as fasting and retreat. In time, this will lead to personal revelations and visions that the subject will intuitively know to be truth. In this respect, Suhrawardi is not elitist, for all of us have what he calls a portion of the 'light of God' (al-bariq al-ilahi). However, what is also important is what one does with these 'apocalyptic lights', and this is where the skills of the philosopher come in, for he or she must then engage in discursive analysis to construct a true science based upon the visionary experiences. While Suhrawardi places great importance on subjective experience, or 'intuition', he also set out to construct a science based upon this illuminative intuition. For Suhrawardi, illumination is as much a science as sensory experience. In the same way the scientist is confronted by 'sense data' – for example, planetary motion through a telescope – and then goes on to use his or her reasoning to develop the science of astronomy, so the illuminationist replaces sense data with personal revelation as the foundation for the science of illumination.

What distinguishes the oriental from the peripatetic is that, for the former, the 'vision' will differ in image from one person to the next; for some, it may be an angel, for others, an historical figure (Suhrawardi often had visions of Aristotle), whereas in the peripatetic view it is described in a less mystical, less personal sense as contact or 'conjunction' (*iitisāl*) with the Active Intellect. This 'conjunction' would essentially be the same for everybody so conjoined, for the Active Intellect is regarded as static and unchanging, and truth cannot change or be different for one person to the next. For Suhwaradi, the vision can be different but the end result – the knowledge gained – will be the same for all.

Suhrawardi wrote four major works of philosophy: *Al-talwihat* (*The Intimations*), *Al-muqawamat* (*The Oppositions*), *Al-mashari' wa-'l-mutarahat* (*The Paths and Heavens*) and the previously mentioned *Hikmat al-Ishrāq* (*The Philosophy of Illumination*). These are all works in Arabic and Suhrawardi stated that he intended them to be studied in the order they were written, as they do progress from a peripatetic, discursive philosophy to the more illuminationist and intuitive. Suhrawardi also wrote, in both Persian and Arabic, collections of symbolic narratives, short treatises and prayers and invocations.

The implications of Suhrawardi's philosophy on our understanding of what we mean by knowledge and truth are immense. In many respects, while firmly within the tradition of Plato and Neoplatonism, he also predates the philosophy of Nietzsche and the existential tradition in recognising the importance of myth, dreams and fantasy in providing us with knowledge of the world that is just as valuable as that provided by, say, physics, regardless of the issues of which is more 'true' than the other. Iluminationist philosophy was very influential among the Shi'a philosophers, including probably that of the highly influential **al-Shirazi** (Mulla Sadra). In fact, to this day, the philosophers of Iran are still labelled as peripatetic or illuminationist rather like philosophers in the West have often been labelled as rationalists or empiricists. In addition, Suhrawardi did much to promote and develop the use of Persian as opposed to Arabic, the *lingua franca* of the time for so many of his contemporaries.

Major works

There is a great deal that has yet to be translated into English. However, the following are available.

The Mystical and Visionary Treatises of Suhrawardi, trans. W.M. Thackson Jr, London: Octagon Press, 1982.

The Book of Radiance: A Parallel English-Persian Text (*Bibliotheca Iranica* Intellectual Traditions Series, No. 1), trans. Hossein Ziai: Mazda Publishers, 1998.

The Philosophy of Illumination, trans. John Walbridge and Hossein Ziai, Hawaii: Brigham Young University Press, 2000.

Further reading

The two major scholars of Suhrawardi's work are Henry Corbin and Hossein Ziai.

Corbin, Henry, *The Man of Light in Iranian Sufism*, London: East-West Publications, 1995.

Ziai, Hossein, *Knowledge and Illumination: A Study of Suhrawardi's Hikmat al-ishraq*, Atlanta, GA: Scholars Press, 1990.

——, 'The Source and Nature of Authority: A Study of Al-Suhrawardi's Illuminationist Political Doctrine', in Charles Butterworth (ed.) *Political Aspects of Islamic Philosophy: Essays in Honor of Muhsin S. Mahdi* (Harvard Middle Eastern Monographs), Cambridge, MA: Harvard University Press, 1992.

——, 'Shihab al-Din Suhrawardi: Founder of the Illuminationist School', in Seyyed Hossein Nasr and Oliver Leaman (eds) *History of Islamic Philosophy*, London: Routledge, 2001.

MUHAMMAD IBN ARABI (1165–1240)

As an illustration of Ibn Arabi's importance to Islamic thought, he is usually known as *Muhyi al-Din* (Renewer of Religion) and later, by the **Sufis** (the mystical branch of Islam) especially, as *Shaykh al-Akbar* ('The Greatest Master'). In the words of James Morris:

> Paraphrasing Whitehead's famous remark about Plato – and with something of the same degree of imagination – one could say that the history of Islamic thought subsequent to Ibn Arabi (at least down to the 18th century and the radically new encounter with the modern West) might largely be construed as a series of footnotes to his work.[1]

Ibn Arabi is, therefore, one of Islam's great spiritual teachers, giving the gnostic (essentially an esoteric religious movement) element of Islam its first fully comprehensive philosophical expression. Although essentially considered a philosopher and mystic, he also wrote an incredible amount beyond that of philosophy (**falsafah**) and Sufism, including fields such as Qur'anic commentary, **hadith** (the sayings of the Prophet Muhammad), jurisprudence, theology (**kalam**) and even some poetry.

Muhyi al-Din Abu 'AbdAllah Muhammad ibn 'Ali ibn Muhammad ibn al-'Arabi al-Hatimi al-Ta'i ibn al-'Arab, to give him his full name, was born in 1165 in Murcia, Valencia (south-eastern Spain). He died in 1240 and was buried in Damascus. He was born into the Moorish culture of Andalucia which, at the time, was the centre of a vibrant cosmopolitan culture of Jewish, Christian and Muslim thought. Consequently, Ibn Arabi was fortunate enough to be brought up in an environment which encouraged and welcomed the most important religious, scientific, theological and philosophical ideas of the time.

From an early age, Ibn Arabi studied the religious sciences. As was the standard practice of any serious scholar, he studied the Qur'an and the Prophetic Traditions. Early on, however, he claims to have received a vision providing him with instructions from Moses, Jesus and Muhammad, that he should pursue a spiritual path. Following on from this he travelled in quest of knowledge from spiritual teachers. He studied at Seville and Ceuta in Spain, and later visited the intellectual and cultural centres of Mecca and Baghdad. Several women especially were of great spiritual inspiration for him and while in Spain he met two very old women saints; Shams of Marchena, and Fatimah bint ibn al-Muthanna of Cordoba. Of the latter, Ibn Arabi says:

> She lived in Seville. When I met her, she was in her nineties. Looking at her in a purely superficial way, one might have thought that she was a simpleton, to which she would have replied that he who knows not his Lord is the real simpleton. She used to say 'Of those who come to see me, I admire none more than Ibn Arabi.' When asked the reason for this, she replied 'The rest of you come with part of yourselves, leaving the other part of you occupied with your other concerns, while Ibn Arabi is a consolation to me, for he comes with all of himself. When he rises up, it is with all of himself, and when he sits it is with his whole self, leaving nothing of himself elsewhere. This is how it should be on the Way.'[2]

His travels and education continued for some three decades in all. In 1202 he performed the pilgrimage to Mecca and spent the next two years of his life there under the tutelage of various spiritual teachers. While in Mecca he received what he refers to as a 'divine commandment' to begin what was to become his monumental work on mystical doctrine, *Futuhat al-Makkiyya* (*Meccan Revelations*), which was to take him the next thirty years to complete. After travelling to Jerusalem, Baghdad, Aleppo and other great cities, he finally settled in Damascus in Syria where he remained for the last seventeen years of his life. He devoted his time in Damascus mainly to teaching and writing. Pupils would come from all corners of the Islamic world to sit at his feet, as he had done before others as a youth. He died in 1240 at the age of 76.

Meccan Revelations consists of 560 chapters and it outlines virtually every known facet of spiritual life in incredible conciseness, including the life and practice (*sunna*) of the Prophet **Muhammad**, the spiritual exegesis of the Qur'an and Prophetic Traditions (*hadith*), the principles of jurisprudence (*usul al-fiqh*), love, worship, cosmology, and politics. It was finally completed in 1231 and modern editions make up some thirty-seven volumes of 500 pages each. If this is not in itself a remarkable achievement, it must be remembered that Ibn Arabi is credited with around three hundred other works, of which half survive.

Debate has surrounded the relationship between Ibn Arabi's work and the influence of Greek philosophy. It is generally considered today that his philosophy is actually rooted within the Islamic and, particularly, the mystical tradition rather than any external influence. In fact, there seems to be little evidence that he read any books of philosophy at all, hardly ever making any mention of philosophers. It is well recorded that he met the Muslim philosopher **Ibn Rushd** when the former was only 15 but, again, there is no evidence he actually read any of Ibn Rushd and, in fact, he refers to him as a scholar of Islamic law rather than philosophy.

In which case, the issue of how Ibn Arabi arrived at his ideas is an interesting one. When he talks about his own methodology, he says that he never set himself a purpose when writing but rather relied upon flashes of inspiration that would so overwhelm him the only way he could rid them from his mind was to put pen to paper. He would write at the command of God which he received either in his sleep or through a mystical revelation. This mystical intuition he describes as his 'unveiling' (*kashf*) and 'opening' (*fath*). Having said that, however, the terminology he uses in his writings is a clear indication that he was very familiar with that used in the Islamic religious sciences.

Ibn Arabi's methodology equally applies to another great work of his, *Fusus al-hikam* (*The Bezels of Wisdom*), which he said he received

as a whole in a dream. The work is essentially an extended meditation on the mystical significance of the major prophets of the Qur'an
and it has proved to be a major influence on subsequent Sufi tradition, inspiring numerous commentaries. It has influenced the
thought of the poet Jalal **al-Din Rumi** and even, it is said, that of
the Italian poet and thinker Dante Alighieri (d. 1321). The far-
reaching influence of Ibn Arabi is summed up by Professor Ralph
Austin, who writes:

> Ibn Arabi gave expression to the teachings and insights of the
> generations of Sufis who preceded him, recording for the first
> time, systematically and in detail, the vast fund of Sufi experi-
> ence and oral tradition, by drawing on a treasury of technical
> terms and symbols greatly enriched by centuries of intercourse
> between the Muslim and Neo-Hellenistic worlds ... all who
> came after him received it through the filter of his synthetic
> expression.[3]

While Ibn Arabi talks of 'unveiling', this should not be interpreted as
a rejection of the role of reason, although he consider the latter to be
inferior to the knowledge that can be attained through Sufi practices.
In fact, Ibn Arabi asserts that reason is necessary in the acquisition of
the true knowledge of things. Central to his thought is the role of
human beings and their potential in actualising within themselves all
of God's attributes. By 'attributes' Ibn Arabi refers to such qualities as
Mercy (*Rahmah*), Wrath (*Ghadab*), Justice ('*Adl*), Beauty (*Jamal*),
Majesty (*Jalal*), and so on. This demonstrates the uniqueness of
human beings as they are created in the image of God. By 'image',
then, Ibn Arabi sees this as synonymous with God's attributes. The
angels, being spiritual themselves and not material, are able to know
God only as a spiritual Being, whereas human beings can know God
as both a spiritual Being, which is pure Reality, but also the manifestation of Reality in terms of creation. The highest manifestation of
Reality is the human, with the archetype of the first man, Adam and
which is also identified as the Perfect Man (*al-insan al-kamil*). Hence
the Perfect Man is actually the visible manifestation of God. As man
has been created by God, he embodies all the perfections of the
universe, as well as those of Divinity. The reason for being, then, is to
strive towards the highest perfection and this is done through the
mystical path. Those who reach this stage are at the 'station of no
station' (*maqam la maqam*) and he calls them the 'Verifier' (*muhaqqiq*)
or 'the possessor of two eyes' (*dhu'l-'aynayn*). With one eye, the

Perfect Man can perceive his own creaturely uniqueness, while with the other, he sees his identity with God.

Ibn Arabi's philosophy is full of seeming reconciling dualities, hence the 'two eyes' reference. The Perfect Man is both near to God and far from him. God's essence is unity and multiplicity, necessity and contingency. Whether such dualities can really be reconciled is a matter of some debate. The fact that Ibn Arabi talks of God's 'attributes' requires God to possess multiplicity and He is not only the Creator but the *created*, in that He is the totality of all things. All of creation partakes of His Being, but he does not adopt a pantheistic approach of going so far as to say everything which exists is therefore God. In his doctrine of the 'unity of being' (*wahda al-wujud*), Ibn Arabi makes a clear distinction between the Absolute One – the indefinable Truth (*Haqq*) – and His creation (*khalq*) or self-manifestation (*zuhur*) which is in constant renewal. The existence of all living things is thanks to the 'breath of the merciful' (*nafas al-rahman*), which flows throughout the universe, giving it existence as a mother gives existence to her children.

The role of reason in all this is that it is innately constituted so as to be able to comprehend distinctions and differentiations and therefore to think abstractly. However, focusing on reason alone causes the thinker to dissect Reality and bypass the underlying unity of all things. What is also required is the quality that, Ibn Arabi argues, the rational philosophers and theologians lack but the Sufi possess, imagination (*khayal*) which allows one to perceive God's presence in all things. Reality is 'unveiled' and bridges the gaps that reason alone cannot bridge. Thus a harmony between reason and imagination is established that allows the person to comprehend all of God's attributes. Philosophers and theologians are useful and necessary, but they have their limits in terms of what can be known and they deceive themselves into believing they can grasp God Essence (*Dhat*) through rational reflection alone. More important are the 'Verifiers' who can see with both eyes God's presence.

The contribution of Ibn Arabi to Islamic thought cannot be overestimated and such a short section here cannot do justice to the wide range of ideas that he discussed and elaborated upon. In particular, the themes of the Oneness of Being, the Perfect Man, and the role of Imagination have all become dominant among thinkers after Ibn Arabi. In fact a whole group of scholars emerged, many calling themselves the 'Verifiers' to distinguish themselves from philosophers and theologians, although there is no specific 'school' or Sufi Order with Ibn Arabi as its eponym. As James Morris points out with reference to writers on Ibn Arabi:

The real philosophic and theological unity and diversity of these writers have not begun to be explored in modern research ... none of the writers are mere 'commentators' of Ibn Arabi ... as with 'Aristotelianism' or 'Platonism' in Western thought, Ibn Arabi's writings were only the starting point for the most diverse developments, in which reference to subsequent interpreters quickly became at least as important as the study of the Shaykh himself.[4]

Major works

A great number of his works are available in English. The Morris translation contains selections of his *Revelations*.

The Bezels of Wisdom, trans. R.W.J. Austin, New Jersey: Paulist Press International, 1980.

Journey to the Lord of Power: Sufi Manual on Retreat, trans. Rabia T. Harris, Rochester, VT: Inner Traditions International, 1990.

The Meccan Revelations, trans. James W. Morris, ed. Michel Chodkiewicz, New York: Pir Press, 2002.

Further reading

The Addas provides the most thorough account of his life while the Chittick is good for his philosophical ideas.

Addas, Claude, *Quest for the Red Sulphur: The Life of Ibn Arabi,* trans. P. Kingsley, Cambridge: Cambridge University Press, 1993.

Austin, R.W., *Sufis of Andalusia: The Ruh Alouds and Al-Durrat Al-Fakhirah of Ibn Arabi,* Berkeley, CA: University of California Press, 1977.

Chittick, William, *The Sufi Path of Knowledge: Ibn Arabi's Metaphysics of Imagination,* Albany, NY: State University of New York Press, 1989.

Chodkiewicz, M., *An Ocean without Shore: Ibn Arabi, the Book, and the Law,* trans. D. Streight, Albany, NY: State University of New York Press, 1993.

Corbin, Henry, *Creative Imagination in the Sufism of Ibn Arabi,* trans. R. Mannheim, Princeton, NJ: Princeton University Press, 1969.

Notes

1 James Morris, 'Ibn Arabi and his Interpreters', *Journal of the American Oriental Society,* 106 (1986), p. 101.

2 Quoted in Austin, *Sufis of Andalusia,* p. 143.

3 Ibid., p. 48.

4 Morris, 'Ibn Arabi and his Interpreters', pp. 751–752.

NASIR AL-DIN TUSI (1201–1274)

Nasir al-Din Tusi was a philosopher, astronomer, and mathematician. He worked as astronomer for the Mongol Khans and proposed a model of the study of planetary motion now known as the 'Nasir al-Din couple'. He was the author of many works on theosophical and theological topics, including the *Tajrid al-I'tiqadat* (*Definition of the Articles of Faith*) and *al-Akhlaq an-Nasiriyyah* (*The Nasirean Ethics*). He is credited with having rescued, consolidated and systematised the best and most enduring aspects of **Shi'a** scholastic learning

Khwajah Nasir al-Din Tusi was born in Tus, Persia, in 1201. His father, Muhammad ibn al-Hasan, was a prominent Shi'a jurist and he provided Nasir al-Din with his early education in the Islamic sciences such as Qur'anic and **hadith** studies, Shi'a jurisprudence, law, logic, the natural sciences, metaphysics, mathematics, and Arabic language and grammar. He then went to the birthplace of the poet Omar Khayyam, Nishapur (or Neyshabur, in the Khurasan province) in north-eastern Iran to continue his studies. At the time, Nishapur was acknowledged as the cultural and intellectual capital of the Islamic world in the east and so al-Nasir al-Din was able to study a number of different subjects under prominent scholars who could trace their pedigree back to the great **Ibn Sina**.

However, while he was studying in Nishapur, the Mongols began their invasion of Khurasan province, but Nasir al-Din was invited by a local **Ismaili** (a branch of Shi'a Islam: see **Al-Mahdi** for a more detailed account of Ismailism) prince to reside in his relatively safe fortress. He spent perhaps as long as eight years here and was able to engage in study as well as his own writing on, especially, astronomy. Another, wealthier, Ismaili prince heard of Nasir al-Din and invited him to his court, which he accepted in around 1234. Keeping in mind the turbulent times one would think Nasir al-Din would have considered himself fortunate to enjoy the patronage of princes. However, he is full of complaint about the conditions which he found 'impossible', although it is not altogether clear what was so difficult for him.

In 1252, the Mongol Khan Mangu sent his brother Hulegu (a grandson of Genghis Khan) to subjugate Persia entirely. It is said that he left with an army larger than that of Genghis Khan himself and, one by one, the Persian provinces surrendered and entered the service of the Mongol warlord. By this time Nasir al-Din was in the service of the Grand Ismaili Master Rukn al-Din Khurshah who, in 1256, also surrendered to Hulegu. Nasir al-Din had been virtually a prisoner under the Grand Ismaili Master, and so the arrival of the

Mongols was, for him, something of a liberation. His library and astronomical instruments were saved from the destruction and he was now part of Hulegu's entourage that was heading next to the *Abbasid* capital Baghdad itself.

His role under the Grand Master was that of astrologer and it was for this reason that Hulegu took him into his service. It was to be a hefty responsibility to say the least as Hulegu relied upon Nasir al-Din's astrological timings as to when to invade Baghdad. If the invasion had not been successful, then Nasir al-Din's life would have been a short one. Fortunately for Nasir al-Din, Baghdad was not in much of a state to resist the Mongol force: it had recently experienced a major flood and there was generally low morale and disorder in the capital. In 1258, the siege began and Nasir al-Din had now become so close to Hulegu's entourage that the Mongol warlord sent him to Baghdad to persuade the Caliph to surrender. The Caliph, after initial resistance, finally did surrender and was executed ten days later. Interestingly, although probably wrongly, Nasir al-Din is given credit for the Caliph's death by some sources: It is reported that the Mongol warlord was reluctant to kill the Caliph – bearing in mind that a Caliph was regarded as God's 'shadow on earth' – in case God should exact revenge. Nasir al-Din promised Hulegu that nothing would happen and, as an insurance, he suggested that the Caliph be put to death by rolling him around in a carpet; should anything start to happen, such as lightning striking, earthquakes, floods, or the like, then the rolling would stop and the Caliph would be saved. Needless to say, the unfortunate Caliph suffered a long and unpleasant death.

Such was Nasir al-Din's power due to the patronage of Hulegu it seemed that, however inaccurate the stories, he nonetheless had power over life and death over others. It is said that he saved the lives of many Muslim scholars in Baghdad, although it is also said that only those scholars who converted to Shi'a Islam were saved; those who remained *Sunni* were executed. For a time, Nasir al-Din remained with Hulegu in Baghdad, advising him how to consolidate his power in the capital, before he set off for the great centre of Shi'a learning, Hillah in central Iraq. Here he met many renowned theologians and jurists. Hulegu, meanwhile, had set up his initial seat of government in Maraghah (Maragheh) in north-western Iran. Nasir al-Din was summoned to the city and here he supervised the construction of what was to become a world-famous observatory (remnants of it still survive today) and was to attract many scientists to the city. In 1256, Hulegu died and was succeeded by his son Abaqa Khan who likewise gave Nasir al-Din patronage. Nasir al-Din became the new leader's vizier and personal physician. While on an official trip to Baghdad in 1273 Nasir al-Din fell ill and died of his illness the following year. His body was buried in the Kazimayn mosque in Baghdad, which holds the tombs of many Shi'a notables.

Due to the patronage of a number of courtly figures, and despite his own complaints, Nasir al-Din was able to produce a prolific amount of material covering subjects from medicine to theology. He wrote at least nineteen treatises on mathematics, and there are about one hundred texts in all attributed to him. Modelling himself on Ibn Sina, he wrote eloquently in both Arabic and Persian. Although the majority of his works were in Arabic, his works in Persian helped to promote the language as a *lingua franca* of philosophical discourse. He saw his philosophical work as closely related to his scientific studies, feeding off each other rather than in any way opposites. This is not uncommon in the ancient Greek tradition. While Nasir al-Din was patronised by many Ismaili Shi'a, and there were many Ismaili ideas in his work, there is some debate as to whether he was actually an Ismaili himself or, more probably, a 'Twelver' Shi'a. His scientific work on trigonometry, and in particular planetary theory, had a great impact. In fact, he has been credited with producing a planetary model that surpassed Ptolemy's in terms of accuracy.

The Mongol invaders were somewhat wary of Islamic religions orthodoxy, but had much greater empathy for mysticism and Shi'ism. Consequently, the Mongols turned out to be liberators, giving Shi'ites prominent positions and allowing them to engage in intellectual and philosophical debate to a much greater extent than had been permitted previously. This intellectual revival was achieved to a large part by Nasir al-Din. He adopted the Neo-platonic teachings of Ibn Sina and **Yahya Suhrawardi**, but, unlike Ibn Sina, he believed that the existence of God is not subject to proof, but rather had to be accepted. He defended the importance of philosophy, of reason, in theological discourse, although he also acknowledged the importance of authoritative teaching. Philosophy, he believed, was the reserve of the intellectual elite, that is, those who were well versed in the language of the discipline. Nasir al-Din was more of an explicator, and a good one at that, of the works of, most notably, Ibn Sina. His originality lies more in the field of logic, particularly in his appreciation of hermeneutics.

Nasir al-Din's political philosophy was something of a synthesis of Aristotelian and Persian ideas. His *Nasirean Ethics* is divided into three parts. The first part is concerned with the individual, the second with the family, and the third with the community. He set out to bring philosophy and jurisprudence together. Whereas Nasir al-Din's concern in philosophy wass concerned with unchanging truths and was considered important for giving us guidance regarding certain natural principles, jurisprudence is more concerned with convention, which can change according to the time and customs of a society. Consequently, his ethics combines, on the one hand, a Platonic conception of universal ethics, with an Aristotelian conception of subjective ethics. So far as *shari'a* (Islamic law) is concerned, there is, for Nasir al-Din, much scope for interpretation and it is not as absolute as Sunni jurists especially would believe. The family is important for Nasir al-Din because he sees the household as the centre of political life and, indeed, essential for human survival. His work examines the relationship between husband and wife, parents and children, but also deals with financial management and the importance of getting on with your neighbours! The central theme is one of mutual respect and responsibility and he gives much space to the importance of a child's education though he thinks it unnecessary for girls to read and write. Interestingly, he cautions against polygamy and gives advice on manners and appropriate behaviour including the right way to drink wine.

The final chapter of the *Ethics* deals with state politics. He starts by discussing why people need civilisation and then considers the different forms of government divided, as Aristotle does, into four types: kingship, domination, nobility, and the community (*jama'ati*). The only virtuous form of government he considered was the community, although by this he did not mean government *by* the community, but rather a community governed by a person of divine inspiration. Therefore, this is no democracy here, but rule by a Philosopher-King or, in *shi'a* terms, the *Imam*. Also, in Aristotelian fashion, Nasir al-Din states that the 'science of politics' (*hikmai-i madini*), which essentially is ethics, is the 'supreme craft' which oversees all other crafts; it is the ultimate end, the 'telos' of humanity. Knowledge, he argued, is fundamental to social order:

> The ordering of cities depends on kingship (*mulk*) and the ordering of kingship on statecraft (*siyasa*) and that of statecraft on wisdom. When wisdom prevails and the true law (*namus e-haqq*) is followed, order (*nizam*) is obtained, as is the attention to the perfection of beings. But if wisdom departs, law (*namus*) is impaired, and when *namus* is impaired the adornment of kingship disappears, and disorder (*fitna*) makes its appearance.[1]

And so the aim of political science, like the analogy with medicine, is equilibrium. The statesman is 'the world's physician' and, as part of his education policy, he believes that every person is duty-bound to study the science of politics in order to achieve virtue and thus perfection. This requirement that everyone should study is an interesting one, particularly in terms of its implications, for it suggests at least the possibility – in a sense not that different from **Mawdudi**'s 'theo-democracy' – that the 'community' may not be limited to an intellectual elite but should be given the opportunity to be intellectual.

Nasir al-Din's *Nasirean Ethics* was very popular and resulted in many imitations. It was particularly well received in, unsurprisingly, Persia and the Ottoman Empire. He was an erudite philosopher and, as a vizier, possessed that rare combination of philosopher-statesman. Aside from his philosophical writings, however, his contribution to the Islamic world is immense, if one were only to consider his role in the building of the Maraghah Observatory and his introduction of scientists and philosophers, particularly from China, which possessed expertise in astronomical and astrological knowledge.

Major works

There are many excellent translations of his works available.

The Nasirean Ethics, trans. G.M. Wickens, London: Allen & Unwin, 1964.
Contemplation and Action: The Spiritual Autobiography of a Muslim Scholar – Nasir Al-Din Tusi, trans. Seyyed Jalal Hosseini Badakhchani, London: I.B. Tauris, 1998.
On God, Destiny and Existents, trans. Parviz Morewedge, Utah: Brigham Young University Publications, 1998.
The Paradise of Submission, trans. Seyyed Jalal Hosseini Badakhchani, London: I.B. Tauris, 2004.

Further reading

Material on Nasir al-Din, in English, is still lacking unfortunately.

Black, Anthony, *The History of Islamic Political Thought*, Edinburgh: Edinburgh University Press, 2001, pp. 145–153.
Madelung, W., 'Nasir al-Din Tusi's Ethics: Between Philosophy, Shi'ism, and Sufism', in R.G. Hovannisian, *Ethics in Islam*, Malibu, CA: Undena, 1985, pp. 85–101.

Note

1 *Nasirean Ethics*, p. 233.

JALAL AL-DIN RUMI (1207–1273)

Jalal al-Din Rumi is one of the greatest mystics and poets of the Islamic world. In its sheer scale, his poetry is incomparable and his life has proven sufficiently enticing for there to be a number of novels and movies about him in recent years. Translations of his work are becoming increasingly popular in the Western world, but he has always held a special place for Muslims, especially in the Persian world where his poetry is seen as encompassing distinctively Persian mystical and philosophical concepts. Known as the 'master' which in Turkish is '*mevlevi*', his writings and actions in life resulted in the establishment of a **Sufi** order known as the Mevlevi, which is known in the West for its characteristic 'dancing' or 'whirling dervishes'.

Jalal al-Din Rumi was born in Balkh in the northern Persian province of Khorasan in 1207. Balkh at the time was a flourishing city and it is recorded that in the ninth century it possessed some forty mosques which was an indication of its size and activity. Many Arabs referred to Balkh as the 'mother of cities'. It was destroyed by the Mongols in 1220 and now it is just a small town. Rumi's family had lived in Balkh for several generations and they were held in high regard as a noble family. His great-grandfather claimed that his family were originally from Arab stock as opposed to indigenous Persian and, in fact, claimed descent from the first Rightly-Guided Caliph **Abu Bakr**. Certainly, his lineage could make claim to a number of jurists and mystics.

The life of Rumi is shrouded in legend. However, in terms of biographical material, his son, Sultan Walad, wrote a long narrative poem on the life of his father called *Ibtida namah* (*Book of Beginning*) which contains some very useful information. There is also a good critical biography by the Persian scholar Badi al'Zaman Furuzanfarr called *Biography of our Master* (*Sharhii hal-i Maulana,* 1932). What is known is that when Rumi was 12 years old, his father, Baha al-Din, took his family and left Balkh in 1219. Various reasons have been given for this exodus, such as Rumi's father – an eminent theologian, teacher and preacher – had received divine inspiration, or perhaps he had a disagreement of some kind with the rulers. However, the fact that Balkh itself was destroyed by the Mongols a year later suggests that many people of the city took the initiative to leave beforehand.

The family were to settle in the city of Konya in Turkey but, prior to that, they travelled to Baghdad, to Mecca and to Damascus before settling in Zarandah, about 40 miles south-east of Konya. There is an apocryphal story that while in Damascus in 1221 Rumi was seen walking behind his father by the great philosopher and mystic **Ibn Arabi** who then exclaimed: 'Praise be to God, an ocean is following a lake!' They stayed in Karandah for some seven or eight years and, during this period, Rumi married and his son, Sultan Walad, was born in 1226. They then travelled to Konya, which at that time was the capital of the Western Saljuk dynasty. It is said that Rumi's father, being of great reputation, was invited by the Saljuk Sultan to also reside in the capital and, as Baha al-Din approached the city, the Sultan left his palace to greet him and led Baha al-Din's horse by hand into the city. At the time Konya was in relative peace and sheltered many fleeing scholars, mystics, and artists from the Mongol invasions. Therefore, it was a stimulating place to be. Because of the Byzantine past of the region, it was called *Rum* ('Rome') among the Turks, and it was because of this that Jalal al-Din came to be known as *ar-Rumi*, 'the man of Rome'. Rumi's father, however, was not to enjoy Konya for too long as he died in 1230.

At around the time of the death of Baha al-Din, a former pupil of his, Burhanu al-Din Muhaqqiq of Tirmidh arrived in Konya and he became Rumi's *Pir* (spiritual master). For the next ten years, until the death of his *Pir* in 1240, Rumi went through all the stages required of the *Sufi* (Islamic mysticism) discipline and so he himself became a *Pir*. Rumi had a strong, charismatic personality and it was not long before he attracted disciples of his own as well as being a spiritual guide and friend of the Saljuk Sultan. Rumi was referred to by his disciples as '*Maulana*' ('Our Master') or, in Turkish, '*Mevlevi*'. In time, under his son especially, the Mevlevi became a well-known Sufi order.

Before that, however, a life-changing event occurred for Rumi at the age of 39. A mysterious, wandering mystic called Shams al-Din of Tabrizi arrived in Konya. Shams was to have a powerful effect upon Rumi and was a major contributor to the maturing of his own spiritual path. Central to Rumi's quest was the need to be associated with a 'Perfect Man' (see **Ibn Arabi** for more of an exposition of this complex phrase). In brief, the Perfect Man (*al-insan al-kamil*) is considered by many mystics to be the living manifestation of God. As man has been created by God, he embodies all the perfections of the universe, as well as those of Divinity. The reason for being, then, is to strive towards the highest perfection and this is done through the mystical path. Those who have achieved the highest perfection can perceive their own creaturely uniqueness as well as see their identity with God. To be associated with such a Perfect Man is, therefore, to be associated with God, to be part of the 'divine light' of God. This theme recurs throughout Rumi's poetry: the Perfect Man is to be seen as a mirror of God's divine attributes and so to be one with the Perfect Man is to be one with God.

Rumi took Shams into his house and for something like two years the two were inseparable, much to the jealousy of Rumi's disciples. In fact, Rumi's followers were so upset by the attachment Rumi showed to Shams that they threatened the latter with violence. Shams fled to Damascus but Rumi sent his son Sultan Walad to seek him out. Rumi's son brought Shams back to Konya and the disciples repented. However, it seems that their repentance was not genuine as Shams once again fled to Damascus and, once again, Sultan Walad brought him back. Finally, in 1247, Shams 'disappeared'. Some reports suggest that he was murdered by some of Rumi's disciples and the body was hidden by being thrown into a well. Sultan Walad in his biographical poem describes how the loss of Shams affected Rumi:

> Never for a moment did he cease from listening to music (sama'), and dancing;
> Never did he rest by day or night.
> He had been a mufti: he became a poet;
> He had been an ascetic: he became intoxicated by Love.
> 'Twas not the wine of the grape: the illumined soul drinks only the wine of light.

In this short passage there are a couple of interesting references. First, to that of Rumi listening to music and dancing. The Mevlevi Order, which was institutionalised by Sultan Walad, is characterised by its religious dance (the sama, or the so-called 'whirling dervishes') to the plaintive accompaniment of the reed-flute. The practice is a form of meditation in which Sufis can attain states of spiritual ecstasy. The suggestion here is that such a practice has its origins with Rumi himself. Secondly, the fact that Rumi now developed from being a *mufti* (essentially a legal functionary or, more generally, a learned Muslim one goes to for advice) into a poet. The reference here seems to be to Rumi's great work, *Diwan-i Shams-i Tabriz* (*Poems of Shams of Tabriz*, and usually referred to as the *Diwan*) which is a voluminous work dedicated to the memory of Shams.

After the disappearance of Shams, Rumi attached himself to another spiritual figure, that of Salah al-Din Fardidun Zarkub. However, this relationship – although meant to be two becoming One – was most likely a reversal of the relationship Rumi had with Shams, for Salah al-Din was Rumi's deputy (*khalifa*) of the Mevlevi

Order and Rumi's charisma was the stronger. Rumi, however, out-
lived his deputy who died in 1261. During the remaining years of
Rumi's life, however, he attached himself to his next deputy, Husam
al-Din Hasan ibn Muhammad ibn Hasan ibn Aki Turk. During this
time Rumi composed his greatest work, the *Mathnawi* (*Spiritual
Couplets*) which he called 'the book of Husam'. Upon the death of
Rumi in 1273, Husam became the Head of the Mevlevi Order until
1284 when Sultan Walad took his place.

The *Mathnawi* is a huge work consisting of 25,000 rhyming couplets and opens with the following well-known lines:

> Hearken to this Reed forlorn, breathing even since 'twas torn
> From its rushy bed, a strain of impassioned love and pain.
> 'The secret of my song, though near, none can see and none
> can hear.
> Oh, for a friend we know the sign and mingle all his soul with
> mine!
> 'Tis the flame of Love that fired me, 'tis the wine of Love
> inspired me.
> Wouldst thou learn how lovers bleed, hearken, hearken to the
> Reed!'[1]

As referred to earlier, the Persian reed-flute (*nay*) has always been
associated with the Mevlevi Order. Symbolically, the devotee of God
is like a reed flute which only becomes a living instrument when it is
torn from the earth. The reed flute is the soul that remembers
the union with God and its music is a longing for a return to this
Oneness.

For Rumi, though also torn from his 'beloved', from God, there is
nonetheless consolation to be found through the forms of God
delivered to him as the Perfect Man, for example, Shams. The
Mathnawi has often been referred to as 'the Qur'an in Persian'
although Rumi himself did not see his poetry as revelation but as a
vehicle for God's expression. Nonetheless, many treat his work as
something complementary to the Qur'an for it is a source of
guidance as well as inspiration. It goes far beyond the scriptural text
and weaves folklore and traditional tales as well as a compendium of
Sufi thought, Neo-platonic, biblical and Christian ideas. Rumi
believed that people should follow divine guidance, whether that be
via the Qur'an or a spiritual master, although he was not enthusiastic about the religious scholars, the *ulama*, as the following
shows:

Learn from thy Father! He, not falsely proud,
With tears of sorrow all his sin avowed.
Wilt thou, then, still pretend to be unfree
And clamber up Predestination's tree? –;
Like Iblis [Satan] and his progeny abhorred,
In argument and battle with their Lord.
The blest initiates know: what need to prove?
From Satan logic, but from Adam love.[2]

The 'Father' in this case is Adam who, according to the Qur'an, repented his sin and wept bitterly. The *ulama*, or the dogmatic theologians, were fond of discussing issues such as predestination and free will (did Adam sin of his own free will or is God to blame?), whereas Rumi is stating that such engagements in logical demonstration only alienate you from God. What matters is Love which Adam possessed.

While the *Mathnawi* is considered more instructional in character, the *Diwan* is more personal and emotional. The appeal of Rumi's poetry lies in its cosmopolitan and universal quality as this well-known passage from the *Diwan* demonstrates:

Tell me, Muslims, what should be done?
I don't know how to identify myself. I am neither Christian nor Jewish, neither Pagan nor Muslim.
I don't hail from the East or from the West, I am neither from land nor sea.
I am not a creature of this world ... [3]

While it has never been so popular with Arabic Sufis, shortly after Rumi's death it was not long before his poetry, and his *Mathnawi* especially, became known all over the Persian world. The Mevlevi Order was institutionalised by Sultan Walad and it spread across the Ottoman Empire, having a particular patronage with the Ottoman Court. There are now many lodges as far away as Egypt and Syria, although in Turkey itself it was suppressed during Kemal Ataturk's secularisation process. Rumi has influenced many poets, was widely read in Iran and had a huge influence in the Indo-Pakistan subcontinent. The Chisti Order of Delhi study the *Mathnawi* and Shams has become a legendary figure in India. Rumi's universal outlook influenced the more pluralistic Mogul Emperors such as **Akbar**, and his writings on the Perfect Man were an inspiration for the poetry and writings of **Muhammad Iqbal**.

Major works

Because of Rumi's immense popularity in the West now, there is certainly
no shortage of translations of his poetry. Probably the best translations of
some of his works are provided here. As a good starter, I suggest the Penguin
book *The Essential Rumi*.

Birdsong: 53 Short Poems by Rumi, trans. Coleman Barks, Witney: Windrush
Press, 1993.
Selected Poems from the 'Divani Shamsi Tabriz', trans. R.A. Nicholson,
London: RoutledgeCurzon, 1997.
The Essential Rumi: Selected Poems, trans. various, London: Penguin, 2004.
The Masnavi, book 1, trans. Jawid Mojaddedi (Oxford World's Classics),
Oxford: Oxford University Press, 2004.

Further reading

Again, there is now a large corpus on Rumi. The Nicholson and Schimmel
are particularly helpful. The Lewis, at seven hundred pages long, is extremely comprehensive and informative.

Lewis, Franklin D., *Rumi, Past and Present, East and West*, Oxford: One-
world, 2000.
Nicholson, Reynold A., *Rumi: Poet and Mystic*, Oxford: Oneworld, 1995.
Schimmel, Annemarie, *Rumi's World: The Life and Work of the Great Sufi Poet*,
Boston: Shambhala, 2002.

Notes

1 Nicholson, p. 31.
2 Ibid., p. 165.
3 From *Diwan*, trans. Cyril Glasse, *The Concise Encyclopaedia of Islam*.

IBN TAYMIYYA (1263–1328)

Ibn Taymiyya was a jurist of the Hanbali (see **Ibn Hanbal**) school of
law and was a very strict Traditionist (those who adhere strongly to
the Traditions of the Prophet and the Qur'an) who railed against
what he saw as the 'innovations' (*bid'ah*) of such authorities in Islam
as **al-Ghazali**, **Ibn Arabi** and the **Sufis** (the mystical branch of
Islam) generally. He emphasised the need to return to what he perceived as the pristine ideals and practices of Islam at the time of the
Prophet **Muhammad**. Often regarded as something of an eccentric,
sometimes as a heretic, his strong opinions nonetheless resulted in
respect from many quarters and his legacy is of a founding figure of

the fundamentalist strand in Islam, and forerunner of the Wahhabi movement (see Abd **al-Wahhab**) in the eighteenth century.

Taqi al-Din Abu al-'Abbas Ahmad ibn 'Abd al-Salam ibn 'Abdalla Ibn Muhammad Ibn Taymiyya was born in 1263 in the ancient biblical city of Harran, Mesopotamia (what is now most of modern Iraq, south-eastern Turkey and eastern Syria). At the age of 5, he went to Damascus in Syria with his father to escape the Mongol invasions that were then overrunning the eastern flanks of the Muslim world. Damascus at the time was an important intellectual and political centre and had been the headquarters of the Sultan **Salah al-Din** (d. 1193) during the Third Crusade, and it was not to fall to the Mongols until 1401 when Tamerlane (d. 1405) pillaged and burned the city. During Ibn Taymiyya's time there, however, he was able to enjoy relative peace among the city's many mosques and religious seminaries. He followed in the tradition of his father by studying with the great scholars who were available to him at the time and as a youth became proficient in most of the Islamic scriptural sciences including scholastic theology (**kalam**) and Qur'anic exegesis (**tafsir**), jurisprudence (**fiqh**) and **hadith** (Traditions of the Prophet), the latter taught to him, it is reported, by the female scholar Zaynab bint Makki. Once he had received his teaching certificate (**ijaza**) at the age of 19, he began a career in teaching. He also began producing his own religious edicts (**fatwa**).

Ibn Taymiyya was never far from controversy as a result of being very outspoken in his opinions, and he was soon being accused of anthropomorphism. Much debate at the time existed as to how literally the Qur'an should be interpreted. A popular school of thought especially of the ninth century were the **Mu'tazilites** ('rationalists'). One of their doctrines was the concept of Allah's unity (**tawhid**) which challenged the popular idea that God could be seen by the faithful in the afterlife. It was an attack on anthropomorphic interpretations of the attributes of God such as the view that He had hands, sat upon a throne, and so on. Many of these views of God could be found in the *hadith* and so it was also an attack upon those who appealed to the *hadith*. Among such 'Traditionists' were Ibn Taymiyya. For the Mu'tazilites, reference to God possessing hands, for example, should be seen metaphorically as, in this case, a reference to God's 'grace'. To suggest that God actually has hands threatens to picture God in too human-like fashion. Although Mu'tazilite teachings were no longer in their ascendancy during the time of Ibn Taymiyya, their influence was widespread and there continued to be suspicion surrounding those who argued for a literalist interpretation.

Ibn Taymiyya was also reflecting the faith of the ordinary Muslims of the early period of Islam who were for the most part encouraged to accept a literal interpretation of faith without delving into the possible hidden meanings. In part this was a defence mechanism against the possibility of Islam becoming watered down or submerged by the various other faiths the Muslims encountered as they expanded. The *hadith*, and much early theology, discourage speculative reflection upon divine attributes and Ibn Taymiyya reflects this view and so is being consistent with his belief that the Muslim must essentially live and breathe the Qur'an and the *hadith*.

At the same time, he was engaged in prolonged polemical activity against various *Shi'a* and Sufi groups. He was particularly critical of the Ittihadiyya School, which taught that the Creator and the created are, to all intents and purposes, one entity. This idea stems from that of the Persian philosopher and mystic **Ibn Arabi** who argued that God is a 'totality' and, as such, is not separate from His creation, hence being both Creator and that which is created. This, for Ibn Taymiyya, smacked too much of pantheism, although Ibn Arabi himself was careful to say that it does not follow that all things that exist are God. At the centre of Ibn Arabi's polemical adventures was his call for a return to the primary sources of Islam: the Qur'an and the Prophetic Traditions which, he argued, if one were to study thoroughly, one would find no support for such 'innovations' engaged in by Sufis, Shi'a and the philosophers.

In 1306, Ibn Taymiyya was summoned before the council of the governor of Damascus to defend the accusations of anthropomorphism levelled against him. He was sent to Cairo to appear before yet another council and was summarily imprisoned in the citadel for eighteen months. It was not long after his release that he was thrown back into prison for denouncing the Sufi practice of visiting the shrines of saints which, he argued, was against Islamic law (*shari'a*). In 1313, he returned to Damascus where he was to spend the rest of his life. He gathered around him a circle of like-minded disciples who were essentially agitators and it was not long before he again offended the authorities because of his campaign against the introduction of a new law that would make it more difficult for a husband to divorce his wife. Ibn Taymiyya was again imprisoned, this time in the Damascus citadel for six months. His last sojourn in prison was in 1326 where he remained until his death in 1328. During this time he was able to write an enormous amount until his jailors deprived him of pen and paper. At his funeral, it is said that some 20,000 mourners followed his bier, many believing him to be a saint. For someone who languished in prison because of his attacks on saint worship, it is ironic that his grave became a place of pilgrimage to seek miracles and favours.

Although he led a more turbulent life than most of his scholarly contemporaries, he was able to produce a considerable body of material covering all the branches of the Islamic sciences. His disciple and ideological spokesman, Ibn Qayyim al-Jawziyya, lists some 350 works by his master. Ibn Taymiyya wrote in the fields of Qur'anic studies and its exegesis, on jusisprudence, theology, logic, ethics, politics, and *hadith* studies. He adopts a measured, sober and precise style throughout his works and his polemical skills are particularly noteworthy. Of particular note is his *al-Kitab al-siyasa al-shar'iyya* (*Treatise on the Government of the Religious Law*) and *Minhaj al-sunna* (*The Path of Prophetic Tradition*), the latter being considered one of the richest works of comparative theology to survive the Middle Ages.

It is somewhat inaccurate to describe Ibn Taymiyya as a strict literalist, although he has often been interpreted that way. As an aid to understanding the sources he endorsed the use of independent reasoning (**ijtihad**) provided it is by a qualified expert (**mujtahid**) and, in fact, advocated a 'happy mean' (*wasat*) between reason, tradition, and free will. However, he is consistent in his view that the reason for what he saw as ignorance, injustice, and a loss of faith and knowledge in the Islamic world was only curable by returning to what he perceived to be the pristine ideals encapsulated in the Qur'an and Prophetic Traditions. Rather than rely upon what he regarded to be erroneous texts written later, the Islamic scholar should 'struggle' (the literal meaning of *ijtihad*) to determine what the original sources have to say. If the Muslims were to emulate the practices as sanctioned by God and contained in the Qur'an and the example provided by Prophet Muhammad, then all would be well. Practices outside of this are 'innovation' (*bid'a*) and, therefore, to be condemned. Such a view was not necessarily restrictive, for Ibn Taymiyya was only concerned with those practices sanctioned by the Qur'an and the Prophet. Activities not referred to in these primary sources were allowed a more flexible approach.

In his main political work, *Treatise on the Government of the Religious Law*, he argues that under the Rightly-Guided Caliphs (the **Rashidun**), the Islamic state achieved a level of moral and political purity and, in fact, this is essentially what the main project of Islamic law (*shari'a*) should be. Rulers since that time have not come up to the mark and so Ibn Taymiyya is aiming for Righteous Rule (*siyasa shari'a*). The ruler should follow, rigorously, the tenets of *Shari'a*, applying it firmly but fairly, and relying on it for all legal opinions and rulings. Those who are ruled should obey the authority of the Caliph provided he, in turn, obeys *Shari'a*. He was insistent that religion cannot be practised without state power. The religious duty of 'commanding good and forbidding evil' (*hisba*) cannot be achieved without a central power and authority and so there is a necessary link between state and religion. Religion and government need one another, an idea explored empirically by the great Muslim philosopher of history, **Ibn Khaldun**. The rulers had high status and great power, but also the people had the right to have high expectations of the rulers that the latter are duty-bound to fulfil.

There are not many Muslim thinkers who have attracted as much controversy and criticism as Ibn Taymiyya has done. His polemical pamphleteering and campaigning made him many enemies among Sufi and Shi'a, scholars of Islamic law, and rulers who found him to be particularly troublesome but were afraid to make a martyr of him for, as his funeral indicates, he had the support of many of the common people. Although controversial in his own lifetime, for a long time after his death he actually had few followers and little influence. A small number of Ottoman scholars studied him in the sixteenth century but it was not until the eighteenth century when Muhammad ibn 'Abd al-Wahhab (d. 1792) took his ideas (or his interpretation of them anyway) down the road to Wahhabism which, together with his military endeavours, led to the creation of the Saudi state. Since that time he has been seen as the champion of revivalism and the founding father of many reform movements which look to the time of Muhammad and the principles inculcated in the Qur'an to counter what is perceived as the threat of modernism. However, his work has not always been fairly understood with a greater emphasis on Ibn Taymiyya as an ultra-conservative rather than his insistence on a 'happy mean' and the importance of independent reasoning.

Major works

In the work below, Ibn Taymiyya sets out to refute philosophical logic. A good translation by Hallaq with useful explanatory notes. A very good scholar of Ibn Taymiyya is Yahya Michot, and his articles – written in French – are being translated in English and becoming more available, especially in the *Journal of Islamic Studies*, for example.

Ibn Taymiyya against the Greek Logicians, trans. Wael B. Hallaq, London: Clarendon Press, 1993.

Further reading

There is not much available in English at present, consisting mostly of entries and overviews.

Rosenthal, E., *Political Thought in Medieval Islam: An Introductory Outline*, Cambridge: Cambridge University Press, 1958.

Lambton, Ann K.S., *State and Government in Medieval Islam: An Introduction to the Study of Islamic Political Thought: The Jurists*, Oxford: Oxford University Press, 1981.

ABD AL-RAHMAN IBN KHALDUN (1332–1406)

Ibn Khaldun was an historian, philosopher, social scientist and jurist who can be credited with being the first Muslim philosopher of history. He led a turbulent and often dangerous political career, but, despite this, was able to produce one of the finest works in Islamic thought, the *Tarikh* (*History*), which goes beyond a mere historical account by looking into what history can tell us about the characterisitics of himan nature and society. It is a monumental work that, more recently, has been recognised for its originality and insight.

Abd al-Rahman ibn Khaldun was born in Tunis in 1332 into a noble tribe who trace their descent to a certain Khaldun who emigrated to Seville in Spain from Hadramut in southern Arabia in the eight century. This Khaldun tribe became very influential especially in terms of their intellectual and political prowess. Shortly before the fall of Seville to Christian control in 1248, the Khalduns had the foresight to migrate to Ceuta in North Africa and thereafter to Tunis where they received a warm welcome due to their strong connections with the ruling dynasty. The Khalduns soon became part of the royal court as administrators and military leaders. However, by the time of Ibn Khaldun's birth, the fortunes of his family were in decline, although they still enjoyed relative wealth and status. Both his father and grandfather, however, had turned their backs on the quest for wealth and power and sought scholarship instead.

As far as can be determined, Ibn Khaldun had only two brothers, an older brother Muhammad and a younger Yahya. He lost both his parents in the plague which struck Tunis in 1347–1348 and so Muhammad became head of the family. Yahya went on to become a successful historian and a high-ranking politician. Ibn Khaldun married the daughter of a general and had seven children by her. It is not known if he had any other wives. His early education was not unlike many of his class. It began with tutoring from his father at home before going to a mosque school and then being taught by specialists, in this case mostly fellow Andalusian migrants. As was customary, he memorised the Qur'an at a young age and studied Arabic. Ibn Khaldun studied in Tunis, where he had spent his childhood and adolescent years, and completed his education in Fez to which he moved in 1354. There he studied under a number of scholars in the fields of mathematics, logic, theology, philosophy, law and the occult. Although he generally received a good education, owing to his family's status and scholarly connections, his formal schooling lasted only until he was 17 years old.

At the time of Ibn Khaldun, the territories of North-West Africa were divided between three Sultanates: the Merinids (Banu Marin) who ruled the Western Maghrib (roughly corresponding to present-day Morocco), the Abd al-Wadids (Banu Abd al-Wad) who ruled the Central Maghrib (approximately present-day Algeria), and the Hafsids (Banu Hafs) who ruled the Eastern Maghrib (also known as Afriqia, approximately present-day Tunisia and Libya). Borders between these three Sultanates were not fixed and each tried to extend its power into the regions of the other. Therefore the era was characterised by continuous inter- and intra-dynastic wars and conflicts. At the same time, the dynasties were vying for the support of the powerful Berber tribes (name given to the language and people of certain indigenous, non-Arabic peoples inhabiting large sections of North Africa).

For over two decades, Ibn Khaldun was an active participant in the turbulent politics of these states, playing the dangerous game of politics and shifting his allegiances when necessary. At the age of 21, he found employment as 'Master of Signature' in the Hafsid court, but, in 1354, deciding that Tunis held little future for him, he accepted an invitation from the most powerful Sultanate at the time, the Merinid Abu 'Inan, to join his inner circle of philosophers, theologians, astrologers, poets and advisors. In 1359–1360, he was appointed Chief Secretary by Sultan Abu Salim, Abu 'Inan's successor. At the death of the Sultan in 1361 Ibn Khaldun set off for Granada where, due to his connections and reputation, he was given a position in the royal court there as an ambassador. But, in 1365, he moved home yet again to the prosperous seaport of Bijayah in eastern Algeria where he was prime minister. He soon fell out of favour, however, and, for about nine years (1365–1374), he operated as an independent 'political expert', mostly recruiting and arranging tribal support, first for Sultan Abu Hammu, the Abd al-Wadid ruler of Tlemcen, and then to the Merinids of Fez. Ibn Khaldun had gained first-hand experience of tribal politics and affairs when he spent two years in their territories during his journey from Tunis to Fez (1352–1354).

Not all of Ibn Khaldun's years in politics revolved around prestigious appointments and high level political activity. In addition to being forced to constantly change his residence whenever falling out of favour with this or that ruler, he intermittently found himself in critical and hazardous situations. He was imprisoned by Sultan Abu 'Inan in 1356 for twenty-one months (released only upon the Sultan's death); arrested by the Moroccan Sultan Abd al-Aziz in 1369–1370; attacked and looted by Bedouins acting on the instigation of Sultan Abu Hammu while on his way from Biskara to Fez in 1372–1373; arrested by the vizier of Sultan Abu al-Abbas of Tunis in 1373–1374, and extradited by the Spanish Sultan Ibn al-Ahmar in the same year.

In 1375, Ibn Khaldun, surrounded by political enemies in the Maghrib, decided to retire altogether from political activities and adventures and devote himself to scholarship. He was 40 years old when he was offered protection by an Arab tribe and he settled with his family in a Sufi shrine known as Qal'at Banu Salama. There, Ibn Khaldun began his monumental history of the world. His *Muqaddimah* (*Prolegomena*), the first version of which was completed in 1377, was the first book in his three-volume *Tarikh* (*History*), and it is this first book that he is most famous for.

Realising that he needed to consult more sources for his work, Ibn Khaldun moved back to his hometown, Tunis, in 1378 after seeking permission from its Hafsid ruler Abu al-Abbas. He settled in Tunis for about four years, teaching jurisprudence in addition to his writing and research work. His stay, however, was interspersed by conflicts with both scholars and conniving courtiers as well as having an uneasy and untrusting relationship with the Sultan. Ibn Khaldun departed to Egypt in 1382, after having obtained permission to make the pilgrimage to Mecca. Whether by accident or design, he ended up spending the rest of his life (1382–1406) in Egypt. Shortly after his arrival he was offered a teaching position at the oldest and most prestigious university in the Islamic world, the al-Azhar. However, in 1383, as he had done on so many occasions in the past, he sent for his wife and family to join him. However, his wife and five daughters perished when a storm struck and wrecked their ship on the journey from Tunis to Egypt.

In Egypt, Ibn Khaldun completed his major work. His *History* bears the full title of *Book of Exemplaries on Historical Narratives Concerning the Arabs, Persians, Berbers and their Contemporaries* (*Kitab al-'ibar wa diwan al-mubtada wal khabar fi ayyam al-'arab wal 'ajam wal barbar wa man 'asarahum min zawi al-sultan al-akbar*). Divided into three books, the famous first book, the *Prolegomena*, outlines his methodology and outlook on history as well as the dynamics of human society. The second book concerns the history of the Arabs and the third deals with the history of the Berbers. This part concludes with Ibn Khaldun's autobiography, *al-Ta'rif bi Ibn Khaldun* (*Acquainting the Reader with Ibn Khaldun*) which makes for colourful reading in itself. Ibn Khaldun has drawn extensively on his predecessors for his sources, although it would certainly not have been the same work if had not been able to draw on his own considerable experiences and travels. Although the emphasis of the *History* is political and focuses on the rise and fall of dynasties, it also offers much more in its analysis of what politics tells us about human nature. The *Prolegomena*, for which he achieved lasting fame, is divided into six chapters. At the beginning of this work he indicates how history differs from other accounts:

> On the surface, history is no more than information about political events, dynasties and occurrences of the remote past, elegantly presented and spiced with proverbs. It serves to entertain large, crowded gatherings and brings to us an understanding of human affairs ... The inner meaning of history, on the other hand, involves speculation and an attempt to get at the truth, subtle explanation of the causes and origins of existing things, and deep knowledge of the how and why of events. History, therefore, is firmly rooted in philosophy. It deserves to be accounted a branch of philosophy.[1]

Having studied philosophy, theology and history, Ibn Khaldun noted that philosophical concepts and reasoning had been applied to theology but not to history. Hence, Ibn Khaldun can rightly be given the status of being the first philosopher of history in the Islamic world. The central theme in the *Prolegomena* is the sociology of human society which he called the science of civilisation (*'ilm al'umran*). To him, *al-'umran* is a science which helps to distinguish truth from falsehood in recording historical events. In other words, studying *al-'umran* would reveal the dynamics of human society, which in turn would enable the historian to sift through historical records and establish fact from fiction. Hence, historical facts are those which correspond to the logic of societies' dynamics and their rules of evolution. At the core of social organisation lies social adhesion or solidarity *asabiyah'*.

To Ibn Khaldun, the power-base of each state depends on its 'asa-biyya, or group solidarity based on family ties and lineage which is to be found mostly among nomadic people and 'savage' nations. Ibn Khaldun argues that the power of each 'asabiyya extends basically to four generations. The first generation, driven by tribal expansionism or religious mission, would conquer the settled nations and establish a powerful state. The second generation would consolidate and expand the state and build its institutions and would still enjoy strong attachment to its 'asabiyya due to its close connection with a tribal ethos. The third generation would enjoy the prosperity of the state and provide support for arts, sciences, and culture, but would have less attachment to their 'asabiyya as a result of their urban upbringing. The fourth generation would be the one to waste the achievements of their ancestors. Confined to a life of palace machinations and pursuit of material gratification, this generation would be mostly concerned with raising money to spend on their welfare and the preservation of their thrones, which would lead to an intensification of the tax burden on the populace. The resulting injustices would lead to the dissolution of the state and the annihilation of its civilisa-tion, and make it vulnerable to invasions from other nomadic or savage groups. The cycle then starts anew.

Despite the monumental achievement of his *History*, Ibn Khaldun's literary output bears no comparison to the encyclopaedic productions of, say, **Ibn Sina** or **al-Kindi**. Aside from his major work, only seven minor works are listed: three on logic, mathematics and *Sufism* (Islamic mysticism) respectively, two commentaries on poems, and two abridgements of the works of theologians. Nonetheless, his *History* alone gives Ibn Khaldun pride of place in any library. It is said that he came at the wrong time and the wrong place, however, to find a European translator or to provide any successors that would lead to a Khaldunian school. It was not until the Ottoman Turks, who translated his *Prolegomena* into Turkish in 1830 that his theories were in vogue. French translation followed in the mid-nineteenth century and he received admiration, although the social sciences were already too well established in Europe by this time for Ibn Khaldun to have any real influence. In his homeland, however, no complete Arabic edition of his history was available until 1867. The first modern Arab to make a study of him was Taha Husayn (1989–1973) who presents Ibn Khaldun as an egoist, and other scholars joined the bandwagon of anti-Khaldunian remarks declaring him anti-Muslim and anti-Arab to the extent that, in 1939, an Iraqi minister of edu-cation suggested that his tomb be dug up and his books burned!

However, since then, he has enjoyed something of a revival, and his contribution to the philosophy of history, together with admiration for his remarkable life, has been duly recognised.

Major works

The Muqaddimah: An Introduction to History, trans. Franz Rosenthal, Princeton, NJ: Princeton University Press, 2004.

Further reading

Ahmad, Zaid, *The Epistemology of Ibn Khaldun*, London: RoutledgeCurzon, 2003.
al-Azmah, A., *Ibn Khaldun: An Essay in Re-interpretation*, Budapest: Central European University Press, 2003.
Enan, M. Abdulla, *Ibn Khaldun: His Life and Work*, New Delhi: Kitab Bhavan, 2000.

Note

1 *The Muqaddimah* (2004).

AL-SUYUTI (1445–1505)

Al-Suyuti was an Egyptian teacher and writer who authored works on a number of subjects, particularly the Islamic sciences. He was a jurist, philologist and an historian. He was recognised as an authority on the **hadith** (Traditions of the Prophet) and, in fact, was given the title of **mujaddid** (renewer), as well as being a **mujtahid** imam (one authorised by his training to arrive at independent legal interpretations). Al-Suyuti has been attributed with playing a very important role in conveying the ideas of many lost or forgotten manuscripts, especially in the field of Arabic language.

Abu al-Fadl Abd al-Rahman ibn Kamal al-Din Abi Bakr ibn Muhammad ibn Sabiq al-Din Jalal al-Din al-Suyuti was born in Cairo, Egypt, in 1445. It is said that his mother was of Turkish origin while his father was Persian. In his autobiography he states that his ancestors derive from Baghdad. His father was a judge of the Shafi'i school of law (see **al-Shafi'i**) and he was brought up in Asyut in central Egypt. At an early age he was taught by a friend of his father who was a **Sufi** (Muslim mystic) and he memorised the Qur'an at the age of 8 which, in fact, was not an unusual enterprise for young

Muslim scholars. He went on to have various teachers who were all recognised experts in their respective fields, notably *tafsir* (Qur'anic exegesis), *shari'a* (law), study of the *hadith*, and Arabic grammar. As was also common among young scholars of the Islamic sciences, he made a point of travelling to other centres of learning to be tutored. He travelled widely, specifically to Damascus, the Hijaz, the Yemen, India and Morocco.

At the age of 18, al-Suyuti became a teacher of *hadith* in Cairo. It is reported that his reputation grew to such an extent that wealthy Muslims and figures of court would offer him money and gifts in return for spiritual endorsements, but he would always reject such offers. Even when approached by the Sultan's envoy, he insisted on maintaining his independence. He argued that pious scholars should distance themselves from their temporal rulers as much as possible and should, therefore, resist gifts and money from them.

At the age of 40, in 1486, al-Suyuti decided to withdraw from public life altogether and so he gave up his teaching as well as his duties as a judge. The reason he gave for this was that he saw a series of signs that had been prophesied by the Prophet **Muhammad** and that these signs urged scholars to withdraw from public affairs and stay in their homes. The kind of signs he meant were more a case of the attitudes of people in his society (and, frankly, most societies one comes across), notably greed, materialism, pride, an increase in false-hood, and great dispute. Much of this he blamed on the ignorance of the religious scholars, the *ulama*. However, he nonetheless continued doing some teaching until 1501 and so this would hardly constitute complete isolation but rather 'semi-retirement'.

In fact, in 1501, his 'retirement' was actually a forced one. It is not entirely clear why he was dismissed from his post as Shaykh, but no doubt his stubbornness towards the Sultan did not help matters and, indeed, his general disinclination towards the acceptance of any kind of political patronage often inevitably leads to the view that if you are not a friend, then you are an enemy. However, he also seems to have made a number of enemies in the academic community, which may be partly due to his own personality; a stubbornness coupled with a self-confidence in his own abilities and his God-given 'mission'. As a result, he was involved in a number of scholarly disputes, mostly over the authenticity of religious opinions (*fatwas*). In spite of official pronouncements he would cause confrontation by promulgating his own opinions. In addition, he would publicly declare that anyone who disagreed with his ideas was ignorant or, worse still, an unbeliever. He was convinced he was living in an age of ignorance and that only his opinions were the right ones. Consequently, he urged his contemporaries to recognise him as a *mujaddid* ('renewer'). According to tradition, based upon a well-known *hadith*, each one hundred years a 'renewer' will come who will restore Islam to its right path, it having, one assumes, veered away. Such recognised 'renewers' include **al-Ghazali**, **Ibn Taymiyyah**, **al-Wahhab**, and **Shah Wali Allah**. These were, for the most part, scholarly and unique individuals. One requirement of being a *mujaddid,* however, is that it is up to the public to recognise him, rather than for the *mujaddid* to declare it himself. Al-Suyuti demonstrated his suitability for the title of *mujaddid* for he was certainly a scholar well versed in the orthodox religious sciences and contributed to the conservation of Islamic knowledge. However, he was not recognised by his contemporaries who found his conceit, pride and impertinence intolerable.

Whatever the reasons for his forced retirement, his reputation was severely damaged by this and his works were condemned. He now withdrew entirely from public life and worked in seclusion on the island of Rawda, near Cairo, until his death in 1505. Despite condemnation during his latter years it was not long after his death before he was rehabilitated in the minds of many and, in fact, gained the status of a saint.

The number of works attributed to him varies depending upon which scholar one refers to, and seem to vary between around 550 and 980. Some of these are brief *fatwas*, which do not exceed four pages. One of his finest writings is considered to be *Al-muzhir fi 'ulum al-lugha wa anwa'iha* (*Exhibiting the Science of Language and its Forms*), which is a compilation of the works of his predecessors and contemporaries on the topic of the Arabic language. This work is divided into fifty sections dealing with the attribution of language, lexicography, semantics, subtleties and witticisms of language, the acquisition of linguistic knowledge, the condition of language and its transmitters, poetry and poets, and, finally, language errors committed by Arabs. The encyclopaedia was largely derived from the works of two predecessors, Ibn Jinni and Ibn Faris. Al-Suyuti was the co-author of *Tafsir al-Jalalain* (*Commentary on the Two Jalals*) with Jalal al-Din al-Mahalli. This was a word-by-word commentary on the Qur'an. His *Itqan fi 'ulum al-Qur'an* (*Mastery in the Sciences of the Qur'an*) is also a well-known work on Qur'anic exegesis. During the years of solitude he wrote *Jami' al-jawami* (*The Collection of Collections*) which was a ten-volume *hadith* work, and *Hadith, Tadrib al-rawi fi sharh taqrib al-Nawawi* (*The Training of the* Hadith *Transmitter: An Exegesis of*

Nawawi's 'The Facilitation') which is a classic commentary on the sciences of the *hadith*.

Al-Suyuti was also an historian and a biographer and wrote a history of the caliphs as well as a history of Egypt, and a large number of biographical collections selected according to the specialities of figures (commentators, traditionists, poets, philosophers and so on). He wrote poetry, mostly praising Prophet Muhammad. Al-Suyuti was a Traditionist, along the lines of Ibn Taymiyya, although he preferred to distance himself from certain aspects of his thought. Nonetheless, he was not fond of Hellenistic logic, and he believed that our knowledge can be derived from the Traditions of the Prophet and the Qur'an. For al-Suyuti, *hadith* scholarship especially was the 'noblest of the Islamic sciences'. This is because it is related to the prophetic model, which for him is the only way leading to God. He believed that the prophetic model cannot be transmitted exclusively by scholarly science, but it must be vitalised from inside, hence his fondness for *Sufism*, the mystical aspect of Islam. He places much cognitive importance – which is echoed in the writings of the illuminationists such as **Suhrawardi** – in visions and claims to have many visions of the Prophet Muhammad.

Al-Suyuti had a prodigious memory and a mind that was able to synthesise many different branches of knowledge as well as engage in the editing and dictating of several works at the same time. From an early age he had desired knowledge and he did not want to be ignorant in any field not, he stated, due to pride, but rather because he saw knowledge as a blessing from God. He led a frugal life and believed he had a mission given to him by God which consisted of assembling and transmitting to future generations Islamic thought before it might disappear as a result of the laxity he saw among his contemporaries. He pre-figures the modern period in some respects in that he was partly an autodidact, presenting to the public manuals which were based on precise themes. However, it is unfair to accuse him of being merely a compiler, for he takes up themes that were usually neglected. His ability to select and abridge works was quite remarkable and he adopted a scientific approach in terms of his methodology, which he always explains in the introductions to his works. Although references to Sufism are peculiarly absent from his canon, he was a practising Sufi and, especially after withdrawing from public life, he adopted the mystic approach to life. He was a member of the Shadhiliyya Sufi order and he believed *shari'a* – Islamic law – and mysticism were not in opposition but rather complemented each other.

Major works

None of al-Suyuti's works are readily available in English.

Further reading

Czapkiewicz, A., *The Views of the Medieval Arab Philologists on Language and Its Origin in the Light of 'As-Suyuti's 'al-Muzhir'*, Cracow: Nakadem Uniwersytetu Jagiellonskiego, 1989.
Sartain, E.M., *Jalal al-Din al-Suyuti*, 2 vols, Cambridge: Cambridge University Press, 1975.

SULEIMAN 'THE MAGNIFICENT' (*c*.1494–1566)

Suleiman was the tenth Ottoman Sultan, and was known in Western Europe as 'the Magnificent' and in Turkey as 'the Lawgiver' (*al-Kanuni*). His reign (1520–1566) is commonly described as the Golden Age of the Ottoman Empire. He reigned over a vast empire and contributed greatly to the promotion of culture, art and the sciences. As Sultans go, he was a cultured figure who wrote poetry and was well read in Turkish and Persian literature. His title, 'the Lawgiver', is due to the fact that he oversaw the most detailed codification of Qur'anic, and Sultanic, law that any Islamic state had ever experienced, while in the West he was considered 'the Magnificent' because of his reputation for his elaborate and grandiose courtly rituals.

Since the early thirteenth century the warrior-like Mongols had spread from the Far East and it was only a matter of time before they reached Muslim borders. It was not long before the heartlands of the Islamic world were under Mongol control, with the Mongols – who 'lacked such a strong religious base' – converting to Islam. The large Mongol states began their collapse in the late fourteenth century and, in Anatolia, small independent states emerged. One of these states was ruled by the Osmanli family which was to grow in power as the power of the Mongols declined. By 1372 the Osmanlis, or 'Ottomans', had conquered much of what was originally Byzantium, establishing their capital at Edirne (Adrianople). Much of their success was due to a well-trained army known as the 'new troop' (*yenicheri* or Janissary) that was essentially a fiercely loyal slave corps. Murad I (1360–1389) became the most powerful Western Muslim ruler of the time, conquering much of the Balkans and, in 1453, during the reign of Medhmed II 'the Conqueror' (1451–1481)

Constantinople itself was conquered and renamed Istanbul. Before this time the Byzantine Empire had always succeeded in rebuffing Islamic incursions, but now there was a new power in town. Whereas previously the Ottoman rulers had ruled like typical military chieftains, in Istanbul they adopted the Byzantine model and established an absolute monarch, the Sultanate. Conquest continued under Selim I (1467–1520) against the Safavids, which brought the whole of Syria and Egypt under Ottoman control. North Africa and Arabia also became part of the empire at this time and, in the 1530s, the Ottoman armies reached as far West as they were ever to go, to the gates of Vienna.

The Ottoman Empire reached its nadir under Selim I's only son, Suleiman 'al-Kanuni' ('the Lawgiver'). It is generally considered that he was born in 1494, although some writers have suggested 1495 or 1496. He was born in Trabzon (or Trebizond), a city in north-east Turkey on the Black Sea. His mother was a slave girl called Hafsa. Before ascending the throne he gained experience as a local governor in the Crimea and at Manisa (Magnesia), an Ottoman *sanjak* (district) north-east of İzmir. On the death of his father, who was on campaign at the time, Suleiman was 26 years old. At his accession, he was described thus:

> He is tall, but wiry, and of delicate complexion. His neck is a little too long, his face thin, and his nose aquiline ... a pleasant mien, though his skin tends to pallor. He is said to be a wise lord, fond of study, and all men hope for good from his rule.[1]

The Ottoman Empire that Suleiman now ruled over was to be the greatest that the empire was ever to know, with a border of some 8,000 miles, and he was feared across the world. In the West, he was known as 'the Magnificent', while among the Turks he was known as 'al-Kanuni', the 'Lawgiver', for his work in overseeing the codification of the laws. He married a slave girl called Ruthenia (known in the West as Roxelana) and, what was most unusual, remained faithful to her. Most Sultans preferred to have a series of concubines, but Suleiman was truly in love with Ruthenia, as his poetry indicates. His poetry is, in fact, highly regarded. He composed over two thousand *ghazals* (poems of five to fifteen couplets) and most of these are addressed to his wife. He was a cultured man who was well read in Turkish and Persian literature.

He was to go to war thirteen times during his long reign which included the taking of Hungary and the island of Rhodes, the latter of which had been considered impregnable. His attempts to take

Vienna, however, failed, though more due to bad weather and bad timing. Nonetheless, he succeeded in pushing the borders of the empire even further than they had been, but it was to be its limit. He could be ruthless when he had to be: He had his best friend murdered and his son, Mustafa, strangled by mutes because he suspected Mustafa was plotting against him. He executed another son, Bayezit, who failed in a coup attempt. He also had Bayezit's own four sons killed. Suleiman left the empire to another son, Selim, who had too much fondness for wine. Despite the number of wars, most of these occurred beyond the frontiers of the Empire and so, within the Empire itself, there was relative peace and considerable prosperity during his reign aside from occasional, manageable disturbances in Syria, Egypt and Anatolia. Much money was devoted to public works: new roads laid, bridges built, as well as aqueducts, mosques, hospitals, schools and universities. Suleiman devoted much money and energy in caring for the important holy and historic cities of Mecca, Medina, Jerusalem, and Damascus, not to mention Istanbul itself where much new building took place under the Christopher Wren of Istanbul, Sinan, including the stunning Suleimaniye Mosque.

His courts were spoken of around the world for their splendour and elaborate rituals. Suleiman's officials were, unlike those in Europe, chosen because of merit rather than nobility. It was possible for a slave to rise to leading positions in the state, although a rise could just as quickly result in a rapid fall if mistakes were made. Suleiman was fortunate to be served by three particularly meritorious Grand Viziers: Ibrahim (1523–1536), Rustem (1544–1553, 1555–1561), and Mehmed Sokollu (1565–1566)

As mentioned, Suleiman was known as 'the Lawgiver', although theoretically, in Islam, only God can 'give' laws. Further, what code of laws existed was largely due to his predecessors. What Suleiman was to initiate was the updating of law codes that were largely produced by Mehmed II. They were then later to be known as 'Suleiman's law code'. Leaving this aside, the law codes were a great innovation and unprecedented in the world of Islam. What came into existence was non-religious law known as 'kanun' which was the law of the Sultan, or Ottoman law (kanuni osmani). They then effectively slotted this into the **shari'a** system and both types of law were administered by the same courts. The book of law codes was first issued by Mehmed II after conquering Rome and updated in 1501, during the reign of Suleiman. Kanun dealt first of all with criminal law and was intended to supplement shari'a by specifying penalties, although the punishments actually tended to replace *shari'a* with harsher punishments. It also dealt with the collection of taxes, land tenure, and so on. Finally, it was concerned with the form of government and the relationships between the various spheres of authority. Because of the integration of *kanun* and *shari'a* the judges implemented secular as well as religious law in Islamic law courts: unique in the Islamic world! And so a judge had to be familiar not only with *shari'a*, the laws of God, but also with *kanun*, the laws of the Sultan. The justification for *kanun* was that *shari'a* simply could not cover everything with regard to social order of such a huge empire with such a diversity of cultures and beliefs and, besides, *shari'a* only applied to Muslims, so another law was required. Both laws, it was argued, were after the same thing, which was public order and justice. Of course the problem was that *kanun* would often conflict with *shari'a* which placed judges in a dilemma as to which law to abide by. However, during Suleiman's reign this did not seem to cause much concern and it was only when the Empire was in its decline that the blame was placed partly on the watering down of *shari'a*.

The authority to produce new laws raises the thorny issue of how much religious leadership a Sultan could legitimately possess. It has been noted that Suleiman, especially in his early years, considered himself to be the 'Master of the Age' (*Sahib-Kiran*), that is the very embodiment of human perfection and thus, a reflection of God Himself. The Moghul emperor **Akbar** had likewise given himself such a title, for it also meant that the ruler saw himself as the *universal* ruler of Islam and responsible for guiding the Muslims along the right path. Suleiman also called himself 'Caliph of the whole world'. The Ottomans had claimed the title of Caliph for some time, especially when Selim I had brought Mecca and Medina into his realm and was thus its guardian. It was believed that the Sultan-Caliph had the responsibility to execute *shari'a* in all parts of the world but it was also claimed that he had the power to interpret the law, hence *kanun* though 'secular' in one sense is, theoretically at least, the product of a ruler guided by divine inspiration.

In 1566, Suleiman set off on his thirteenth and final campaign, once again – for the seventh time – against troublesome Hungary. His army besieged and took the fortress of Szigetvár but Suleiman died before it fell. He had been sick with dropsy and probably died as a result of a heart attack following an attack of dysentery. As was the practice, the news of his death was kept secret from his army until Selim II was present to assume control. Suleiman was seen as the model of a just ruler, although he was fortunate to inherit a position of such power gained by his predecessors. In fact, some scholars have argued that the decline that was to follow Suleiman's death was in part due to Suleiman overreaching himself in the territories he conquered, causing insurmountable administrative problems for any successor. He has also been regarded as a pillar of orthodoxy, although it was only perhaps in the last twenty years of his life that he adopted a more pious and austere existence.

Further reading

There is a wealth of material on Suleiman and the Ottomans.

Clot, Andre, *Suleiman the Magnificent*, London: Saqi Books, 2005.
Goodwin, Jason, *Lords of the Horizon*, London: Vintage, 1998.
Rogers, J.M. and Ward, R.M., *Suleiman the Magnificent*, London: British Museum Press, 1998.

Note

1 Goodwin (1998), pp. 81, 82.

AKBAR (1542–1605)

The third Mughal emperor of India (reigning from 1556 until his death in 1605), and considered the true founder of the Mughal Empire, Akbar achieved distinction as both soldier and administrator. Based upon his study of not only Islam, but also especially Hinduism, Christianity, and Zoroastrianism he founded his own syncretistic cult which was known as 'Divine Faith' (*Din Ilahi*), although this apparently did not spread beyond his own court.

Akbar (which means 'the greatest') was the son of Emperor Humayun and the grandson of the Mongol clan leader Babur (d. 1530), the founder of the Moghul dynasty. Babur had been an ally of Shah Ismail and had fled as a refugee to Kabul in the Afghan mountains during the wars between the Safavids and the Uzbeks. He established a power base in north India which was consolidated to a greater extent by Akbar's father Humayun. Akbar was descended from the great Mongol military rulers Tamerlane and Genghis Khan. He was born in Umarkot in Sind province, which is now in Pakistan. He succeeded to the throne at the age of 13, but being too young to rule independently the country was effectively governed by a regent,

Bairam Khan, who was himself successful in recapturing territory that had been usurped at the death of the young emperor's father. However, in 1560, at the age of 18, he took control of the government.

Akbar expanded the empire from its original territories, making extensive conquests to the west, east and south. He successfully won the allegiance of the Rajputs, the honourable, yet belligerent caste-based group who, at the time, were in a dominant position in northern and Western India. Akbar demonstrated his shrewdness by marrying two Rajput princesses and giving Rajput princes positions of authority in his government. He established an efficient administration of what was a huge multi-credal empire.

Akbar's ambitious aim was to create a single community of **Sunni** and **Shi'a**, Muslims, both **Sunni** and **Shi'a** and Hindus living in an environment that inculcated religious toleration and equality of status. Such a policy had, in fact, been initiated by Babur, and Akbar's father had also little truck for religious sectarianism within Islam itself. Such a project was no doubt helped by the fact that this was India; a nation of mostly Hindus who had long accepted religious variety. In addition, the Mughals had always been less inclined to impose Islamic law, especially in respect of civil matters. The religious scholars, the **ulama**, had less power in central Asia and India, and the Moghuls had more empathy with **Sufism** (Islamic mysticism). Consequently, in this region, religious leadership rested with Sufi masters who had much in common with the Yogic strand in Hinduism.

The Moghul emperor was incredibly open-minded in both philosophical and religious concerns; although this was no doubt a pragmatic realisation that ruling over India required a large degree of compromise so far as religious belief was concerned. It was inconceivable that such a small minority of Muslims could impose their religion on the Hindu tradition which had such a long and entrenched tradition. However, Akbar was naturally inquisitive about the beliefs of other religions and he was constantly seeking religious guidance from sages whom he would invite to his palace. Such a sage was Abu'l-Fadl (1551–1602) who had received a philosophical and religious education from his father, and who held the view that, 'there is no creed that may not be mistaken in some particular, nor any that is entirely false'.[1] Abu'l-Fadl came to be a good friend and adviser to Akbar and guided him in his spiritual quest. He wrote *A'in-i Akbari* (*Regulations of Akbar*) which not only provides an interesting narrative on Akbar's life, but also presents Akbar's views on government and religion. As Akbar was himself illiterate, such a work is invaluable. It records, for example, how, in 1578, Akbar, 'experienced "the sublime joy" of the "attraction of the cognition of God"'. This seems to be a form of illumination which led Akbar to believe his kingship was to be guided by divine inspiration, but,

> Now that the light of truth has taken possession of our soul, it has become clear that ... not a single step can be taken without the torch of proof, and that that creed is profitable which is adopted with the approval of wisdom.[2]

And so Akbar was now to be guided in his political decision by the 'torch of proof' which resulted in Akbar's quest to find out as much as possible on what each religion has to offer. Abu'l-Fadl ordered translations of, for example, the *Laws of Manu* and the *Mahabharata*. At the same time, while bowing to the wisdom of revelation, it gave Akbar himself infallible authority as the source of the 'cognition of God', for he regarded himself as the Perfect Man (*insan-i kamil*), not unlike the Platonic Philosopher-King. The concept derives from the philosopher and mystic **al-Arabi** (see also **Rumi**) and was adopted by the Ismailis as well as Sufis. The highest manifestation of Reality is the human, with the archetype of the first man, Adam, and which is also identified as the Perfect Man. Hence the Perfect Man is actually the visible manifestation of God.

Akbar encapsulated both the political ruler and the spiritual teacher and, 'what really changed the emotional climate, and gained increasing solidarity and strength for the Mughal throne, was the Sufic ideology of the Perfect Man propounded by Abu'l-Fadl which appealed both to Hindus and Muslims'.[3] Consequently, the kind of spiritual guidance lay especially with a combination of divine inspiration through spiritual exercise and dialectical reasoning, rather than the observance of Islamic law (*shari'a*) as dictated by the *ulama*. Akbar rejected much of *shari'a*, partly because he was not convinced that much of it came from reliable sources. Legitimacy, rather, did not come from obedience to *shari'a* (see, for example, **Ibn Taymiyya** who argued that rulers are only legitimate if they follow *shari'a*) but rather a more direct access to God's will via divine inspiration. Naturally, many orthodox scholars were suspicious of this approach – and hence their wariness of Sufism generally – for it seemed too much like revelation which, it is traditionally considered, ended with the Prophet **Muhammad**.

Akbar presented himself as the supreme religious authority within the Islamic community, regardless of whether he was addressing Sunni or Shi'a Muslims. In 1579 he produced the quite remarkable 'infallibility decree' which stated that on points for which religious jurists (the **mujtahids**) differ, Akbar will himself decree which opinion was correct and it would from thenceforth be binding upon all Muslims. More than this, Akbar could also initiate new laws which all must abide by, provided, he states, they do not go against injunctions of the Qur'an. However, Akbar was effectively bypassing a thousand years of the development of *shari'a*. This is clearly an indication of the authority Akbar possessed as he was able to get the *ulama* to sign up to the decree. One justification for the religious authority given to the ruler was that, 'the rank of a just sultan is higher in the eyes of God than that of a *mujtahid*'.[4] The idea of the 'just sultan' (*sultan-i adil*) was the title given by the Shi'a to a ruler who, in the absence of an *Imam*, upheld religious values. Akbar, in fact, claimed to be the 'Imam of Islam and the Muslims', as well as the 'lord of the age' (*sahib-i zaman*) and hence chosen at this particular time to rid religion of its differences. In terms of the authority of the Caliph, who at this time resided in Istanbul, the seat of the Ottoman Empire, Akbar considered him to be merely 'Caesar of Rome' (*Qaiser-i Rum*), whereas Akbar was Caliph of the Age. He was given the additional title of Emperor of Islam (*Badshah-i Islam*) and was pronounced an even greater hero than **Salah al-Din**, because he was reconciling the differences between Sunnis and Shi'ites.

Akbar, however, went far beyond uniting the different sects within Islam itself. He repealed laws that discriminated against other religions. Hindus were permitted to repair their temples, as well as to build new ones. In addition, conversion to Islam by force was prohibited and those who had previously been converted by force were allowed to return to their religion. He also abolished the discriminatory poll-tax (*jizya*) against non-Muslims. Positions of authority were given on merit, rather than on religion, and many Hindus rose to very high rank in government and society. It would actually not be an exaggeration to say that Hindus and Muslims lived together on an equal footing, at least for a time.

No doubt Akbar was aware of the advice of his father and Babur himself who had seen differences within a religion as a weakness. What was important was stability and order and so Akbar had no patience with sectarianism. He believed in looking beyond what he saw as the pettiness of the *ulama* and instead focused on the underlying sameness of religious belief *per se*. To this end, during the mid-1580s, both Akbar and Abu'l-Fadl constructed a whole new religion, the Divine Faith' (*Din Ilahi*), of which Akbar himself was its spiritual master. The structure followed that of a Sufi order, with Akbar as *Pir*, and with his senior officials as his disciples, thus establishing a spiritual patronage as well as a political one. It was a new religio-political order in which his disciples took part in an initiation ceremony repudiating traditional, orthodox Islam, for they were required to say:

> I liberate and dissociate myself from the traditional and initiative Islam which I have seen my fathers practice ... and join the religion of God of King Akbar, accepting the four degrees of devotions, which are sacrifice of property, life, honour and religion.[5]

Needless to say, this was seen as heresy by most orthodox Muslims, although it did have some links with elements of Islamic thought, notably the Sufic concept of leadership, and that of **al-Farabi**'s Platonic conception of rule. The Divine Faith was also presented just before the new Muslim millennium (1591–1592) when there were expectations of the coming of a 'just ruler' a *Mahdi*, especially among Shi'a. It was also an amalgamation of Sassanian, Zoroastrian and Hindu ideas of kingship. Most importantly, however, was that Akbar saw his role as very much a part of his Mongol heritage. Abu'l-Fadl took great pains to present a sacred lineage of divine light that had been transmitted to Akbar through fifty-two generations from the first man, Adam. Akbar's predecessors such as Tamurlane and Genghis Khan saw themselves not just as local rulers but also *world* conquerors.

Akbar's new religion, however, barely stretched beyond his court. His inclusivist policies were continued by the next two emperors, Jahangir (r. 1605–1627) and Shah Jahan (r. 1628–1658) whose Taj Mahal combines Muslim and Hindu ideas of architecture, with the Divine Faith being extended somewhat to include Muslim and Hindu nobility, but the opposition of the orthodox Muslims led to the new religion's eventual abandonment. Akbar had brought relative peace to the region during his reign and his religious tolerance was quite remarkable for any age. He had his critics, however, most notably the Sufi Ahmad Sirhindi (d. 1625) who, aside from proclaiming himself to be the Perfect Man of the age, argued for the importance of observing *shari'a*. However, it was the Emperor who came after Shah Jahan, Aurenqzebe (1658–1707) who despised pluralism and set about destroying Hindu temples, imposing heavy taxes upon non-Muslims, and suppressing both non-Muslim and Shi'a festivals. At the death of Aurenqzebe, the empire was in a dire state with many revolts and regions breaking away. It was never to recover the golden era that it had under Akbar and, during the eighteenth century, the position of Indian Muslims was fragile indeed, leading to the views of the Sufi thinker Shah **Wali-Allah** (1703–1762) who echoed those of Sirhindi.

Further reading

Alam, Muzaffar and Subrahmanyam, Sanjay (eds) *The Mughal State 1526–1750*, Delhi: Oxford University Press, 1998.

Fazl, Adu'l, *The Akbar Nama of Abu-L-Fazl: History of the Reign of Akbar Including an Account of His Predecessors*, trans. H. Beveridge, Lahore: Sang-e-Meel Publications, 2005.

Rizvi, A.A., *The Religious and Intellectual History of Muslims in Akbar's Reign with Special Reference to Abu'l Fazl*, New Delhi: Munshiram Manoharlal, 1975.

Streusand, Douglas E., *The Formation of the Mughal Polity*, New Delhi: Oxford University Press, 1989.

Vanina, Eugenia, *Ideas and Society in India from the Sixteenth to the Eighteenth Centuries*, Delhi: Oxford University Press, 1996.

Notes

1 Vanina (1996), p. 64.
2 Rizvi (1975), p. 380.
3 Ibid., p. 361.
4 Alam and Subrahmanyam (1998), p. 141.
5 Streusand (1989), p. 150.

SADR AL-DIN SHIRAZI 'MULLA SADRA' (*c*.1572–1640)

A remarkable intellectual, Muhammad ibn Ibrahim al-Qawami al-Shirazi, known as 'Mulla Sadra' to many Muslims, is considered to be one of the most influential and revered philosophers in Islamic thought. His works represent a synthesis of a thousand years of Islamic thought which preceded him and he was expert in Islamic philosophy, theology, mysticism, Qur'anic interpretation, and history. His familiarity with the Qur'an and the sayings of the Prophet **Muhammad** (*hadith*) as well as that of the *Shi'a Imams* was unequalled, as was his intimate knowledge of the schools of Islamic philosophy, not to mention his mastery of the doctrines and practices of mystical Islam.

Al-Shirazi was born in Shiraz in southern Persia in around 1572 to a wealthy family. His father, Ibrahim Shirazi, was a minister in the royal court of the Shi'a Safavid dynasty and was also a recognised scholar. After completing his elementary studies in his native city, al-Shirazi pursued his education in Isfahan, the seat of Safavid rule and one of the most important centres of learning in the Islamic world in the sixteenth century. He studied there under some of the most influential and original Islamic thinkers of the time, including Astarabadi (better known as Mir Damad). Apparently, Asterabadi was very impressed with al-Shirazi's knowledge and expertise in constructing philosophical arguments and readily sung his praises. Within a few years of beginning his studies at Isfahan, the intellectually gifted al-Shirazi was a recognised master in all branches of formal learning and excelled that of many of his teachers. He became expert in what are regarded as the two branches of Shi'ite learning: the transmitted and the intellectual. The 'transmitted sciences' (al-'ulum al-naqliyyah) relate to jurisprudence, Qur'anic interpretation and hadith scholarship. The 'intellectual sciences' (al-'ulum al-aqliyyah) included philosophy and mysticism. His expertise rested especially in the philosophical and mystical school of Illumination (hikmat, see **Suhrawardi**).

Upon completing his studies he withdrew from society and lived in seclusion in the small village of Kahak, near the holy city of Qom. During this time, al-Shirazi became increasingly preoccupied with the life of contemplation and asceticism which, like Suhrawardi before him, he believed to be necessary experiences for the acquirement of knowledge. In this respect, he believed that knowledge cannot be merely theoretical but is also experiential.

However, al-Shirazi's fame as a scholar resulted in many invitations from Isfahan to take up a position within the royal court. For his part, however, he shunned the opportunity for such wealth and status, and was also not enamoured by the inevitable court intrigues and scholarly jealousies of the city. Instead he returned to Shiraz to teach at a new religious school, far away from what he saw as the corrupting influences of big city life. It is reported that he made the pilgrimage to the holy city of Mecca on foot seven times and died in Basra on his way back from his seventh pilgrimage.

Al-Shirazi's literary output is considerable, with more than fifty works attributed to him. He wrote commentaries on the works of Suhrawardi and **Ibn Sina**, as well as original short treatises on theological and philosophical topics, on Islamic jurisprudence, Qur'anic commentaries and hadith scholarship. His major works, however, are al-Mashha'ir (Apprehensions), Kasr Asnam al-Jahiliya (Breaking the Idols of Paganism) and al-Asfar al-arba'ah al-'aqliyyah (Transcendental Wisdom, better known as The Four Intellectual Journeys). In his Four Journeys, al-Shirazi expresses concern over the neglect paid to philosophy, and argues for the compatibility of philosophy with religion. Both, he believes, present the same single truth of the nature of the world, a truth that was revealed to the first man, Adam, then transmitted to the prophet Abraham and the other prophets, the Greek philosophers, the Prophet Muhammad, the Muslim mystics, and finally the philosophers of more recent times. It is interesting to note that al-Shirazi does not distinguish between the knowledge acquired by the prophets and that of the philosophers, for, so far as al-Shirazi was concerned, as there is but one truth, there can be no distinction. However, it can be understood how this levelling of the playing field between the Greeks and prophets, including Muhammad, would offend many orthodox Muslims who accused al-Shirazi of blasphemy and atheism. Al-Shirazi stated that such philosophers as Empedocles, Pythagoras, Socrates, Plato, Aristotle and Plotinus are all, in his words, 'pillars of wisdom' who have received the 'light of wisdom' from the 'beacon of prophethood', hence his view that they all share the same outlook on such issues as the unity of God (**tawhid**), the creation of the world, and of resurrection. Such a view, of course, is rather far off the mark from reality.

Al-Shirazi produces an imaginative synthesis of **Sufism** (Islamic mysticism) with that of Shi'a Islam. He pictures a philosophical history in which the prophetic stage of history comes to an end with the death of Muhammad as the Seal of the Prophets, but this is then followed by the Imamate stage of the twelve Shi'ite Imams which will continue until, as is accepted teaching for Shi'a Muslims, the twelfth Imam returns from his temporary occultation (**ghaybah**). These Imams are not prophets but 'executors' in that they execute the truth as revealed by the prophets. In fact, al-Shirazi believed, these executors have a longer history than the twelve Imams; there have been other 'executors' going right back to Sheth who was executor to Adam. When the Twelfth Imam, the *Mahdi*, comes out of occultation at the end of time, mankind will return to a pure monotheistic state that existed at the time of Abraham.

At the centre of al-Shirazi's philosophy is his view on Being as Reality. Whereas in our everyday experience we are aware of objects that exist, al-Shirazi had a vision in which he experienced a single Reality (*wujud*) which gives the appearance of a multiplicity of existent things. This emphasis on existence in itself is what the German philosopher Heidegger calls *Dasein* some three hundred years later. This single Reality is something that can be comprehended only through extensive mental preparation as well as practices of purification; such an experience of Reality is an understanding of its unity (wahdat al-wujud); a doctrine associated especially with the philosophy of **Ibn Arabi**, from whom al-Shirazi borrows heavily. For al-Shirazi, an analogy is that whereas the unity of being is the sun itself, the manifestations of many existent things are the rays of the sun, which bears a similarity with the Neo-platonic idea of the rays of the sun as emanations of the Active Intellect. In this sense, Reality itself is God, and the exiting things are emanations of God. Hence there are degrees of being or 'gradation of being' (tashkik al-wujud). Being is like light in that it possesses degrees of intensity while being a single reality and so there is a chain of being from the simplest of molecules to God.

Interestingly, al-Shirazi saw the Qur'an, as it is the word of God, as the same as Being itself and so it should be of no surprise that perhaps no other Islamic philosopher has devoted so much attention to the Qur'an as a source of philosophical knowledge as well as producing so many detailed commentaries. He has written interesting commentaries, some of which are now available in English, on a number of chapters and verses of the Qur'an including The Opening, The Throne Verse, The Light Verse and The Event. Al-Shirazi is always at pains to stress the harmony between revelation and reason, rather than any opposition of the two and, in fact, regards the intellect as humanity's 'inner prophet'. However, this is dangerous territory for those who would argue that no humans since Muhammad could possibly measure up to the Prophet in terms of knowledge of God. So far as interpreting the Qur'an, al-Shirazi was opposed to the literal or 'outer' approach which reads a text as it is without considering its inner meaning. However, he was likewise not impressed by those who concentrated on only the inner meaning without appreciating its outer elements. Rather, the best approach is to explore the inner meaning without going against the external sense of the words.

No other Islamic philosopher has dealt in as much detail as al-Shirazi with the concepts of resurrection and eschatology. He devoted various works to these topics: in particular, the fourth book of his *magnum opus The Four Intellectual Journeys* goes into considerable detail on the philosophy of the soul (*nafs*). This work describes the spiritual path as being at first a journey in which one becomes detached from the physical world and seeks extinction in the Divine. On the second journey, one reaches the degree of Divine Names and Attributes, which is the station of sainthood and in which he now sees, hears and acts through God. Third, is the end of extinction and the individual is transformed. In the final journey, the saint then returns to the world and acts as a guide for others along the spiritual path. In relation to the soul, upon death al-Shirazi supports the orthodox view that there is bodily resurrection, but that the body is 'subtle', and so not the same in form or matter as the body one was born with. Curiously, al-Shirazi presents a view of resurrection reminiscent of Eastern conceptions of karma. After death the individual is not simply a disembodied soul but possesses bodies which are 'woven' by the actions that the person engaged in during earthly life and, likewise, they enter a world that reflects the life they have led. Therefore, someone who has committed evil in life will enter hell simply because that has become the nature of his soul.

Despite al-Shirazi's impact on Islamic intellectual history, there is little yet available in the way of comprehensive studies in the Western world. More recently, however, Henry Corbin, James Morris, Seyyed Hossein Nasr, and Fazlur Rahman have produced the most detailed works on al-Shirazi available in the West, while Rahman's work on his metaphysical philosophy is the most thorough work on the philosopher to date. Nonetheless, his contribution to Islamic thought influenced Persia during his time and after, as well as India. More recently, and certainly since the 1950s, his writings have been influential among religious scholars in Iran.

Major works

Very little is available in English at present.

Wisdom of the Throne: Introduction to the Philosophy of Mulla Sadra (Princeton Library of Asian Translations), trans. A.K. Morris, Princeton, NJ: Princeton University Press, 1981.
The Hermeneutics of the Light Verse of the Qur'an, London: Islamic College for Advanced Studies, 2003.

Further reading

Moris, Zailan, *Revelation, Intellectual Intuition and Reason in the Philosophy of Mulla Sadra: An Analysis of the Al-Hikmah Al-'arshiyyah*, London: Routledge, 2001.
Rahman, Fazlur, 'The God–World Relationship in Mulla Sadra', in G.F. Hourani, *Essays on Islamic Philosophy and Science*, Albany, NY: State University of New York Press, 1975.

SHAH WALI-ALLAH (1703–1762)

The Indian Muslim Shah Wali-Allah was a religious leader of the Naqshbandi *Sufi* (Islamic mysticism) Order. While incorporating ideas to be found in the work of **Ibn Taymiyya, Ibn Arabi** and Muhammad **al-Wahhab**, he was also an extremely innovative and original thinker, particular in his ideas on natural law and its relation to *shari'a* (Islamic law). He came at a time when Muslims were experiencing an identity crisis as Mughal supremacy was in decline and Hindus and Sikhs were in constant revolt against Muslim authorities. Wali-Allah responded to this in his call for reform in Islam and the need for a strong Islamic state that lived according to *shari'a*. For this reason he is considered to be the father of Islamic modernism.

Before we can consider the life of Wali-Allah, we need to understand his importance in the context of what was happening before and during his life. During the reign of the Moghul emperor **Akbar** in the sixteenth century, India experienced a time of relative peace, prosperity and religious and social tolerance. Akbar, though a Muslim, had little time for adherence to *shari'a* or for sectarianism between **Shi'a** and **Sunni** Muslims. He believed that he was the 'Perfect Man' (*al-insan al-kamil*, see Ibn Arabi for explanation of this concept) who received divine revelation. Akbar's ambitious aim was to create a single community of Sunni and Shi'a, Muslims and Hindus living in an environment that inculcated religious toleration and equality of status. Akbar encapsulated both the political ruler and the spiritual teacher. Consequently, the kind of spiritual guidance lay especially with a combination of divine inspiration through spiritual exercise and dialectical reasoning, rather than the observance of Islamic law as dictated by the **ulama** (the religious scholars). Akbar rejected much of *shari'a*, partly because he was not convinced that much of it came from reliable sources. Legitimacy, rather, did not come from obedience to *shari'a* (see, for example, Ibn Taymiyya who argued that a ruler is only legitimate if he follows *shari'a*) but rather a more direct access to God's will via divine inspiration. Naturally, many orthodox scholars were suspicious of this approach. During the mid-1580s, Akbar introduced a whole new religion, the 'Divine Faith' (*Din Ilahi*), of which Akbar himself was its spiritual master. This was seen as heresy by most orthodox Muslims. His inclusivist policies were continued by the next two emperors, Jahangir (r. 1605–1627) and Shah Jahan (r. 1628–1658).

Many Muslims, as well as Hindus, found such religious reforms insufferable and sought to retreat within their own traditions. The consequences of seeking universality within society is that it can disguise the underlying differences between them. Akbar criticised the caste system, to the chagrin of Hindus, and criticised the *ulama* and *shari'a* to the annoyance of orthodox Muslims. The group that was at the forefront of the reaction against this pluralism was a Sufi order called the Naqshbandi which was a relatively recent order in India and had enjoyed the patronage of Akbar (who believed that Sufism had a more universal approach to religion than what was considered orthodox Islam) in his later years when it was headed by Shaykh Khawaja Baqi-billah. It grew in strength and activity during the reign of Emperor Jahangir when the order was headed by Shaykh Ahmed Sirhindi (1564–1624). Not unlike Akbar himself, Sirhindi claimed that he was, in fact, the Perfect Man which resulted in a spell in prison for the latter.

Sirhindi was critical of those teachings of Sufism that promoted the mixing of Hinduism and Islam, for example Ibn Arabi's 'unity of being' (*wahda al-wujud*) which some commentators (Indians especially) interpret as a form of pantheism which would fit in nicely with forms of Hinduism. Sirhindi's concern was that Indian Islam, being very much the minority in India as well as a much newer religion, would become submerged into just one expression of Hinduism. He argued that Sufi orders, which were the most powerful forms of Islamic expression in India, should abide strictly by *shari'a*. Sirhindi agreed with the Muslim philosopher and theologian **al-Ghazali** who argued that although mystical experience was important, it is still necessary to engage in 'outer acts' (*zahir*), especially the rituals associated with Islam such as pilgrimage, prayer, ablutions, alms, fasting, reading the Qur'an, following the *shari'a*, and so on. Sirhindi presented the theology of 'phenomenological monism' or 'unity of witness' (*wahda al-shuhud*). The very subtle difference here between 'unity of witness' and 'unity of being' is that Sirhindi argued for a clear distinction between Creator and created, whereas Ibn Arabi argued that God is both, being a 'totality'. Sirhindi argued that the *ulama*, who were to a large extent ineffectual in India at that time, should have supremacy over the *pirs* (Sufi saints). Islam and 'disbelief' (*kufr*), which in this case meant Hinduism, were irreconcilable opposites and, as such, Muslims should not even be friendly or mix in any way with non-Muslims

Shah Wali Allah was another Naqshbandi shaykh who essentially continued the work started by Sirhindi, promoting *shari'a* particularism over Muslim universalism. He argued that unbelievers, and again he was, like Sirhindi, referring specifically to Hindus, should not be accorded the same social status as Muslims and, in fact, should be agricultural labourers at best who should also pay a poll tax (*jizya*) for Muslim protection. Shah Wali Allah was alive during a very unstable period: a time when the Moghul Empire was in decline and a feeling was present among the small Muslim minority that their identity and very existence were being threatened by the rise in power of both Hindus and Sikhs. Islam within itself was also lacking unity, with conflict between Sunni and Shi'a, the *ulama* and Sufis. Shah Wali Allah had gone on a pilgrimage to Mecca which lasted two years (1730–1732) during which time he received some education in other reform movements, particularly that of Muhammad ibn Abd al-Wahhab, who was his contemporary. Although adherence to *shari'a* was vitally important, Wali Allah, like al-Wahhab, who took as his model Ibn Taymiyyah, did not believe in blind adherence to the Qur'an and the **hadith** (the sayings of Muhammad). Al-Wahhab's writings are a good example of **ijtihad**, of engaging in active reasoning and interpretation of *hadith* to ensure it is conducive to understanding the message of the Qur'an. The point of reform was to turn the Muslims away from engaging in practices or beliefs without actually understanding the reasoning behind such activities and beliefs. So while al-Wahhab emphasised the importance of obedience to *shari'a*, it was also important that Islamic law should be in accordance with the Qur'an, that is, the word of God, and this required a degree of interpretation. Al-Wahhab did not want Muslims to follow *shari'a* merely because it is the law, but rather because it was in tune with the word of God.

Wali Allah was in entire agreement with al-Wahhab on the issue of *ijtihad*, but where the former differed was in his less confrontational approach towards what al-Wahhab would have regarded as un-Islamic and heretical. Al-Wahhab's militant approach led to the destruction of Sufi orders under the military command of Ibn Saud, whereas Wali Allah sought the reform of Sufism. He also did not see 'unity of belief' and 'unity of experience' as distinctly different, but merely a matter of semantics. He was, in fact, more accurate in interpreting Ibn Arabi as not promoting pantheism; the fault lay with his interpreters rather than with Ibn Arabi himself. Like al-Ghazali before him, Wali Allah called for 'balance' (*tawazun*), which was not unlike the Aristotelian doctrine of the mean: a middle way that is in accordance with the time and circumstance. *Ijtihad*, therefore, was essential in this enterprise, for without independent reasoning it is impossible to determine what the middle way is. It does not make sense to adopt the attitude of blind imitation (*taqliq*) of the rulings of past scholars and implant a collection of rules set in stone upon a completely different community. Rather, religious law could, and should, vary with the times and this Wali Allah developed in line with a remarkable theory of natural law that, up until that time, had been absent from Islamic thought.

For Wali Allah, human beings are unique in that they possess three distinctive qualities. First, a universal outlook; second, an aesthetic sense; and, third, what he calls '*irtifaqat*' which is an innate ability to discover 'supports' for civilisation. He develops what he means by '*irtifaqat*' by dividing this into four stages: The first stage, which is achieved by all civilisations, is that of language, agriculture, building, clothing, female monogamy, and tool-making. The second stage is in the actual *application* in society of the fields referred to in stage one; that is the establishment of laws and general rules of conduct, conventions, contracts, and so on. This, he argued, was common among only sedentary societies. The third stage is the development of political science which arises out of the necessity of those urban societies where people are in close contact with one another. Consequently, states, or city-states, require strong kings to rule over them. The final stage, then, is the need for a ruler, a Caliph, who oversees and acts as arbiter among the often quarrelling kings. The model Caliph, for Wali Allah, was the Prophet **Muhammad**.

Wali-Allah's account of the development of social organisation is basically naturalistic. It is in the nature of humans to form societies and for societies to form laws. Legal systems differ from one community to the next, but this is also natural because it is in accordance with variations in temperament, habit, and so on. Differences between religions arise because prophets have a high regard for the cultural norms and conventions, provided the universal outlook is not lost. Consequently, *shari'a*, as in religious law, is based on, first, human nature, and second, the cultural and social norms of a particular time and place.

Given these views, it is perhaps surprising that Wali-Allah was so intransigent towards non-Muslims, but his tolerance only extended to Muslims and he was concerned with Muslim identity and survival as much as Sirhindi was. Wali-Allah was an advocate of Islamic reform and the establishment of a traditional Islamic state, not the watering down of Islam within a pluralistic society. From this perspective, Wali-Allah undoubtedly considered Islam to be superior to that of its non-Muslim counterparts.

Wali-Allah's teachings resulted in a revival of Islamic thought in India. His son, Abd al-'Aziz (1746–1824) promoted his father's teachings by encouraging local communities to elect their own *imams* and adhere to them rather than be subject to the increasing presence of British rule at that time. A disciple of Wali Allah's son, Sayyid Ahmad Barelewi (1786–1831) went further in ushering in a ***jihad*** movement against both the Sikh armies and the British. In 1826, with his holy warriors, he defeated an army of Sikhs at Balakot in what is now the Northwest Frontier Province in Pakistan. He established what proved to be a short-lived religio-political state based on *shari'a* with himself as leader. Barelewi was killed in battle in 1831, but his *jihad* movement continued to harass the British.

Wali-Allah has been regarded as the father of Islamic modernism. He was a purist like Ibn Taymiyya, but he also believed in conciliation, at least among Muslims. He contributed greatly to the belief that if Islam was to survive at all in India, it not only had to reform but also to establish an Islamic state separate from non-Muslims and hence we have the germ of the idea that was to become Pakistan in 1947. His understanding of *ijtihad* influenced many reformers such as **Sayyid Ahmad Khan**, **Muhammad Iqbal** and **Mawlana Abul Ala Mawdudi**.

Major works

There is very little currently available in English.

The Conclusive Argument from God (Islamic Philosophy, Theology and Science: Texts and Studies), trans. Marcia K. Hermansen, Leiden: Brill, 1995.

Further reading

The Hardy is good for what occurred after Wali-Allah, for example with Barelewi.

Baljon, J.M.S., *The Religion and Thought of Shah Wali-Allah Dihlavi*, Leiden: Brill, 1986.
Hardy, P., *The Muslims of British India*, Cambridge: Cambridge University Press, 1972.

MUHAMMAD IBN ABD AL-WAHHAB (1703–1792)

A theologian and founder of the Wahhabi movement, al-Wahhab modelled himself on the Hanbali thinker **Ibn Taymiyya** (d. 1328) in that they both possessed an uncompromising dislike for what was perceived as non-Muslim innovations which contaminated the purity of Islam. Such 'innovations' (***bid'a***) and idolatry (***shirk***), such as the celebration of Prophet **Muhammad**'s birthday and the visit to *Sufi* (Islamic mysticism) shrines, al-Wahhab saw as the cause for the decline of Islam. Out of his beliefs emerged the militant Wahhabism, in particular; the aggressive techniques employed by the group were to influence militant movements in the twentieth century. His movement gave rise to a state known as Saudi Arabia and the military and political impact of Wahhabism, more so than its intellectual force, is significant.

Wahhabism reflects some of the most important trends in eighteenth-century Islamic thought and should not be considered as merely an historical aberration. Importantly the movement emerged as a result of internal conditions as opposed to external, Western influence, which usually signifies the movements of the nineteenth century. Although these conditions are 'internal' they were nonetheless regarded as foreign innovations, such as distinctively Egyptian religious ritual and belief. However, in terms of doctrine and organization, the Wahhabi shared much with the 'modern' movements and, in fact, is a precursor of them.

Al-Wahhab was born in 'Uyaynah, in Arabia (now in Saudi Arabia) in 1703 to a family of religious judges and scholars into the Tamim branch of the Banu Sinan tribe. He had a formal education in the holy city of Medina in Arabia and then as a youth travelled to other parts of the Middle East where he met a number of distinguished scholars who helped to shape his own beliefs. Also during this time he compiled and published numerous works on such subjects as innovation and superstition. He taught for four years in Basra in Iraq, and in Baghdad he married a wealthy woman whose property he inherited when she died. In 1736, in Iran, he preached against what he regarded as innovation, particularly the practices of Sufis such as the veneration of dead saints. He also travelled to Persia where he is reported to have studied Neo-platonic philosophy as well as Sufism despite his own distaste for Sufi practices. He then moved to Qum where he became a strong advocate of the conservative law school of **Ibn Hanbal**.

On returning to Uyaynah he wrote *Kitab at-tawhid* (*The Book of Unity*) which became the central text for the Wahhabi movement. Consequently, his followers referred to themselves as the 'Unitarians' (*al-Muwahhidun*), while the term 'Wahhabi' was initially used by non-Muslims and opponents. The people of the movement, especially in the early period, saw themselves as pursuing true Islam, rather than the teachings of an individual in particular. However, as the term 'Unitarian' has often been associated with a series of diverse and, in many cases now defunct, organisations, the term 'Wahhabi' is more common.

Initially, al-Wahhab's puritanical and traditional teachings met with much resistance in Arabia itself (including from both his father and brother). The ruler of Uyaynah, Uthman ibn Muammar, made al-Wahhab welcome and was sympathetic to his teachings, but Uthman himself received death threats for his support and so reluctantly expelled al-Wahhab from the province in 1744. He came to the village of Dir'iyyah, some 40 miles away, in the Najd desert (near present-day Riyadh) where he was well received by an Amir by the name of Muhammad ibn Sa'ud. The people of this province welcomed the teachings of this reformer and the prince and theologian formed an alliance. As a way of cementing this alliance, al-Wahhab's daughter was married to Ibn Saud's son. Thus, the pact was sealed by a marriage and a traditional oath of allegiance and from then, they set out to conquer the Arab world under the ideology of al-Wahhab and the organisation of Ibn Saud. Together they engaged in military expansion, leading to a state in central Arabia and the Persian Gulf declared independent of the Ottoman regime and living under the guidance of *shari'a*. The Wahhabi conquest proceeded rapidly under the leadership of Abd al-Aziz, the son of Ibn Saud. In 1802 the Wahhabis captured Karbala in Iraq, the site of Husayn's tomb (the third **Imam** of **Shi'a** Islam), and in 1803 they seized Mecca. It was not until 1932, however, that the region was renamed Saudi Arabia.

In what was the cradle of Islam many people believed that the deterioration of Islam, signified by the decline in power of the last great Muslim empire, the Ottomans, was also signified by internal factors such as the adoption of beliefs and rituals from other religions like the veneration of saints and the belief in their intercession. People had adopted what were perceived as superstitious practices such as spitting in a particular way or wearing charms to ward off evil. Such activities were seen as characteristic of the time before the coming of Muhammad and the Qur'an; the period of **jahiliyah**. It is perhaps inevitable that reformers would call for a return to what was perceived as the time when Islam was pure, during the time of Muhammad and his **Companions**. Of particular concern was that such activities seemed to be evidence of idolatory, or '*shirk*', which went completely against the central Islamic precept of 'unity' (**tawhid**) and the belief in one God: there are to be no intermediaries. Al-Wahhab was not working in a vacuum; a number of reform movements existed that shared the same concerns and were working towards the same logical conclusion that Islam needed to rid itself of what was seen as foreign innovation. What made al-Wahhab distinct was not so much his teachings, which were by no means original, but the support he was able to gain from the militant Ibn Saud. Adherence to *tawhid* had implications beyond private religious belief; it should also be reflected in the public domain by being the centre of the political system. It was for this reason especially that a number of the provincial princes were hostile towards al-Wahhab. However, Ibn Saud obviously recognised the power of such a unifying message in terms of military conquest. Coupled with adherence to *tawhid* was putting into place the central tenets of Islam as inscribed in Islamic law, *shàri'a*. Hence, any such movement required the enforcement of *shari'a*. It should be noted that such teachings did not necessarily require violence or the military overthrow of contemporary regimes, for many more moderate elements believed that the return to a more 'pure' Islam could be achieved from the bottom up via education and welfare reform.

Al-Wahhab, it should be stressed, like his model Ibn Taymiyyah, did not believe in blind adherence to the Qur'an and *hadith*. His writings are a good example of ***ijtihad***, of engaging in active reasoning and interpretation of *hadith* to ensure it is conducive with the message of the Qur'an. The point of reform was to turn the Muslims away from engaging in practices or beliefs without actually understanding the reasoning behind such activities and beliefs. So while al-Wahhab emphasised the importance of obedience to *shari'a*, it was also important that *shari'a* should be in accordance with the Qur'an, that is the word of God, and this required a degree of interpretation. Al-Wahhab did not want Muslims to follow *shari'a* merely because it is the law, but rather because it was in tune with the word of God.

Although there was always some independent jurist in the Islamic world who interpreted Islamic law through reasoning, the 'gates of *ijtihad'* had to a great extent been closed since **al-Shafi'i** in the thirteenth century. The guidelines and teachings of the legal scholars became so enshrined that judges would rarely dare do anything other than imitate (***taqlid***) these predecessors. What was questioned was whether a work by a legal scholar could really be authoritative for another age; whereas the Qur'an was eternal and universal, the rulings of mere men were not. It was this treatment of legal rulings as being as authoritative as the Qur'an that was of concern for al-Wahhab.

In theory, at least, Wahhabism allowed that anything that is not explicitly forbidden in the Qur'an or in the **sunna** was therefore permitted. However, in practice, the more militant element of the movement resulted in actual physical attacks on any actions that were perceived as 'innovation' such as the visit to tombs of the saints. This could be regarded as polytheistic in that it seemed to allow mediation

MUHAMMAD IBN ABD AL-WAHHAB

between God and man. The Wahhabis, in fact, only allowed pilgrimages to the 'three mosques' (Mecca, Medina, and the Al-Aqsa mosque in Jerusalem) as prescribed in those recognised as authentic *hadith*. Further, al-Wahhab stated that constructing buildings over graves and shrouding them with flowers and other decorations was un-Islamic. He prohibited the burning of candles over graves as well as the setting up of stone inscriptions. He did not approve of such actions as the kissing of graves or encircling them. Other such innovations which were condemned included celebrating the birthday of Muhammad, decorating mosques, shaving one's beard, and smoking tobacco. He condemned the practices of the Sufi orders, and the militant Wahhabis set about their destruction, as well as burning down and destroying many mosques and shrines. The Shi'a in particualr have never forgotten the destruction of shrine of Husayn at Karbala by the Wahhabis as well as the massacre of its inhabitants. Alongside Sufi practices, the Wahhabis regard Shi'a Islam as un-Islamic with its cult of Imams and pilgrimage practices.

The watchword for Wahhabism became simplicity, and this was evident in simple tomb markers at graveyards and the most basic furnishings in mosques, relieved of any ornaments or even minarets. Aside from laying the ideological foundations for the Saudi state, al-Wahhab's legacy has spread beyond Arabia. A form of Wahhabism put down roots in India as well as Central Asia. In India attempts were made to rid the country of Hindu practices and a similar movement was set up in 1837 in Sumatra where attempts were made to prohibit the use of opium, tobacco and betel nut. In Africa, Usumanu Dan Fodio (1754–1817) preached Wahhabi teachings and he mobilised enough support to found the powerful Muslim emirate of Sokoto and the Fulah kingdom (later to become Nigeria under the British).

While the Wahhabis did preach a return to *ijtihad*, they nonetheless rejected rational speculation and preferred to adopt more violent means to achieve their ends. Hence, *ijtihad* has proved largely ineffectual despite continuing calls for it. While the original Wahhabis banned music, dancing, poetry, silk, and all jewellery and more modern equivalents have also condemned the use of the telephone, radio, television and other technology as un-Islamic, the nature of the power and wealth of the Saudi princes has meant they face little opposition from the **ulama** in introducing such modern conveniences. The ideology of Wahhabism is still, nonetheless, enforced against political opposition and has become more of a religious police force than a mover for renewal and reform.

Major works

Al-Wahhab's *Book of Unity* is currently available in English from the IIPH.

The Book of Tawheed, Saudi Arabia: International Islamic Publishing House (IIPH), 1998.

Further reading

The Rentz, though very recently published, was originally a well-acknowledged doctorate thesis from 1947 and an interesting read.

Algar, Hamid, *Wahhabism: A Critical Essay*, North Haledon, NJ: Islamic Publications International, 2002.

Natana, J. and DeLong-Bas. *Wahhabi Islam: From Revival and Reform to Global Jihad*, Oxford: Oxford University Press, 2004.

Rentz, G.S., *Birth of the Islamic Reform Movement in Saudi Arabia: Muhammad B. 'Abd Al-Wahhab (1703/4–1792) and the Beginnings of Unitarian Empire in Arabia*, Saudi Arabia: Arabian Publishing Ltd, 2005.

SIR SAYYID AHMAD KHAN (1817–1898)

The Indian Muslim Ahmad Khan was an influential modernist thinker who, rather than shun the Western lifestyle, adopted it wholeheartedly. His importance rests in his realisation that Islam needed to reform if it was to survive, although he has remained a controversial figure due to his collaboration with the British who occupied India at the time, as well as being a strong anglophile himself, which was reflected in his dress and lifestyle.

Sayyid Ahmad Khan himself was descended from a prominent family of Mughal administrators. The title 'Sayyid' is an honorary one given to those who can trace their ancestry back to the family of the Prophet **Muhammad**. In Ahmad Khan's case this is through Persian ancestry via Muhammad's son-in-law and cousin **Ali** (the fourth Righly-Guided Caliph) and his wife Fatima. He was born to a wealthy family, although at the time Mughals were in decline as British supremacy increased. Of a big influence in his early life was his maternal grandfather, Khwajah Farîd, who died when Ahmad Khan was eleven. Khwajah Farîd saw the importance of the British East India Company and made a point of finding fruitful employment with them, often at the expense of the crumbling Mughal dynasties. It was during the decade of the 1860s, that Ahmad Khan developed his ideas of a 'modern Islam' and a Muslim polity living under the British rule. During this time, he wrote *A History of Insurrection in*

Bijnor District, and *Causes of the Indian Revolt*. Of the latter work he sent five hundred copies to the India Office in London. In 1860–1861, he published *Loyal Mohammedans of India* in which he claimed that the Indian Muslims were the most loyal subjects of the British Raj because of their kindred disposition and because of the principles of their religion. He also wrote a commentary on the Old and New Testaments. He spent his career working for British administrators and served in the British East India Company. He was knighted for his services in 1888.

In 1857, many Muslims and Hindu troops 'mutinied' as a result of pent-up resentment against British rule. Some Indian historians have referred to this event as the first war of independence, and it proved to be a turning point in Indian relations with Britain. The revolt was bitterly suppressed and the Mughal Empire was replaced by direct crown government. Further, the British blamed the Muslims for the revolt, although Hindus were also involved, and the **ulama** (the Islamic scholars), for their part, did nothing to alleviate the British suspicions by declaring them the 'enemies of Islam'. Ahmed Khan's reaction to this was a pragmatic one: to accept and, indeed, collaborate with the British. Under British rule, Muslims were on the whole protected – given their minority status compared with the number of Hindus – and **shari'a** (Islamic law) was applied.

His main concern was in educational reform and in this respect his contribution was highly visible. In 1856 he founded the National Mohammadan Association and, in 1863, the Mohammadan Literary Society. This was followed by the *Anjuman-i Islam* of Bombay as well as the establishment of new religious schools in Dacca and Chittagong. He sponsored the translation of English scientific works into Urdu and, in 1864, founded the Ghazipur Scientific Society. In 1869, Ahmad Khan visited England (funded by mortgaging his ancestral house in Delhi) for seventeen months. While he was impressed by the culture and civilisation of British society he was shocked by the ignorance of Islam he encountered. He attended Charles Dickens' last public reading, met the influential social critic Thomas Carlyle and visited Cambridge, Oxford, Harrow and Eton. It was the visit to the universities and public schools that formed an important impression on Ahmad Khan and he returned to India determined even more to produce an educated Muslim elite that would take over the reins of administration. In 1875, he founded the Muhammad Anglo-Oriental College in Aligarh (now the Muslim University of Aligarh) in India which taught European arts and sciences (in English) as well as traditional Islamic studies. It was more conservative, and less 'Islamic', than Ahmad Khan would have liked but, ever the pragmatist, he realised that its survival and funding required that it had the approval of the British overlords. What it did do, however, was to produce many young Muslims who were more self-confident and possessed values of community and leadership skills.

Sayyid Ahmad Khan was a great believer in the need for Islam to modernise and he saw in Western thought, especially in the realm of science, a force that should not be regarded as antithetical to Islam. His pro-Western stance in terms of adopting Western dress as well as singing the praises of the British was heavily criticised: **Al-Afghani**, for example, accused him of being a materialist and even the Anti-christ! Ahmad Khan was also associated with '*nechari*' ('nature') because of his post-Darwinian views that nature – in terms of cause and effect – operated independently of God's power. This view was antithetical to many conservative Muslims who preferred to see God as omnipotent in every respect, including being the manager of nature.

Like his *Salafiyyah* (Islamic revivalist movement) counterparts in the Middle East (see **al-Afghani**, **Abduh** and **Rida**) he believed that the survival of Islam required the abandonment of *taqlid*; the blind imitation of the medieval interpreters of the Qur'an. He undertook the reinterpretation of the Qur'an, believing the more obscure passages had to be interpreted symbolically, allegorically or analytically in order to reveal their true meaning. He believed that reason played a very important part in this process and that the focus should be on the main principles contained within the Qur'an that, he believed, were in tune with scientific progress and reason in accordance with nature. Like **Ibn Rushd** ('Averroes'), Ahmad Khan believed Islam was the religion of reason and nature and in this belief he was heavily influenced by nineteenth-century European rationalism and natural philosophy.

He drew heavily on both the reformism of Shah **Wali Allah** (d. 1762) and the rationalism of *Mu'tazilites* (see **al-Zamakhshari**) and the *Ikhwan al-Safa* (the Ismaili-influenced 'Brothers of Purity'). He argued that Muslims have the right to engage in unrestricted personal *ijtihad* (independent reasoning), although based on a good understanding of the text. In practice, therefore, he admitted that the understanding of the Qur'an by the masses would be at a different level than for those educated in Islamic studies. In concentrating on the main principles contained within the Qur'an, the more specific references to such things as angels are to be interpreted within the legendary context of the time: they are 'properties' of things which encourage man in his struggles in life. Likewise the *jinn*, or 'demons', are symbolic of evil desires.

Ahmad Khan believed that God's laws are identical to the laws of nature and that all morality and social ethics derive from these natural laws. This view was often criticised by some Muslim scholars as the logical conclusion was that morality can be determined through the rational study of nature and, therefore, why was there a need for revelation? Ahmad Khan was critical of what he called 'unrecited revelation', that is the writing of **hadith** collectors, but maintained that the 'recited revelation', the Qur'an, was the only authority. However, by limiting the Qur'an to general principles – essentially the following of the *five pillars* – it allowed for a great deal of interpretation as to what constitutes a Muslim: such flexibility has both its advantages and disadvantages and failed to please the conservative *ulama* who relied upon the accretion of centuries of Muslim law in defining what constituted a good and bad Muslim and were not prepared to abandon literalistic interpretations of the divine texts to accommodate a scientific world-view.

On the one hand, Ahmad Khan strived to show his fellow Muslims that Islam allowed for scientific advances while, on the other, he also set out to show the West, and Britain in particular, that Islam was a rational religion capable of relating to the modern world and deserving of admiration and respect. His concern was with cooperation, not conflict, and he took pains to explain the theological intricacies on such issues as polygamy, slavery and the role of women – issues that were not only controversial but frequently misunderstood by foreign observers.

Ahmad Khan's loyalist approach was submerged by an increased aggression among Indian Muslims towards British rule, not least due to Britain's own somewhat negative attitude towards India, as well as the increasing power of Hindus and their own religious revivalism that threatened Muslim identity. The younger generation of Muslims were less accommodating than Ahmad Khan and his supporters and Muslim militancy increased in the early twentieth century. While the legacy of Ahmad Khan's encouragement of an educated elite was that many young Muslims were now more self-confident and able to express themselves, the anachronism of the pursuit of such a small elite of educated Muslims among a mass of Hindu revivalism was not lost. Consequently, Islamic revivalism in India became more concentrated on promoting mass political support rather than the education of a few in the ways of Western etiquette. In time this led to the movement for a separate Muslim country spearheaded by such eminent spokesmen as **Muhammad Iqbal** and Abu Ala **Mawdudi**.

Major works

A Series of Essays on the Life of Muhammad and Subjects Subsidiary Thereto, London: Trubner & Co., 1870, reprinted by Lahore: Premier Book House, 1968.

Writings and Speeches of Sir Syed Ahmad Khan, ed. Mohammed Shan, Bombay: Nachiketa Publications, 1972.

History of the Bijnor Rebellion, trans. Hafeez Malik and Morris Dembo, Ann Arbor, MI: Asian Studies Center, Michigan State University, n.d.

Further reading

Malik, Hafeez, *Sir Sayyid Ahmad Khan and Muslim Modernism in India and Pakistan,* New York: Columbia University Press, 1980.

Baljon, J.M.S., *Reforms and Religious Ideas of Sir Sayyid Ahmad Khan*, Lahore: Ashraf, 1970.

SAYYID JAMAL AL-DIN 'AL-AFGHANI' (1838/9–1897)

Sayyid Jamal al-Din 'al-Afghani' ('the Afghan') was a modernist, reformer and co-founder of the *Salafiyyah* with Muhammad **Abduh**. The name '*Salafiyya*' derives from the phrase *salaf as-salihin* ('the pious ancestors') and seeks to reform Islam by referring to the lives and teachings of the Prophet **Muhammad** and his **Companions** as the primary source for guidance. Al-Afghani was also a controversial political activist and agitator, travelling around the Muslim world in his mission to encourage Islamic states to reform and to unite against what he saw as the European (British especially) threat to Islamic identity. Al-Afghani was a highly influential orator and pamphleteer and, some would argue, an original thinker who systematized Islamic philosophical and mystical traditions with contemporary political thought.

Although nicknamed (by himself) the 'Afghan', he was actually an Iranian **Shi'a** (the minority Muslim group as opposed to the **Sunni**) born in Asterabad near the city of Hamadan (where lies the tomb of **Ibn Sina**) in Western Iran. In Iran he received a traditional Shi'a education and became well versed in Islamic philosophy. In his early twenties he spent his time in India where he was influenced by the modernist views of Sayyid **Ahmad Khan** (1817–1898), while rejecting the pro-Western stance of Khan. Many scholars, however, consider him to be more an activist than a thinker, and during the period 1866–1868 he started his career of political agitation by going to Afghanistan to encourage Azam Khan, the military ruler of Kandahar province, to form an alliance with Russia against the British. During this period, al-Afghani claimed to be of Turkish (and Sunni) origin in order to procure a more sympathetic reception among the Sunni Muslims. It was for this same reason he began later to refer to himself as 'the Afghan'. He then went to Istanbul and joined the *Tanzimat* reformers, but his lectures proved to be so controversial that he was expelled in 1871 and he moved to Cairo. It was during this period that he collaborated with Muhammad Abduh, the latter being more the disciple, but al-Afghani was expelled from Egypt in 1879 for taking part in nationalist movements.

From 1879–1882, al-Afghani resided in India once more, where he collaborated with followers of Ahmad Khan, although in 1881 al-Afghani wrote, in Persian, the pamphlet *Refutation of the Materialists* which unfairly attacked Ahmad Khan among other 'materialists' (by which he means those lacking in religiosity, citing such people as Democritus, Marx, and Darwin) for their rejection of religion in favour of science. From around 1882 until 1885, he lived mostly in Paris and was joined by Muhammad Abduh in 1884. Together they published an Arabic-language periodical *The Strongest Link (Al-'Urwa al-Wuthqa)* which attacked the British and promoted reformist and liberalist attitudes. Unlike Abduh's more nationalistic stance, however, al-Afghani adopted the pan-Islamic cause. In 1885, he went to Tehran where he attempted to convince the Shah that he should make a stronger alliance with the Russians against British influence in Iran and, failing in this attempt, al-Afghani himself spent the next two years in St Petersburg (at that time the capital of Russia), conspiring against the British before again returning to Iran. Eventually the Shah was compelled to expel him and he settled in London to continue propagandist methods of pamphleteering and speeches aimed at the religious authorities in Iran, which included the call to depose the Shah. In fact, in 1896, one of al-Afghani's disciples, Mirza Reza, assassinated the Shah. Iran demanded al-Afghani's extradition but he found refuge in Istanbul and died the next year of cancer.

A central concern for al-Afghani and, indeed, for the *Salafiyyah* movement generally, was the seeming decline in the power of the **umma**, the Muslim community, corresponding with an increase in the supremacy of the Western world. This concern was not just a matter of economic and political status – important though this undoubtedly was – but also a genuine fear that religion itself was being eroded. The whole basis for a coherent understanding of the world and of God and Man's place in the world was being threatened by Western secularisation and modernisation. Many of the **ulama**, the religious scholars, either adopted a passive attitude to this Western encroachment or became more conservative in their stance in an attempt to protect the Islamic tradition. Others believed that Islam had essentially failed and that Westernisation should be encouraged. Al-Afghani, however, while believing that modernisation was essential, also believed that this project was compatible with Islam, rather than in opposition to it. In this respect al-Afghani was a relatively enlightened individual for his time and was open to new ideas in comparison to the huge majority of Islamic thinkers who preferred to cling to the past. Al-Afghani saw the benefits of science and reason, but sought it from the point of view of an Islamic position rather than a Western one; hence his criticism of Ahmad Khan whom he believed represented someone in the pockets of the Western powers (Ahmad Khan was knighted for his services to Britain).

Al-Afghani took full advantage of his own culture and education to argue, like **Ibn Sina** and other before him, that prophecy, mysticism and the rational tools of philosophy are all expressions of the one truth. Science was not a European phenomenon but, he argued, an *Islamic* one in its origins. Al-Afghani recognised the power of science to rule the world and cited Islam's own history of the time when, at its zenith, the Islamic community led the world in science. Where the problem lay, then, was in the fact that the Islamic community had closed the gates of **ijtihad** ('independent reasoning') and allowed the Western world to overtake it. Islam, rather, was a religion of reason and the Qur'an should be interpreted by reason and open to new interpretations by scholars of each new generation, rather than blindly imitating ('**taqlid**') the views of scholars from primarily the Middle Ages.

Social activism was the keystone of al-Afghani's thought, and he blamed the decline of Islam on the fatalism, passivity and decadence that permeated all elements of Muslim society, but most significantly among the *ulama* who, he argued, had become backward and lacked the skills necessary to engage in the contemporary world from an Islamic viewpoint. Al-Afghani also placed blame on **Sufism** – the mystical aspect of Islam – for its 'other-worldly' attitude. A 'return' to the Islam of Muhammad and his Companions did not mean imitating this period, for that would be impossible anyway, but rather meant making use of the vigour and spirit of that reformist time to guide one's view of the modern world. In this sense, al-Afghani stresses the importance of the human psyche as the motor for progress.

Al-Afghani agreed with the view of many Western Orientalist scholars that the Islamic world had an anti-scientific attitude, but where he disagreed was that this had always been the case or that it was a necessary consequence of religious belief. Rather, he believed, the decline in independent reasoning was not the result of religion as such, but rather political despotism. So al-Afghani was not only calling for an intellectual revival within the religious tradition, but he also had a political agenda that attacked forms of tyranny. Al-Afghani cast himself as a Lutheran character who called for an Islamic Reformation that allowed the Muslim people to think for themselves without fear of oppression. Religion for its part, and by religion he meant the Islam that existed at the time of the 'pious ancestors' (i.e. the Prophet Muhammad and the Companions especially), was perfectly in tune with intellectual and critical rigour, as well as providing social cohesion and a positive community ethic. What al-Afghani saw as virtues in the Western world, those of rationality, science and patriotism, he saw as the same virtues as the essence of Islam.

What this meant in real political terms was the adoption of constitutional or republican government in which the citizens partake in political affairs. Whereas at times al-Afghani sought a pan-Islamic ideal, he also frequently made use of nationalistic terminology as a tool against European encroachment. While this comes across as contradictory, it also demonstrates al-Afghani's desire to make use of whatever means seemed necessary to rid the Muslim world of Western domination. However, one result of this flexibility of response was that al-Afghani has not always been taken seriously by scholars and has been viewed with suspicion by many of his contemporaries, being perceived as an opportunist rather than someone with intellectual weight. He presents a chameleon figure who at times seems a radical libertarian and at others a conservative. This impression was not helped by his association with a mixed bag of powerful individuals, a number of whom could hardly have been sympathetic to al-Afghani's mission yet al-Afghani himself was not beyond seeking their patronage, the Ottoman Sultan Abdulhamid being the most notable example here. His political agenda was not dissimilar to that voiced by the European Renaissance, and lacked the intellectual detail of how such a republican system would work in relation to religious authority. Muhammad Abduh, who was to break away from al-Afghani and pursue a more balanced and considered intellectual path, at least saw the need for an authoritarian political structure to be in

171

place if Islam was to initially reassert itself. Considering the weakness and uncertainty of political authority that existed at the time, it is difficult to see how a republican system could so readily be put into place.

Nonetheless, al-Afghani's importance lies in his vision of the possibilities of a united Islam and for a role for religion in the modern world, as opposed to being antagonistic or incompatible with it. He was a major catalyst in the struggle to bridge the ever-widening gap between secular modernism and religious traditionalism. He still possesses a degree of hero worship, and was certainly a charismatic figure, and he has influenced the writings of such thinkers as the scholar and poet **Muhammad Iqbal**, as well as Shi'a political theology. His anti-colonial sentiment inspired much of early twentieth-century Islamic political thought and he is regarded as a great inspiration for the beliefs of the Muslim Brotherhood (see **al-Bana** and **Qutb**).

Major works

Unfortunately, none of his works have, as yet, been translated into English.

Further reading

There are many good books on al-Afghani and this particular period. The Kedourie is particularly contentious as it argues that al-Afghani (with Muhammad Abduh) was part of a subversive atheist movement and may even have been a Russian agent!

Ahmad, Aziz, 'Sayyid Ahmad Khan, Jamal al-Din al-Afghani and Muslim India', *Studia Islamica* 13 (1960): 55–78.

Algar, Hamid, *Religion and State in Iran, 1785–1906*, Los Angeles: University of California Press, 1969.

Hodgson, Marshall G., *The Venture of Islam*, vol. 3, *The Gunpowder Empire and Modern Times*, Chicago: University of Chicago Press, 1974.

Keddie, Nikki R., *An Islamic Response to Imperialism: Political and Religious Writings of Sayyid Jamal al-Din 'al-Afghani'*, Berkeley, CA: University of California Press, 1968.

Kedourie, Elie, *Afghani and Abduh: An Essay on Religious Unbelief and Political Activism in Modern Islam*, London: Frank Cass, 1966.

Kramer, Martin, *Islam Assembled: The Advent of the Muslim Congresses*, New York: Columbia University Press, 1985.

MUHAMMAD ABDUH (1849–1905)

Together with his friend and colleague **al-Afghani**, Muhammad Abduh is the founder of the modernist movement known as *Salafiyyah* (although considered modernist, the movement 'looks back' to the time of **Muhammad** and his *Companions* as a guide to the right way to live) and together they were the most influential spokesmen for Egyptian Islamic modernism in the nineteenth century. Abduh's writings have had an immense and lasting influence on the Muslim world. His most distinguished follower was the Syrian Rashid **Rida**. Abduh and Rida are considered the great synthesisers of modern Islam.

Abduh was born in 1849 to a poor but educated rural family in Egypt. At the age of 13 he went to Tanta (a city in north-eastern Egypt) to study at the prestigious Ahmadi mosque and, from 1869–1877, received his education at the famous al-Azhar University in Cairo. However, he was unhappy with the education he received there, with its emphasis on rote-learning and an unwillingness to engage in critical thought, and this was a catalyst for his life-long dedication to educational reform. His intellectual development was shaped by two charismatic figures. In his early years his maternal uncle, Shaykh Dawash – a *Sufi* master of the Shadhili Brotherhood – taught him the moral and ethical disciplines of that order which remained with Abduh throughout his life. More significant was the influence of the reformer and activist al-Afghani whom Abduh first met at al-Azhar University. It was under al-Afghani that Abduh became politically active.

In his early years, reflecting al-Afghani's views, Abduh was more radical and an activist. He gained a university teaching position which he lost in 1880 due to his controversial stance. He then took up journalism, writing articles promoting the nationalist cause and participated in nationalist demonstrations against British control of Egypt which led to his exile from 1882 until 1888. Abduh went first to Beirut, and then joined al-Afghani in Paris in 1884. It was during this period that Abduh and al-Afghani founded the *Salafiyyah* movement and collaborated on an Arabic-language periodical *The Strongest Link* (*Al-'Urwa al-Wuthqa*) which attacked the British and promoted reformist and liberalist attitudes. Abduh returned to Beirut to teach at a Muslim school and it was during this period that much of his more mature intellectual development was formed.

In 1888, Abduh was allowed to return to Egypt but was not permitted to resume a teaching position. Rather, he assumed a career in public service. He was appointed judge and, later, the Grand Mufti (the chief judge of Islamic law) of Egypt from 1889 until his death in 1905. As Mufti, Abduh was in the powerful and controversial position of being in charge of the whole system of Islam law in Egypt.

However, by returning from exile, Abduh was giving implicit acceptance to British rule, and from then on he adopted a less revolutionary, more conciliatory approach to European dominance.

Abduh certainly appreciated much of European science and culture and encouraged a broad-minded liberalism not unlike that of the Indian Muslim reformer Sayyid **Ahmad Khan**, although he did not go so far as to adopt a European lifestyle as Khan did. He was an *ulama* (religious scholar) of a traditional education but was not averse to modernising Islam provided it remained within strict Islamic limits. Interestingly, Lord Cromer, the British Consul General in Cairo and effectively the ruler of Egypt from 1883 until 1907, described Abduh as an 'agnostic', which perhaps to some extent is a reflection of Cromer's (and many Europeans') concept of Islam as strictly traditionalist and an antonym to modernism. For Abduh, the British occupation was a necessary evil until Egypt could stand on its own two feet through a process of modernisation and, most importantly, education. Abduh's more mature moderate and intellectual views contrasted therefore with al-Afghani's militancy.

Unlike the pan-Islamist ideas of al-Afghani, Abduh possessed a strong nationalist temperament and, indeed, represented the generation in which the ideas of nationalism became explicit among not only Egyptians, but also Turks, Arabs and Tunisians especially. In the case of Egyptian nationalism, it emerged as a result of British occupation during the 1880s, although it did not become an effective force until the early twentieth century. The nationalist tendencies can be simplistically divided into two schools: those who called for a complete withdrawal of British occupation, and the school to which Abduh belonged, those who thought that the Egyptians could profit from the British presence in the quest for Islamic modernism.

Abduh was far more a theologian than a social activist and, like **Ibn Khaldun** and **Ibn Rushd** before him, he regarded religion as an essential ingredient of social cohesion and fulfilment. One of Abduh's major works, based on the lectures he gave in Beirut, was *Risala al-tawhid* (*The Theology of Unity*) which argued that religion and reason were complementary. Like Afghani, Abduh believed that the truth claims of religion and science can be harmonised, and this view is consistent with his own attempts to reconcile the apparent conflicts between the successes and superiority of the West with its scientific knowledge and the comparative weakness of Muslim Egypt with its traditionalist views on religion and the prevalence of what he considered to be un-Islamic practices such as visiting the shrines of saints. The compromise lay not in rejecting the truth claims of Islam and, as a result, embracing 'Western' knowledge, but rather in remaining firmly within the Islamic fold by demonstrating that science and reason are, in themselves, Islamic.

While Abduh would not go as far as the **Mu'tazilites** (the 'rationalist' school of philosophy), he believed reason should be exercised to determine legal decisions. As a Mufti he regularly engaged in **ijtihad** ('independent reasoning') and his reformist ideas were incorporated in his legal rulings and presented in his influential journal *The Beacon* (*al-Manar*, also translated as *The Lighthouse*), which he published with his disciple Rashid Rida. Like many of the modernists, his main criticism of Muslim society was its reliance on **taqlid** ('blind imitation') of traditional scholarship. A principle adopted by Abduh was *talfiq* ('piecing together'), according to which decisions can be made by comparing the views of the four legal schools (see **Abu Hanifa, Malik ibn Anas, al-Shafi'i**, and **Ibn Hanbal**), and then going behind them to the Qur'an, the **hadith** (the sayings of the Prophet Muhammad) and, importantly, the *salaf al-salih* ('the pious ancestors'). In fact, Abduh's approach to *Salafiyyah* was to call for the dissolution of the four legal schools altogether and instead to use the 'pious ancestors' (that is, the Prophet **Muhammad** and his Companions primarily) as the 'beacon' for guidance, but in line with man's rational capacity. He stressed that while those laws that governed worship such as prayer, fasting, pilgrimage, and so on, were unchangeable, the vast majority of legislation, such as regulation on family law, penal codes, and so on, was open to change according to the social and cultural traditions of the time.

In theory, then, a *Salafiyyah* approach to Islam should allow for independent reasoning, although there is always the danger that, in the way that some Muslim scholars have been reluctant to contradict the rulings of traditional legal scholars, likewise, the 'fundamentalist' or conservative element – which to some extent can be evidenced in Rida's approach – could be unwilling to adopt anything other than a literal approach to the 'pious ancestors' and the Qur'an. Abduh, for his part, was not averse to interpreting the Qur'an to accommodate modern conditions, and, in fact, saw no contradiction between the truths of revelation and that of science. In some ways, this is a rather naïve and outdated view of science as essentially 'discoverable facts' that are in some sense 'out there' as opposed to a continual process of discovery that needs to be constantly revised or rejected as new theories come about. It is not surprising that the *Salafiyyah* movement has to a large extent run its course, although this is not to deny its immense influence on Islamic modernism.

Politically, Abduh believed that Islamic doctrine does not prescribe any specific form of government, provided it follows the general principles of consultation (*shura*) as well as supporting the Maliki principle of *maslaha* (public interest) as the basis for legal decisions. He stressed the importance of education so that the public will be informed (in the sense of possessing the knowledge of what is and is not Islamic) to issue opinions. Later he was less optimistic that the Islamic public were yet ready for any kind of representational government and, until they achieve the necessary education, a 'just dictator' would be required who would work towards educating the population in the art of rule. If this despot – who, theoretically at least, should be constrained by Islamic law – failed to do this, then the people had the right to overthrow him

His progressiveness lay in his call for the modernisation of Islam, as well as the need for greater educational opportunities, especially for women, and his criticism of what he regarded as backward – and unnecessary – laws such as polygamy. He essentially established modern reformism as a force in Egypt, as well as spreading al-Afghani's ideas to other parts of the Muslim world.

Major works

Only one of his major works is available in English:

Abduh, M, *The Theology of Unity*, trans. I. Musa'ad and K. Cragg, London: Allen & Unwin, 1966.

Further reading

Donohoe, J. and Esposito, J. (eds), *Islam in Transition: Muslim Perspectives*, Oxford: Oxford University Press, 1982.
Haddad, Y., 'Muhammad Abduh: Pioneer of Islamic Reform', in A. Rahnema (ed.) *Pioneers of Islamic Revival*, London: Zed Books, 1994.
Kedourie, Elie, Afghani and Abduh: An Essay on Religious Unbelief and Political Activism in Modern Islam, London: Frank Cass, 1966.
Kerr, M., Islamic Reform: The Political and Legal Theories of Mohammad 'Abduh and Rashid Rida, Berkeley, CA: University of California Press, 1966.

RASHID RIDA (1865–1935)

Muhammad Rashid Rida is part of a trio with **Jamal al-Din al-Afghani** (1838–1897) and **Muhammad Abduh** (1849–1905) of the great synthesisers of modern Islam and the founding intellectual fathers of the **Salafiyyah** movement. The name 'Salafiyyah' derives from the phrase *salaf as-salihin* ('the pious ancestors') and seeks to reform Islam by referring to the lives and teachings of the Prophet **Muhammad** and his **Companions** as the primary source for guidance. Whereas Afghani was more a politician than a theorist, and Abduh more a theorist than a politician, it could be said that Rida was skilled in both the arts.

Rida was born near Tripoli in Lebanon (not the Tripoli in Africa) in 1865 and studied at the state school, the *Madrasa Watiniyya*. At this time, Lebanon was part of the Ottoman Empire. However, he soon left to attend the National Islamic School, which was run by followers of the then nascent *Salafiyyah* movement. This is an indication of the aims of the *Salafiyyah* to reform Islamic society through, among other things, education. This school, however, was later closed by the Ottoman authorities and Rida had to return to a traditional state education. Nonetheless, the influences of the *Salafiyyah* had their impact on the rest of his life.

Rida did not venture abroad until he was in his thirties, and restricted himself to a brief spell of travelling during the winter of 1897–1898 to mostly Muslim countries. Unlike Abduh, he had little interest in learning languages or spending time in the West, making only a brief visit to Europe in 1921. Rather, Rida was less influenced by Western ideas and instead focused more on what he considered to be essentially Islamic teachings.

The turning point in Rida's life came when he moved to Cairo in Egypt in 1897 to work with Abduh. In fact, Rida became his acolyte and in 1898 they both began a periodical called *The Beacon* (al-Manar, also translated as *The Lighthouse*) which became the mouthpiece of their *Salafiyyah* movement and of which Rida took over the reins after the death of Abduh, in 1905. In fact, *The Beacon* existed for thirty-five years; an indicator of its success and importance. However, while Rida always said that *The Beacon* was a vehicle for the teachings of Abduh, it later reflected Rida's more conservative attitude. Aside from the work on this periodical, Rida also published a hugely influential **tafsir** ('interpretation') of the Qur'an. In this *tafsir*, Rida argued for a rationalistic approach to interpreting the Qur'an. By 'rationalistic', he aimed to dissolve any claims to a miraculous aspect of the Qur'an, aside from its divine origin of course, but he also was not content – as many traditional Islamic scholars were – to leave certain aspects of the Qur'an without interpretation by using the argument that they are beyond human understanding. On the contrary,

Rida believed, man has been given reason for the very purpose of using it in understanding the Qur'an.

His theoretical work in the sphere of Islamic politics is also extremely important. As a result of defeats in the First World War, the Ottoman Empire had effectively collapsed and, in November 1922, the position of the Sultanate was abolished and, as a result, the Ottoman dynasty ceased to exist, to be replaced a year later by the Republic of Turkey. This is an extremely significant series of events in the formulation of Rida's political views, particularly his thoughts on the caliphate (the role and function of the **caliphs**, or Muslim rulers). The Ottoman sultans frequently assumed the title of caliph as well, or in some cases appointed a separate caliph, and so claimed to represent a continuation in the line of caliphs that had ruled over the **umma** (the Islamic community) since the very first caliph **Abu Bakr**. After the abolition of the Sultanate, the position of caliph remained as a purely spiritual position so as not to offend the conservative element in Turkey. However, this caliph proved to be more powerful than the new Turkish president, Kemal Ataturk (1881–1938), would have wished and so that position also was abolished in March 1924. The question of the role of the caliphate remained and its abolition had a huge psychological impact on the Muslim world. Aside from this, the political implications were equally significant and recognised by such interested parties as the British, echoed in the writings of T.E. Lawrence ('Lawrence of Arabia'), that with the abolition of the caliphate, chances of Muslim unity became ever slimmer.

Rida, however, also recognised that the abolition of the caliphate would only weaken the unity of Muslims and cause them to fall prey to the Western world more easily. In *al-Khalifa* (*On the Caliphate*), written in 1922, when the caliphate still existed in a nominal sense, Rida argued for the preservation of the caliphate, but went much further than a call for its mere preservation. Rather, he saw the future caliph as a great 'renewer' (**mujtahid**) who would be able to modernise Islamic law – **shari'a** – without causing its dilution. Like his counterparts al-Afghani and Abduh, Rida was convinced that Islam was perfect and fully equal to the achievements of the West, while also holding fast to the traditional concept of the **umma** (the Muslim community) and that *shari'a* could unite all Muslims.

He saw the caliph as a leader who would preside over a 'commonwealth' of Islamic states, and cited the papacy as a model. However, this raises serious questions as to how much power the caliph would effectively be able to exercise. Rida argued that the successors to the first four Rightly-Guided Caliphs (the **rashidun**), did not exercise the role of the caliphate in a valid and sensible manner. Therefore, the only true caliphate were, as their title implies, the 'rightly-guided'. He blamed this decline on the religious scholars, the *ulama*, who failed in their historic duty to exercise their role of guiding the community and calling on them to disobey unjust rulers. The failure of the *ulama* to exercise their responsibility was, according to Rida, a result of their reluctance to engage in independent legal reasoning, or *ijtihad*.

The power of the caliph, then, would be more of a supervisor for the development of *shari'a*, but in close consultation with the *ulama*. In fact, Rida emphasised the importance of consultation (a principle in Islamic political philosophy referred to as '*shura*') which he argued was abandoned after the death of the fourth caliph. The *ulama*, then, would be the ones who would exercise considerable power, but provided they are skilled enough to exercise the principle of *ijtihad*. Obviously, Rida felt that the *ulama* of his contemporary world were ill-equipped for such a duty and his aim was to establish a seminary where students would be taught the principles of international law, sociology, world history, organisation of religious students, Western science and, of course, *shari'a*.

The position of the caliph would be more of a figurehead than having as much power as the first four caliphs exercised. Rida refers to such duties of the caliph as organising religious education and the laws of personal status, but aside from that, there seems little else under his control. It seems that Rida sees the caliph as more of a charismatic figure than an actual implementer of law, but it raises the question as to how the Muslim world is able to always determine such rare individuals. Certainly, in Rida's own time, there did not seem to be any suitable candidates. In fact, his suggestions for possible candidates for the caliph represent a curious bunch, eventually putting forward an Iman from Yemen of the *Zaydi* branch of **Shi'a** Islam. The Zaydis, also known as 'Five-Imam Shi'ites', represent some 40 per cent of the Yemen population, but are much smaller in numbers than the 'Twelver' Shi'a of mostly Iran and Iraq. The choice of a Shi'a to represent all Muslims is in itself a curious one, and then to also suggest a Zaydi would hardly meet with the approval of the *umma*.

He is very critical of the traditional ways of applying Islamic law, which involved little more than a blind imitation (*taqlid*) of the rulings of the four great law schools. He encouraged the great Islamic jurists of his day to gather together and produce a definitive book of *shari'a* that is relevant to the modern world and, in fact, his writings in *The Beacon* represent a challenge to *shari'a* as it stood, containing many legal rulings on such important issues as the role of women, rules for a just war, and usury.

Rida represents a curious amalgam of conservatism and modernism. On the one hand he is a great advocate of consultation in the political process as well as supporting the Maliki principle of *maslaha* (public interest) as the basis for legal decisions. However, on the other hand, who can decide what is in the interest of the public seems to be limited to a trained elite, and does not seem too dissimilar to the concept of rule adopted by Ayatollah **Khomeini**. While his writings often reflect Shi'a ideas, not to mention his enthusiasm for a Zaydi Shi'a Imam, he is also very critical of the role of Shi'a Muslims in history and succeeded in offending many Shi'a thinkers.

His conservatism seems to have increased in his latter years. In 1925, Rida travelled to Saudi Arabia and this drew him closer to the Hanbali law school (see **Ibn Hanbal**) which is generally considered the most traditionalist of the four schools of law and dominates Saudi society, although Rida himself was careful to make a distinction between Hanbali rulings on religious practice and the need to practise *ijtihad* in social affairs. He also became a staunch supporter of the ultra-conservative Wahhabis (see **al-Wahhab**) and argued that they were the true defenders of Islam. Needless to say, this view angered many Muslims, especially as the Wahhabis were intent on ridding Islamic society of *Shi'a* and *Sufi* influences. This ambiguity was one failing. However, Rida was a hugely influential figure, who is important in countering the trend among some Muslim intellectuals who argued not only for the abolition of the caliphate, but also for greater secularisation. Rida stressed the importance of consultation, public interest, and modernisation of the legal system, while attempting to maintain what was traditional about Islam. However, it is debatable how successful this would be in practice. Nonetheless, his views and actions had a major impact on his spiritual heir, Hasan **al-Bana** (1906–1949), the founder of the Muslim Brotherhood.

Major works

None of his major works are currently available in English

Further reading

Kerr, M., *Islamic Reform: The Political and Legal Theories of Mohammad 'Abduh and Rashid Rida*, Berkeley, CA: University of California Press, 1966.

Shahin, Emad Eldin, *Through Muslim Eyes: M. Rashid Rida and the West*, Singapore: Federal Publications, 1993.

SIR MUHAMMAD IQBAL (1877–1938)

Born in India, to this day, Iqbal's writings remain an important influence not only in South Asia but also in the Middle East. He is renowned and admired for his passionate poetry, which has inspired millions, but he was also a philosopher, political thinker and spiritual father of Pakistan. His importance lies primarily in his awareness of the problems faced by Islam when confronted with so-called modernity; in particular, the failure of the Muslim world to respond to Western encroachment both in the political and social sphere, but also in the technological and scientific arenas. He wrote in three languages: English, Urdu and Persian

Muhammad Iqbal was born in November 1877 in Sialkot, in the Punjab, to a middle-class family whose origins lay in Kashmir. His father was a tailor by trade, but was well versed in Islamic theology and mysticism. Not unlike many Islamic reformers, Iqbal's education consisted of a mix of both Islamic and Western. He went to modern schools and attended the grammar school, the Scotch Mission College in Sialkot and then, from 1889–1893, the Murray College. After completing his high school studies he left Sialkot, and from 1893–1897, studied at Lahore's Oriental College. He was a particular expert in Arabic and English and continued to study for his Master's in Philosophy. Upon graduation in 1899 he was appointed to the McLeod Readership in Arabic at the Oriental College, but soon gave this up to teach Philosophy at the Government College in Lahore.

While teaching in Lahore, Iqbal established a friendship with the noted British Orientalist T.W. Arnold who encouraged Iqbal to travel to Europe. This he did between 1905 and 1908, where he studied in both Britain and Germany. In London he joined Lincoln's Inn and qualified for the Bar, after which he studied at Trinity College, Cambridge University with the *Sufi* specialist R.A. Nicholson and the neo-Hegelian John M.E. McTaggart. He then went to Heidelberg and Munich where he completed his doctorate entitled *The Development of Metaphysics in Persia* in 1908.

In 1908 he returned to Lahore to teach briefly, but he had already established a reputation as a poet and preferred to devote his energies to this while pursuing a profession in law. Iqbal's poetry reflects a synthesis of Eastern and Western influences, frequently combining the thoughts of Muslim reformers, jurists and mystics such as the Sufi poet **Rumi**, with that of Western philosophers such as Hegel, Bergson and Nietzsche. His underlying concern, which was reflected in all his output, was with the revival of Islam. Preceding his political activism he wrote books on economics in Urdu and regularly published poems on subjects related to nature, religion and politics in the Urdu journal *Makhazan*, which was founded in 1901.

During his time in Europe, Iqbal's poetry reflected a nationalist stance. He wrote a eulogy to the Prophet **Muhammad** which describes the golden age of the Islamic empire and laments its subsequent decline. The message of the eulogy was that the fate of the Muslim world was in the hands of the Muslims themselves rather than being enslaved to external factors. His poem *Portrayal of Pain* (*Taswir-dard*) expresses his anger over the sufferings of the Indian people under colonial rule. In particular, his nationalist poems are concerned especially with the Muslim community in India and hopes of ending not only colonialism, but also the conflict between Muslims and Hindus in India itself.

His philosophical views on the notion of the self as a dynamic force – in line with the influence of Nietzsche's *Übermensch* – meant that he rejected the quietism that seemed to be prevalent among colonised Muslims, not only in India but further afield. Ultimately he places the blame for this complacency on Muslims themselves for they are not fulfilling their God-given purpose to be His vice-regent on Earth. Rather, Muslims have relinquished this authority. In his controversial poem *The Complaint* (*Shakwa*) he does level a complaint against God for allowing Muslims to be subjected to poverty and humiliation. However, he still lays the blame squarely on the Muslims themselves for the political unawareness, factionalism and lack of activism in the political sphere. Because of the controversy the book raised, Iqbal made a point of writing another poem, *The Answer to the Complaint* (*Jawab-i-shakwa*) in which he attempts to reply to those critics who accused him of complaining to God!

In later life Iqbal shifted politically to pan-Islamism, and his poetry became more philosophical and mystical. In terms of his poetry, the more philosophical works culminated in his great work *Secrets of the Self* (*Asrar-i-Khudi*) where he writes of the need for Muslims to reawaken their soul and act. His rejection of territorial nationalism was based on his belief in the *umma*: a community of like-minded individuals that existed beyond national boundaries. He saw in the Prophet Muhammad the exemplar of the Muslim community; a Prophet-Statesman who founded a society based on freedom, equality and brotherhood reflected in the central tenet of 'unity' (*tawhid*). In the practical sense, Iqbal believed that a requisite of being a good Muslim was to live under Islamic law which acts as the blueprint for the perfect Islamic society as envisioned by the Prophet Muhammad. In 1937, Iqbal sent a letter to Muhammad Ali Jinnah, the leader of the Muslim League and future founder of Pakistan, in which he emphasised the importance of Islamic law if Islam was to remain a force in the region.

Aside from the need for Islamic law, *shari'a*, to exist in any Islamic state, Iqbal also stressed the importance of absolute equality. He believed democracy was the best form of government in terms of allowing the individual to emerge, whereas aristocracy suppressed such individuality. When he looked to Indian Muslim society, he saw only sectarianism and a caste system that he believed was worse than in Hindu society! He also argued that democracy was not merely a pragmatic form of government but was also rooted in Islam itself and he looked to the early years of Islam, the time of Muhammad and his **Companions**, when the small society, in Iqbal's eyes, operated on the basis of largely egalitarian principles and unity. This system was soon destroyed, however, as Islam expanded rapidly resulting in factionalism and the adoption of non-Islamic forms of government.

It should be noted that when Iqbal talked of democracy, he was not referring to Western forms of democracy which give the franchise to any individual over a certain age regardless of educational level. In this sense, Iqbal shared a view of democracy not dissimilar from his compatriot **Mawdudi**: democracy is only for those who are sufficiently learned to know what they are voting for! The logic of this was based on the belief that the best person to rule the Islamic state should be the best Muslim, not someone who may be particularly good at rhetoric or play the popularity card. Therefore, only those who have a level of expertise in what it means to be a good Muslim, i.e. have knowledge of Islamic law, history and so on, are equipped to vote. Education, therefore, is an essential component before democracy can be entertained. However, the contentious issues that are explored in more depth when looking at Mawdudi remain: what level of education is required before one can vote and what of the rights of non-Muslims? These are issues that Iqbal failed to address.

The influence of Nietzsche is particularly evident when Iqbal talks of the intermediate stage before mass democracy can become a reality, in terms of addressing the question of who should rule. It was essential, given the decay of the Muslim society, that it should be

[SIR MUHAMMAD IQBAL]

ruled by a particularly charismatic and learned individual who can provide the model for those to follow. Here, again, Iqbal was making close reference to how he perceived the early Muslim state under the charisma of the Prophet Muhammad. He believed that like-minded individuals do emerge from time to time during the course of human history. This theme is not only taken from Nietzsche and his 'Superman' or *Übermencsh*, but was also a belief within Islam itself, based on a well-known **hadith**, that there would, every new century, emerge a 'renewer' (*mujaddid*). Such acknowledged 'renewers' in the past include **al-Shafi'i** and **al-Ghazali**. In addition, Iqbal is drawing upon Sufi concepts of the Perfect Man (*insan-i-kamil*) which includes not only past prophets but the Sufi saints. The Sufi poet Rumi, in particular, wrote a great deal on the notion of the Perfect Man and his life was dedicated to his search for such. Again, such thorny questions as to how this Perfect Man is to emerge and to be recognised as such are not adequately addressed.

Importantly, and like so many other reformers, Iqbal called for the re-opening of the gates of **ijtihad**, of the need for independent reasoning in the making of laws. While he wrote of a utopian ideal, he claimed that his ideal society would not be a static ideology, but one that could readily adapt to change and progress while remaining firmly embedded in the fundamental principles of the Qur'an and the life of Muhammad. These Islamic sources of authority were to be seen as paradigms, or beacons of light, rather than set doctrine. This view is in line with his theological belief in God as a creative and dynamic force, as the unfolding of inner possibilities. Therefore, *shari'a* is also open to change while remaining a blueprint. The view that *shari'a* was fixed and sacrosanct he blamed on the conservative religious scholars, the **ulama**, hence his call for education in more modern affairs. Again, however, Iqbal's vision raises more questions than providing answers, for in practical terms it is difficult to determine the extent to which parts of *shari'a* are sacrosanct and parts are not.

In 1924 he joined the National Liberal League of Lahore and, in 1926, he was elected to the Punjab Legislative Council. He was an active member, speaking on land revenue and taxation and advocating compulsory education and better sanitation for the villages. Iqbal's apparent pan-Islamism in his writings did not always coincide with his nationalist activities for he also promoted provincial autonomy for Islamic India and separate elections for Muslims and Hindus. The motive for this was partly to see Islam return to the pure ideals he envisions in his poetry, but he was also pragmatic in that he could not believe that an India could be created which could treat all creeds equally especially in the case of the Muslims who were such a minority in comparison to the Hindus. In 1930, Iqbal was elected president of the Muslim League and in his presidential address he laid down his vision of Pakistan. He attended the second and third round-table conferences on the future of Pakistan held in London in 1931 and 1932 respectively, and, in 1932, he was knighted for his services.

Iqbal's writings can often come across as confused and contradictory. At times, he calls for democracy, while at other times he warns people to steer well away from it. He talks of egalitarianism, but is elitist in terms of who has the right to be enfranchised. In addition, his later life seems to reflect pan–Islamism in his writings yet he devoted his energies to the formation of an independent Muslim state separate from India. In all these cases, however, a distinction does need to be made between Iqbal's vision of the Muslim society as an ideal, and his pragmatic attitude to the state of Islam in his time. In one of his writings he states that all Muslim societies must first of all become independent before they can then merge under one *umma* under one caliph. Iqbal's thought, then, must be divided into the immediate and the long-terms goals. His impact on the thought of Ali Jinnah and Mawdudi especially and, in turn, the formation of the independent Islamic state of Pakistan is particularly noteworthy.

Major works

There are a number of Iqbal's work available in English. The following are enlightening:

Reconstruction of Religious Thought in Islam, Littlehampton: Apex Books Concern, 1980.

Shikwa and Jawab-i-Shikwa (Complaint and Answer): Iqbal's Dialogue with Allah, trans. Khushwant Singh, New Delhi: Oxford University Press, 1991.

Tulip in the Desert: A Selection of Iqbal's Poetry, trans. Mustansir Mir, Montreal: McGill-Queen's University Press, 1999.

The Secrets of the Self: Asrar-I-Khudi, trans. R.A. Nicholson, New Delhi: Kitab Bhavan, 2000.

Further reading

A more up-to-date book on Iqbal's life and thought is well overdue. Schimmel's is a work I particularly recommend, especially in relation to Iqbal's more 'mystical' side.

Dorraj, M., 'The Intellectual Dilemmas of a Muslim Modernist – Politics and Poetics of Iqbal', *Muslim World* 85(3–4) (1995).

Hussain, R., *The Politics of Iqbal*, Lahore: Islamic Book Service, 1977.

May, L.S., *Iqbal: His Life and Times*, Lahore: Ashraf, 1974.

Schimmel, A., *Gabriel's Wing: Study into the Religious Ideas of Sir Muhammad Iqbal*, Lahore: Iqbal Academy, 1989.

SAYYID RUHOLLAH KHOMEINI (1902–1989)

Khomeini has become a legendary revolutionary figure for millions of *Shi'a* Muslims and he signifies the power religion can muster against what is perceived as materialist oppression. He came to embody both a popular conservatism and the strong desire for spiritual renewal which was so longed for by an Iranian population that had spent years under a puppet regime engaged in rapid modernisation and capitalism that seemed alien to the spiritually inclined masses. This charismatic, yet contradictory figure, acquired the necessary authority to lead the 1979 Iranian revolution that toppled the Shah of Iran and resulted in the establishment of a Shi'a Islamic state. If **Ali Shariati** was the ideological father of the revolution, Khomeini was its living symbol and guide.

Ruhollah al-Musavi was born in the Iranian provincial town of Komein, hence the name 'Khomeini' which he adopted in his student years. His family came from a strong religious tradition, for both his grandfather and his father were religious scholars (*Mullahs*). Khomeini was able to possess the title of respect 'Sayyid' ('lord') because his ancestry could be traced back to the Prophet **Muhammad** through his daughter Fatima and her husband (and Muhammad's cousin) **Ali**, who is also acknowledged as the First *Imam* of the Shi'a. It also so happens that Khomeini was born on the birthday of Fatima. Such facts only help to accentuate his mythical qualities. His father was killed the same year Ruhollah was born and so he was brought up by his mother and aunt who themselves died when he was just 16

However, Khomeini displayed a keen interest in religion and, at the age of 17, he went to Arak, then known as Sultanabad, in Western Iran to study religious sciences. He became a pupil of Shaykh Abdul-Karim Haeri who not only taught him the intricacies of Shi'ite scholarship, but also the importance of political activism as central to Shi'a belief. In 1922, Haeri moved to the sacred city of Qom to head the religious seminary there and Khomeini followed him. Khomeini excelled in his studies, in particular Islamic philosophy, and became a good teacher himself, earning the title of *mujtahid* in the early 1930s. A *mujtahid* is someone who has earned the status of being learned enough to make independent legal interpretation, that is to engage in *ijtihad* (independent reasoning). Whereas in Sunni Islam, *ijtihad* had been almost completely replaced by *taqlid* (imitation), it was still exercised in Shi'a Islam.

In 1943, Khomeini wrote *Kashf al-asrar* (*Revealing the Secrets*) which was a defence of Shi'ite orthodoxy, including such popular customs as veneration of the saints and requests for their intercession, mourning the martyrdom of various Imams, and the right of the Shi'a clergy to teach others in Islamic knowledge as well as veto legislation if considered un-Islamic. This book was a response to a work called *Secrets of a Thousand Years* by Ahmad Kasravi, an Iranian intellectual of the 1930s and 1940s, who had attacked the clergy as being superstitious and ignorant. Khomeini also attacked Reza Pahlavi (the Shah of Iran from 1925 until 1941) in his work for being a tyrant. However, at this time, Khomeini did not believe that the clergy itself should be involved in the day-to-day running of politics, regarding politics as a sullying influence. The *Secrets* proved to be very popular and, by the early 1960s, Khomeini had risen to the rank of Grand Ayatollah, an acknowledgement as one of the most powerful religious leaders in Iran.

In 1963, Khomeini publicly protested against the secularising reforms under the so-called 'White Revolution'. He was arrested for his involvement and, in 1964, sent into exile, first to Turkey and then on to Iraq. In the Shi'ite religious centre of Najaf in Iraq, where he spent the next fifteen years, Khomeini was able to sermonise against the Iranian regime and these powerful lectures were taped and distributed in the streets of Teheran. Khomeini was just as much a force abroad as he was at home. His lectures were published as *Islamic Government: Guardianship by the Clergy* which formulated the role of the clergy in government with specific reference to the contentious concept *vilayat-i faqih* ('guardianship by the clergy'). During the 1970s Khomeini became a central figure for militant religious opposition to the government. In 1977 his eldest son died in mysterious circumstances and, in January 1978, a newspaper attack on Khomeini helped spark violent demonstrations in support of Khomeini with many referring to him as an Imam. Khomeini was expelled from Iraq and he went to Paris for refuge but he returned to Iran in February 1979, after the Shah had fled, and took the reins of government as both religious and political leader, presiding over an Islamic revolution that attempted to rid Iran of all Western influence, as well as all possible opposition to the clerical regime.

A central theme of Khomeini's writings was the concept of the Perfect Man (*insan-i kamil*). This concept owes much to **Ibn Arabi**'s concept of the Perfect Man which, in turn, was drawn from *Sufi* notions that were also developed by the Indian poet and reformer, **Muhammad Iqbal**. Likewise the Iranian scholar and contemporary of Khomeini, Ali Shariati, made use of the concept with reference to his 'theomorphic being'. The idea centres on the question of what constitutes the perfect Muslim, with usual reference back to the Prophet Muhammad as the paradigm. In Shi'a Islam, other examples would include the Imams, most notably **Ali** and Husayn. In *Sunni* Islam, references to the Perfect Man are sometimes linked to the belief that in every century a 'renewer' (*mujtahid*) will emerge: a charismatic leader who will return Islam to its right path, whereas, in Shi'a Islam there is an almost messianic belief that the Twelfth Imam, or the *Mahdi*, will one day return. In the meantime, however, leadership fell into the hands of the 'guardians', the ayatollahs. Among this select group of ayatollahs it was theorised that a Perfect Man would emerge who, while not possessing the spiritual status of the *Mahdi*, would be a pious and charismatic leader who would be infallible. It is interesting that whereas Ali Shariati saw the Perfect Man as an empowerment of the masses in an existential sense, Khomeini saw it in a hierarchical elitist sense and it is no surprise that many of Khomeini's followers saw him as this Perfect Man if not the *Mahdi* himself: an observation Khomeini neither denied nor admitted to.

In his writings and lectures, Khomeini argued that if Islam was to be rejuvenated it needed to look towards the Perfect Man for guidance and he set out the kind of qualities required. He argued that monarchy is incompatible with Islam and rejected Iranian nationalism in favour of an Islamic universalism, albeit of the Shi'a variety. By the 1970s Khomeini was arguing that in the absence of the Imam the clergy should do more than simply advise the government on how Islamic their legislation is; rather, they should rule directly. This doctrine of 'rule by the jurists' (*vilayat-i faqih*) had little Qur'anic support, not to mention a rejection by virtually all of the Shi'a clergy. However, for Khomeini the concept of rule by jurists was a logical conclusion to the much more widely held view that an Islamic state, if it were to be truly Islamic, must be governed by *shari'a*. It was believed that Islamic law amounted to a complete social system, providing regulations for all aspects of life. If it is indeed the case that *shari'a* is all-encompassing, there is therefore no need for any kind of human legislation for it has all been provided for by God. However, the problem rests in interpreting divine law so that it may adapt to changing circumstances. Shi'a Islam has a long tradition of independent reasoning or '*ijtihad*' and Khomeini argued that those best qualified for *ijtihad* are the jurists, the *Mullahs*. Khomeini presents a view of his Republic of Iran not unlike Plato's hypothetical 'Republic': a state ruled by Philosopher-Kings who naturally should rule as they have access to moral truths. Likewise, the 'Guardians' or the ayatollahs had access to God's law by nature of being the most learned. Even better if, among them, should emerge a Perfect Man with near infallibility in his decision making.

Khomeini cited historical evidence to demonstrate that Islamic law left in the hands of politicians usually results in a spiritual morass, and this certainly seemed to be the case in Iran which also suffered poverty and oppression. Here he was being pragmatic, stressing the need for good government in a nation that had lost its way. Khomeini went much further than the other clerics, however, in arguing that authority should not only be religious but also political because otherwise knowledge of divine law would be ineffectual if they did not have the power to enact it.

Khomeini's view that the state should be ruled by a group of experts in *shari'a* would have remained nothing more than an academic debate if it had not been for the 1979 revolution that effectively put Khomeini in power and allowed him to insert *vilayat-i-faqih* as a central tenet of the new constitution. When Khomeini assumed power, there was much opposition to his views not only from secularists and Islamic modernists, but from a number of the clergy who believed that politics was too much of a dirty business for clerics to be directly involved with. However, Khomeini successfully suppressed these elements in a not-altogether bloodless manner and his clerical followers took over the reins of power in parliament, the judiciary, the military, the Revolutionary Guards, and the media. Khomeini ruled supremely for another decade and in that time a doctrinaire ideology was incorporated into every aspect of Iranian life, from the news and media, to the universities and the home. All evidence of the 'corrupting West' was eliminated and many dissenters were exiled, imprisoned or executed. Khomeini did not succeed, however, in exporting his revolution to other Islamic countries, despite some efforts at insurgency in such countries as Saudi Arabia, Bahrain and, of course, neighbouring Iraq which has a Shi'a majority.

Khomeini was an original thinker who created a state with a unique constitution: an attempt to incorporate revelation with democracy, although the democratic element – the National Consultative Assembly (*majlis*) – was subject to the scrutiny of the Guardian Council which was made up of six religious jurists. Khomeini, unusually for a high-ranking cleric, specialised in mystical philosophy and his views closely reflect those of **Sadr al-Din Shirazi** ('Mulla Sadra') in that both stressed the importance of philosophical values being integrated into normal society rather than separate or aloof from it. However, Mulla Sadra rejected the notion that *mujtahids* should take on the role of interpreters for the masses whereas Khomeini made this a central tenet of the constitution. While Khomeini often spoke of social justice, once in power he engaged in social coercion and clamped down on freedom of thought. However, in terms of his legacy, the current state of Iran is still in the process of finding a new identity for itself that allows both for an expression of its religious values as well as that of democratic values and, in this respect, it is proving to be a vibrant and fascinating place.

See also: **Abd al-Karim Soroush**.

Major works

A number of his speeches and writings are available in English.

Islam and Revolution I: Writings and Declarations of Imam Khomeini (1941–1980), trans. Hamid Algar, Berkeley, CA: Mizan Press, 1981.
The Sayings of Ayatollah Khomeini, New York: Bantam Books, 1985.
Islam and Revolution, London: Kegan Paul International, 1985.

Further reading

The activities in Iran since 1979 occupy countless shelves.

Dabashi, H., *Theology of Discontent: The Ideological Foundation of the Islamic Revolution in Iran*, New York: New York University Press, 1992.
Moin, B., 'Khomeini's Search for Perfection: Theory and Practice', in A. Rahnema (ed.) *Pioneers of Islamic Revival*, London: Zed Books, 1994.
——*Khomeini: Life of the Ayatollah*, London: I.B. Tauris, 1999.
Brumberg, D., *Reinventing Khomeini: The Struggle for Reform in Iran*, Chicago: University of Chicago Press, 2001.

SAYYID ABUL ALA MAWDUDI (1903–1979)

While Egypt was an important intellectual bastion for Islam in the twentieth century due, primarily, to the activities of the Muslim Brotherhood, another vital centre for resurgence was India. Here emerged Sayyid **Ahmed Khan**, the poet and philosopher **Muhammad Iqbal** and, undoubtedly the figure who has had the greatest impact, Mawdudi. As head and founder of the political movement

Jamaat-i-Islami – the Indo-Pakistan equivalent of the Muslim Brotherhood – Mawdudi was the most controversial and significant Islamic thinker and activist in the region until his death. He was renowned for possessing incredible energy, which he poured into his political and religious activities, including speeches and writings. In fact, his writings, much of which has been translated into numerous languages including English, are extraordinary in terms of topics covered and quantity. Nonetheless, the primary focus determined from all his works is a genuine concern for the future of Islam coupled with the call for an Islamic state and how this might be constituted. Further, he believed that Islam could achieve this through its own ideology which he considered to be self-sufficient and distinct from Western values. In many respects, his views echo those of the **Salafiyyah**. Undoubtedly, Mawdudi's writings and activities contributed greatly to the founding of Pakistan in 1947. Today, Mawdudi continues to be read, studied and respected by Muslims across the world and is constantly referenced in relation to modern themes of Islamic resurgence.

Mawdudi was born on 25 September 1903 in Aurangabad, part of the state of Hyderabad (now the Indian province of Andhra Pradesh). On his father's side he was descended from the Chisti line of **Sufi** saints, and he was nurtured in religion from an early age. He received much of his religious education from his father and a variety of teachers that his strict father employed so that Mawdudi was well versed in Islamic teaching, history and literature. However, he had little in the way of a formal education in terms of what was being taught in modern schools and, unlike many twentieth-century Muslim reformers, was isolated from the knowledge of Western culture and thought.

In 1918, he entered journalism by contributing to an Urdu newspaper and, at the age of 17, became the editor of the weekly paper *Taj* in Jabalpur. In 1920, he went to Delhi as editor of *Muslim* until 1924 when he edited *al-Jamiah*. Both these papers were part of the *Jamiyat-i Ulama* organisation which introduced Mawdudi, at such a young age, to the foremost Indian Muslim scholars. Consequently he became more involved with politics, becoming a member of *Tahrik-i Hijrat*, a group opposed to British rule in India which urged Muslims to migrate to Afghanistan to maintain their identity. Mawdudi also wrote his first major work, *al-Jihad fil al-Islam*, which consisted of a collection of articles he had written for *al-Jamiah* and was well received by such notable figures as Muhammad Iqbal, and contained the main themes in nascent form that were to occupy all his future writings.

Central to Mawdudi's writings is his audience: aimed at the edu-cated, leading classes of India. His concentration on the leadership, rather than the common man, is reflected in his doctrine of *al-Jihad fi-l Islam*, by which the character of a social order flows from the top down. This necessarily implies a form of authoritarianism: he believed that practical social change was impossible unless the theo-retical views held by the leadership changed first. On this further point, he frequently makes reference to the authority of the Prophet **Muhammad**, the Rightly-Guided caliphs (**Rashidun**), and the great jurists as prime examples of forces for transformation. A significant change of direction in his works took place from 1937 when he began for the first time to concern himself specifically with the political problems of Muslim India. This period was one of great change in the area of India as it was on the verge of achieving inde-pendence. Mawdudi was fearful that Muslim identity would be sub-merged by the Hindu majority. From 1937 until 1941 he published in *Tarjuman al-Quran* a series of essays dealing with the political con-sequences of this. The stance of the Indian National Congress, which affirmed that all Indians constitute a single nation and that a future government in India must be democratic and secular, in particular warned Mawdudi of possible risks to Islamic identity. This led him to address issues of secularisation and Muslim identity, particularly emphasising that Muslims had a 'nationality' of their own which is the polar opposite of 'nationalism'.

Mawdudi greatly feared Western-style democracy, which he believed to be nothing more than majority rule, whether its views are right or wrong: majority rule was not a moral imperative, merely the tyranny of the majority. In Mawdudi's writings, the term employed to translate 'secular' (*la dini*) in fact literally means 'reli-gionless': he believed that a secular society, such as was envisaged for an independent India, would really be an oppressor of minority groups (i.e. Muslims) and partisan towards the religious majority (i.e. Hindu). As a result, he believed that Muslims should constitute their own 'nation'; not in the sense of having physical boundaries, but in the sense of the **umma**. His beliefs here are largely affected by the situation in India at the time where Muslims constituted a small minority.

Mawdudi considered an Islamic form of government to be a moral imperative; it is the system by which the laws of God are given form. He appeals to the primary source, the Qur'an, to support his thesis. Following on from Mawdudi's assumption that the authority for the state rests with the will of God, the question of how one is to find out this will beyond the Qur'an must be addressed. Mawdudi looks to the Prophet Muhammad as the ideal statesman and Medina as the ideal Islamic State; an age of unity between the religious and the secular with Muhammad as its Head. Many Islamists, Mawdudi among them, make reference to a 'golden age' of Islam; a period that is portrayed as a pure Islamic State. In appealing to traditional **hadith** and histories, the Islamist sees ultimate authority resting with the Rightly-Guided caliphs. They are seen as ideal Islamic rulers, by and large, who governed an ideal Islamic State. Mawdudi does not detail exactly how much authority the rulings of past 'great jurists' would have in his Islamic state, nor does he specify which rulings. He has moved on from the sources of purportedly 'objective knowledge' (i.e. the *'ilm* of the Qur'an and the **sunna** of the Prophet) to one of subjective understanding; the **fiqh** of the scholars: although how much trust Mawdudi is prepared to place in them is debatable.

Mawdudi portrays his vision of the Islamic State as a workable proposition by dividing the organs of the state into three: the Legislature, the Executive and the Judiciary and defining their powers and functions accordingly:

1 *The Legislature.* For this, Mawdudi uses the old Islamic terminology *fiqh* – 'the body which resolves and prescribes' (*'Ahl al-hal wa'al-'aqd'*). As it is limited by the Divine Code, it cannot legislate in contravention of the directives of God and His Prophet.

2 *The Executive.* The institution of the Executive in Mawdudi's Islamic State (which he compares with the *Ulul-Amr* in the Qur'an) would engage in the actual enforcement of the rules and regulations put forward by the Legislature. The Executive must be obeyed 'on the condition that it obeys God and His Prophet and avoids the path of sin and transgression'.

3 *The Judiciary.* These courts of law are established to enforce the Divine Code.

At first glance, the 'democratic principles' of consultation do indeed suggest democracy, but when one digs a little deeper, there are serious limitations placed on the citizen. Apart from the fact that no mention is made here of non-Muslims, Mawdudi's reference to 'only Muslims' would not include women either. Mawdudi then proceeds to allocate powers of **ijtihad** (independent legal reasoning) to those Muslims 'who have achieved the capability of interpretation'. According to Mawdudi's own calculations, the percentage of Muslims with any true knowledge of Islam is no more than 0.001 percent!

Thus, although he makes allowance for *ijtihad*, this authority would be limited to a very small minority indeed. Mawdudi's 'limited popular sovereignty' does not imply democracy in the sense of power to the masses, despite his theo-democracy claims.

In his book *Purdah and the Status of Woman in Islam*, Mawdudi begins by painting what he sees as a dark, satanic picture of the status of women in Western society with members of the same sex involved in homosexuality, and magazine articles providing contraceptive information! In the same way that Mawdudi looks at history in an attempt to justify his notion that no nation has prospered under a woman ruler, he now states that no woman's genius is as great as the likes of such men as Aristotle, Kant, Hegel, Shakespeare, Napoleon, **Salah al-Din**, and so on. For Mawdudi, men are naturally generals, statesmen and administrators, and women are wives, mothers and housekeepers.

Mawdudi – like many other writers – fails to accommodate religious pluralism politically. His isolationist policy for non-Muslims is reminiscent of Byzantine 'protection' of the Jews, and the 'millet' in the old Ottoman State. Non-Muslims, or **zimmis,** who have, nonetheless, affirmed their loyalty to the state are classed as citizens, and would, therefore, have citizens' rights. However, Mawdudi distinguishes the *zimmi* from the Muslim and is not an adherent of 'equal rights', believing such ideals are the resting place of hypocritical nations that fail to practise what they preach. So, rather than attempt to achieve the ideal of equality, Mawdudi would prefer to avoid being accused of hypocrisy and so states quite categorically that non-Muslims would not be treated with equal status in his state: only Muslims would be given the 'burden' of running the state. Islam enforces only its laws of the land on non-Muslims and gives them equal rights with Muslims in all 'civil matters', that is, criminal and civil law are the same for both Muslims and non-Muslims. Mawdudi goes so far as to state that *zimmis* can follow their own laws, such as make and sell alcohol (to fellow non-Muslims, of course), and raise and sell pigs (again, only to fellow *zimmis*.) A *zimmi* cannot, of course, be the head of state, nor a member of its *Shura* (Consultative Assembly). However, he may be allowed to participate in the legislative assembly on the condition that he does not adversely affect the ideological basis of the state.

In Mawdudi's Islamic state, authority – the body to which the power to make and enforce laws is given – would rest with a small number of individuals, acting as representatives of God. This conception of authority is reminiscent of medieval European societies rather than any modern democratic system. Mawdudi's claim that his Islamic society would be a 'theo-democracy', therefore, seems to beg the question: where is the democracy?

Mawdudi's outline of the state is authoritarian in the sense that political coercion is required to implement Islamic philosophy throughout all elements of life. Reforms, Mawdudi argued, that Islam wants to introduce cannot be introduced just by preaching. To implement them, political power is needed. Mawdudi has shown throughout his writings a lack of trust in general human will and has, therefore, chosen to exclude it as a weakness and a distraction from his political aims: his objective is not to organise a society on the basis of equity and justice – which would seem entirely 'Islamic' in spirit – but to interpret the sovereignty of God as the submission of the individual will to the coercive power of the state apparatus. As such, Mawdudi has remained ignorant of the twentieth-entury political arena where all political philosophies are necessarily influenced by the international context and the socio-economic conditions that are prevalent at the time. The fact that it may be conceivable to organise a society on a level that would allow individual free will is a concept that Mawdudi distrusts entirely. Having said that, Mawdudi's influence continues to be immense and no doubt this is due to consistent determination to keep to the Islamic teachings of early Islam rather than face any possibility of its 'watering down'. Whether such a 'theo-democracy' is really possible continues to be a matter of considerable debate.

Major works

The Islamic Foundation, largely under the auspices of Khurshid Ahmad, has provided English translations of much of Mawdudi's work; most are in short pamphlet form.

Human Rights in Islam, trans. Khurram Murad, Leicester: Islamic Foundation, 1980.
The Islamic Movement: Dynamics of Values, Power and Change, trans. Khurram Murad, Leicester: Islamic Foundation, 1984.
Witnesses Unto Mankind: Purpose and Duty of the Muslim Ummah, trans. Khurram Murad, Leicester: Islamic Foundation, 1986a.
The Islamic Way of Life, trans. Khurram Murad, Leicester: Islamic Foundation, 1986b.

Further reading

Khurshid Ahmad has written a number of studies of Mawdudi's life and work. However, a more critical work has yet to be produced, although the

Nasr is interesting as he sees Mawdudi's revivalism as not so much a response to the West but also a result of the need to establish a distinct Muslim identity in India.

Ahmad, Khurshid (ed.) *Islamic Perspectives: Studies in Honour of Sayyid Abdul A'la Mawdudi*, Leicester: Islamic Foundation, 1979.
——(ed.) *Mawdudi: An Introduction to His Life and Thought*, Leicester: Islamic Foundation, 1979.
Nasr, S.V.R., *Mawdudi and the Making of Islamic Revivalism*, Oxford: Oxford University Press, 1996.

HASAN AL-BANA (1906–1949)

Hasan al-Bana was the founder of the most important reform movement of the era, the Muslim Brotherhood (*al-Ikhwan al-Muslimun*), and a respected writer on Islamic jurisprudence. Ideologically, al-Banna is associated with the **Salafiyyah** (a movement of modernisation but 'looks back' to the time of the Prophet **Muhammad** and the **Companions** for inspiration and guidance) and shares many ideas with his predecessors, **al-Afghani, Rashid Rida** and **Muhammad Abduh**. He was a highly effective organiser and a charismatic leader who proved an inspiration for many Islamic movements that were to follow.

Al-Bana was born in October 1906 in the small town of Al-Mahmoudiyya, which is some 90 miles north-west of Cairo. Therefore, al-Bana was not brought up in a cosmopolitan environment. His father, Sheikh Abdul Rahman, was the prayer leader, the imam, at the local mosque. Rahman was a learned figure himself and a Hanbali scholar (see **Ibn Hanbal**), having studied at the prestigious Al-Azhar University in Cairo, and, naturally, proved to be a huge influence on the life and thought of al-Bana. Al-Bana's education was similar to Rida's in that he experienced the dualistic educational approach of, on the one hand, attending a traditional Qur'an school from the age of 8 where he was taught to memorise the entirety of the Qur'an, and then moving to a government-organised modern primary school where he was taught under a more contemporary, 'Western', curriculum. At this school he displayed an early talent for organisation and leadership. At the age of 10 he organised the Society for Moral Behaviour in which he had other pupils on the look-out for misbehaviour.

In 1923, al-Bana moved to Cairo to study at Dar al-Ulum, the very first teacher-training college to provide a higher education in the sciences. At the age of only 16, al-Bana recounts how shocked he was by the sights of the big city; by the dominant British presence, the neglect of Islamic morality, the streets rife with gambling and the consumption of alcohol, and the general indifference shown towards religious matters. Significantly, al-Bana also became seriously involved in a **Sufi** (the mystical branch of Islam) order known as the Hasafiya. This is important for although al-Bana's predecessors al-Afghani and Rashid Rida were initially involved in Sufism, they later repudiated Islamic mysticism as essentially 'un-Islamic'. Al-Bana, on the other hand, remained a Sufi all his life and his organisational methods are directly borrowed from those of Sufi orders. Indeed, al-Bana himself preferred the title of *murshid* (literally 'guide' or 'instructor') for himself which is frequently given to spiritual teachers of Sufi orders. In his memoirs, al-Bana talks of his love of the writings of the great Sufi scholar **al-Ghazali**, particularly his major work *The Revival of the Religious Sciences* which inspired al-Bana to pursue what he considered to be his religious duty to restore Islam to its former glory through action rather than be a closeted scholar. During this period he continued to lead and organise by establishing the Society for the Prevention of the Forbidden and also participated in founding the Hasafiya Society for Charity, for which he acted as secretary. It was during his time in Cairo that, in 1924, the **caliphate** was finally abolished under the Turkish President Ataturk. Although the caliph had long ceased to have any significant political power, he had remained an important symbol of Islamic unity even if the Muslim world in reality was not united. With the abolition of the caliphate, that symbol of unity had gone and the result was a huge psychological blow to many Muslims, al-Bana included.

Al-Bana graduated from teacher training in 1927 and took up his first teaching post in Ismailia in the Suez Canal Zone. Ismailia contained the largest contingent of British troops in Egypt and this time and place proved to be an important milestone in al-Bana's life. The Suez Canal itself was largely a British enterprise that they protected jealously. To understand al-Bana's stance, it helps to have a picture of the historical and political context. Al-Bana remarks in his memoirs that Cairo during this period was rife with anarchy and moral degradation which he blamed on the historical events of the time and, most pointedly, the lack of unity among Muslims. He witnessed first-hand the contrast between the luxury homes of the British, and the hovels many of the Egyptians lived in. The people suffered from low morale and felt humiliated by events in their own country. Egypt had been under British occupation since 1882 and had been a British protectorate since 1914. The outbreak of he First World War led Britain to declare Egypt a protectorate and it severed all ties with Turkey (Egypt was still nominally part of the Ottoman Empire) which had entered the war on the side of Germany. The war caused considerable hardship and resentment among the *fellahin*, the Egyptian peasants, who were conscripted to dig ditches and had their livestock confiscated. Also, Egypt suffered greatly financially as their resources were drained for the war effort. Britain, as a salve, promised that former Ottoman territories would be allowed self-determination once the war was over but back-tracked on these promises. After the war, a new nationalist movement in Eygpt, the *Wafd* ('Delegation') was established but met harsh resistance from the British. Finally, in 1922, Britain declared Egypt an independent monarchy but Britain still reserved the right to intervene in Egyptian affairs if their own interests were threatened. As a result, Egypt was in the unstable position of a struggle for power between the king, the British ambassador and the *Wafd*, which was the only grass-roots party.

However, the *Wafd* was often accused of being too closely associated with British interests so that when al-Banna founded the Muslim Brotherhood (*al-Ikhwan al-Muslimun*, also translated as the 'Society of Muslim Brothers') in March 1928 it soon became the primary source of Islamic radicalism and, essentially, its importance lies in being the ancestor of most Islamic movements on an international level. However, it should be stressed that during al-Bana's lifetime the Brotherhood was not a political party and did not, therefore, contest elections. In fact, al-Bana disapproved of political parties as he believed politics perpetuated disunity among the Muslim community. Theoretically at least, the Muslim community, the **umma**, should have no need of separate parties with differing ideals. The Brotherhood itself started off as a small group of colleagues, mostly students from the Dar al-Ulum, to engage in ways to alleviate what was perceived as the illness of Muslim society. These small groups of benevolent societies were not an uncommon feature in Egypt at that time. It is notable that membership of such groups consisted mostly of laypeople and young religious students. Generally, the **ulama** (the religious scholars) were absent from their ranks. In fact, these moralistic societies were partly a response to the ineffectiveness of the *ulama* to fulfil what was considered their moral, religious and social duty. Al-Bana became increasingly active, preaching in the coffee houses where he gained a huge following. It made sense to target the coffee houses rather than the mosques, as the latter already contained the more religiously inclined, although conservative element, while the former were occupied by the younger, disenchanted classes. In 1927, in Cairo, another organisation was formed, the Young Men's Muslim Association, which is modelled on the Young Men's Christian Association. Al-Bana's father was involved with the YMMA and the two organisations merged to form a much larger Brotherhood. In 1929, the Brotherhood had only four branches, in 1938 three hundred branches, and by 1948 there were two thousand branches with a total membership of some two million. In 1932, the Brotherhood moved its headquarters from Ismailia to Cairo and, by 1939, the organisation could be said to stand out clearly from the mass of charitable organisations in terms of the complexities of organisation, its number of members, and its clearly articulated programme.

In terms of the aims of the Muslim Brotherhood, it was stated at a conference in 1933 that the organisation should devote itself to the reinforcement of Islamic knowledge and culture, and so education was a primary part of their programme. The first step was to rebuild the Muslim community, the *umma*, and to redress the balance of power between Islam and the West, and so a 'call' (*da'wa*) was made to all Muslims to return to their faith. A publication house was set up to propagate the aims of the Brotherhood, as well as publish al-Bana's own writings. Although the Brotherhood was not a political party as such, al-Bana stressed that there was no separation between religion and politics. Rather, Islam is an integrated and comprehensive system that, in the tradition of the *Salafiyyah*, should be understood exclusively from the Qur'an and the **Sunna** (tradition of the Prophet Muhammad) and be applicable to all times and places.

The Brotherhood was organised on military lines, with sub-groups known as 'battalions'. Members would meet once a week for prayer and spiritual instruction and there was much emphasis on the avoidance of such temptations as alcohol and gambling. The organisation built schools for boys and girls, and established the 'Rovers', which was not unlike the Boy Scouts. Night schools were run for workers, trade unions, clinics and hospitals were founded and members worked to improve sanitation and welfare for the poor. In many respects, the Brotherhood behaved like a state within a state and obviously this raised the suspicions and concern of the Egyptian government as it only highlighted their own failings in terms of welfare and education. Al-Bana, however, set out to demonstrate that Islam could be progressive and that welfare was based on Islamic principles.

The Brotherhood had no definite notions about the kind of polity the future Islamic state should have and al-Bana felt that discussions about an Islamic state were premature as there was still much work to do at grass-roots level in terms of the struggle against illiteracy and poverty. To a large extent, the Brotherhood was anti-intellectual and intolerant of dissension in the ranks. Al-Bana's charisma and leadership skills were both a blessing and a curse as he insisted on obedience and was reluctant to delegate, so that, upon his death, there was a leadership vacuum. Of greater concern, however, was the emergence in 1943 of a terrorist unit of the Brotherhood known as 'The Secret Apparatus' (*al jihaz al-sirri*) which was so clandestine that little is known about it and, most likely, few members of the Brotherhood even knew of its existence. Al-Bana himself frequently referred to *jihad* (literally 'struggle', but in the sense al-Bana meant it, 'holy war') as an important religious duty and it is not clear to what extent al-Bana was implicated in the activities of the Secret Apparatus.

After the Second World War, disenchantment with the British increased even more as well as the 'disaster' (*al nakhbah*) of 1948 when five Arab armies were defeated against Israel, and led many to resort to terror for results. From then on the Secret Apparatus started a campaign of violent raids and bombings of the Jewish district of Cairo, and the Prime Minister, Nuqrashi Pasha, was assassinated. The Brotherhood denied involvement in the killings and al-Bana himself expressed horror over the murder of al-Nuqrashi, but the new Prime Minister − al-Hadi − set out to eliminate the Brotherhood. The Brotherhood was declared illegal and many of its members were arrested and tortured. By July 1949, some 4,000 were in prison and in February of the same year al-Bana himself was shot dead in the street, and almost certainly the Prime Minister was involved in his assassination.

Al-Bana's legacy cannot be underestimated. He essentially put the flesh on the bones of the work of his *Salafiyyah* predecessors and, in the Muslim Brotherhood, set about establishing a new type of Muslim community. Its originality lay in it being the first mass-supported and well-organised grouping that was in touch with the demands of a modern urbanised world and its ideological base, which was further developed by Sayyid **Qutb** (1906–1966), provided a model for countless Muslim organisations. The Brotherhood continued to act as a counter to government activities after the death of al-Bana, although frequently subject to harassment from the government, as well as not being averse to terror tactics which included an alleged assassination attempt on the Egyptian President Abdel Nasser in October 1954. The Brotherhood still exists in Egypt and other parts of the Arab world, often under different names and not always unified.

Major works

None of his major works are currently available in English.

Further reading

Bari, Zohurul, *Re-Emergence of the Muslim Brothers in Egypt*, New Delhi: Lancers Books, 1995.

Chasdi, Richard J., *Tapestry of Terror: A Portrait of Middle East Terrorism, 1994–1999*, Lanham, MD: Lexington Books, 2002.

Choueiri, Youssef M., *Islamic Fundamentalism*, rev. edn, London: Pinter, 1997.

Davidson, Lawrence, *Islamic Fundamentalism: An Introduction*, rev. and updated edn, Westport, CT: Greenwood Press, 2003.

Esposito, John L., *Unholy War: Terror in the Name of Islam*, Oxford: Oxford University Press, 2002.

Hussain, Asaf, *Political Terrorism and the State in the Middle East*, London: Mansell Publishing, 1988.

Kepel, Gilles, *Muslim Extremism in Egypt: The Prophet and Pharaoh*, trans. from French by Jon Rothschild, Berkeley, CA: University of California Press, 1985.

SAYYID QUTB (1906–1966)

Qutb was an active reformer and a leading Islamic intellectual who formulated a distinct ideology of the radical reform movement, the Muslim Brotherhood. Although he was not the head of this organisation, he exemplified its radical trend. Hence he is regarded as the intellectual heir of the Brotherhood's founder, Hasan **al-Bana**. His writings are highly regarded as literary works. He spent a number of years in prison where he concentrated on his writing, producing such well-known works as *In the Shade of the Qur'an* and *Milestones*. As part of the campaign of the Egyptian president, Jamal Abd al-Nasser, against sthe Muslim Brotherhood, Qutb was executed in 1966 on the charge of conspiracy against the government. His execution has given him the status of martyr (*shahid*).

Sayyid Qutb was born in the province of Asyut in Upper Egypt in 1906. His father, although not a scholar, was known for his piety and learning. Qutb's life has a number of parallels with his compatriot Hasan al-Bana. Like al-Bana, Qutb left the village to live in Cairo and this proved to be of pivotal importance due to the impression city life gave him; in particular the obvious social imbalance, political corruption, and the presence of the British. However, unlike al-Bana, Qutb seemed less concerned with the religious indifference that was so evident. In fact, Qutb himself in his early years displayed little in the way of religious adherence. Qutb's early career in teaching also paralleled al-Bana's as he enrolled in the same teacher-training college, the Dar al-Ulum. He studied there from 1929 until 1933. Upon graduation he was appointed, as his mother always wished, as a teacher in a primary school. He also, however, dedicated his time to writing literary criticism, short stories and novels, although primarily on such themes as romance rather than religion.

In 1940, Sayyid Qutb was moved to the Directorate of Public Culture Supervision in the Ministry of Education. He also worked as an inspector in primary education. At around this time he joined the *Wafd* ('Delegation') Party, the oldest existing political party in Egypt and the only major oppositional force during that period. Although his reputation as a literary critic improved, it earned him little financially and with his subsequent decrease in interest in literature he commenced writing social and political articles. In 1948, Qutb received a government scholarship to travel and study for a Master's degree in Education at the University of Northern Colorado. He spent three years in Colorado, travelling little, and it was here that Qutb encountered first-hand what he regarded as excessive materialism, sexual permissiveness and racism (Qutb himself was very dark-skinned and encountered racism personally), in particular, comments on what he perceived as a pro-Zionist slant of the US media. When the leader of the Muslim Brotherhood, Hasan al-Bana, was assassinated – most likely at the behest of the Egyptian government – in 1949, the US media seemingly treated this event with delight.

Qutb's writings started to have an Islamic orientation, and he produced numerous articles on artistic imagery found in the Qur'an. Qutb found the Qur'an to be an important spiritual resource, and he focused his attention on the importance of Islamic research and Qur'anic studies. In the same year that al-Bana was killed, Qutb's work *Al-'adala al-ijtima'iyya fi al-islam* (*Social Justice in Islam*) was published. This attracted the attention of many scholars and Islamic activists and its originality lies in his perception of Islam not only as a spiritual resource, but also as an integrated system of social and economic justice. Qutb considered himself a *Salafiyyah* (a movement of modernisation but 'looks back' to the time of the Prophet **Muhammad** and the **Companions** for inspiration and guidance; aside from al-Bana, see also **al-Afghani**, Muhammad **Abduh**, and Rashid **Rida** for more on this movement). He idealised the first four Rightly-Guided caliphs (*rashidun*), and argued that this period represented, on the whole, a time of full social justice, although Qutb caused some controversy and criticism by admitting that the third caliph, Uthman, especially did not always come up to the mark.

Qutb became disillusioned with the ideology and activities of the *Wafd* Party as a result of widespread corruption among its leadership and accusations of being too closely associated with British interests. The primary source of Islamic radicalism now rested with the Muslim Brotherhood, which al-Bana had founded in 1928. With his death in 1949, leadership had transferred to the more 'respectable' Hasan al-Hudaibi. As soon as Qutb arrived back in Egypt he resigned from the Ministry of Education. The Brotherhood was attracted by Qutb's revisionist writings and a mutual sympathy grew which led to his membership in around 1952. He wrote regularly for their magazine, *Al-Da'wa* (*The Mission*) where he developed the ideas that were to become central to the ideology of the Brotherhood. The Muslim Brotherhood possessed a mass following, but, unlike the *Wafd*, was not a political party and so did not engage in elections. A much smaller oppositional force was the Communist Party, which – despite its secularist credentials – united with the Brotherhood against what both perceived as the common enemy and so-called 'Anglo-American stooge', President Nasser. It was Sayyid Qutb who took charge of the role of liaising with the Communists. In November 1954 an assassination attempt was made on Nasser, and the Brotherhood was blamed. Although some have argued that the failed assassination attempt was staged, it gave Nasser the excuse he needed to clamp down on opposition. There followed a series of arrests, show trials and executions. Qutb, together with Hudaibi and a number of other members, was arrested. Seven were sentenced to death, although Hudaibi's execution was commuted due to old age and ill health. Qutb, for his part, was sentenced to sixteen years in prison.

During his time in jail which, in fact, was to constitute virtually the whole of the rest of his life, Qutb wrote some of his finest works. He wrote a commentary on the Qur'an, *In the Shade of the Qur'an* (*Fi dhilal al-Qur'an*). In this work, Qutb sees the Qur'an as an integrated whole rather than adopting the usual atomistic approach of dissecting each verse. Qutb is not interested in small theological details, but rather the major themes, and what is most interesting is that he wrote the commentary without access to the corpus of traditional sources, that is past commentaries. As a consequence, the Qur'an is perceived through the prism of his own perceptions and experiences and not 'weighed down' by preceding scholarship.

Another important work during this time is *Milestones* (*Ma'alim fi al-tariq,* also translated as *Signposts on the Road*) for which the central theme is that the problem with the Islamic community, as Qutb saw it, was not so much the encroachment of the West, or autocratic government, but rather what he refers to as the *jahiliya* of society as a whole. The term '*jahiliya*' is mentioned in the Qur'an as a reference to the state of Arabia before the coming of the Prophet Muhammad and the message of Islam. In this sense, then, it is the 'age of ignorance' when the people lacked divine guidance. Qutb's use of the term *jahiliya* was popularised by his Pakistani contemporary **Mawdudi** and refers to the state of the Muslim community at the present time. He remarks that he saw his present society in a state of *jahiliya* similar to, or even worse than, that which existed before the time of the Prophet. The community, in terms of its beliefs, traditions, culture, laws, politics and so on are all essentially un-Islamic in character in that, in true *salafi* tradition, they do not reflect the community that existed at the time of Muhammad and the Rightly-Guided caliphs. There are echoes of the Wahhabism of Saudi Arabia here (see **al-Wahhab**) but whereas Wahhabism is critical of 'Muslims' individually in the sense that non-Wahhabis are non-Muslims, Qutb's concern is, again, less atomistic in that it is more to do with how society is structured.

While Qutb claimed that Islam could provide the answers to all the ills of society, the influence of Western thought on his ideas cannot be ignored. In fact, Qutb himself makes reference to a work by the French surgeon and author Alexis Carrel (1873–1944) whose work *Man, the Unknown* (*L'homme, cet inconnu*,1935) had a great impact on Qutb. Carrel writes of the demoralising effects of material progress and that what was needed was a new ascetic and mystical elite to rescue mankind from the degradation caused by democracy. These views are in some respects echoed in other Western philosophers such as Friedrich Nietzsche, and Qutb's writings are also Kierkegaardian in his individualism. Qutb also talks of the need for a new elite among the Muslim youth that would act as a clandestine 'vanguard' against the modern *jahiliya*, mirrored on the Prophet and the Companions as the archetype. Qutb is not specific in what this elite would actually do, and seemed to have a somewhat romantic and naïve notion of a group of ascetic individuals that, once they know the truth of Islam, could simply come into being and take over the reins of state rule which would then require no earthly laws or regulations.

Qutb is little concerned with what form a Muslim state would take, leaving the actual organisation to the *umma* once they are capable of it. He makes use of another term borrowed from Mawdudi, that of *hakimiyya*, or 'divine governance'. Essentially, provided society is governed according to God's will – which can be determined via the traditional sources of the Qur'an and the **Sunna** (tradition) of the Prophet – then all will be well. He does not see religion as prescriptive, but more as an aesthetic-psychological experience, a view that shares much with the Western existential approach. It relies upon intuition in that the believer will simply 'know' what to do in the circumstance. Again, similarities can be observed with Nietzsche's *Übermensch* ('Superman'), the **Sufi** mystic's experience of the divine, or even Martin Luther's idea that the authority of the religious text can be grasped intuitively by the individual without the need of a hierarchical structure of scholarship.

Nonetheless, the government interpreted this call for a vanguard of believers as conspiracy against the state and, after being released from prison in December 1964 he was re-arrested in August 1965 and hanged on 29 August 1966. Qutb's influence on, especially, what are referred to as 'fundamentalist' or 'revivalist' militant groups has been especially significant. His own martyrdom has provided a model for many as has his dualistic vision of the world as divided between the 'party of God' (*hizb Allah*) and the 'party of the devil' which has to be converted through *jihad*. While Qutb often referred to *jihad* in relation to missionary teaching (*da'wa*), he also argued that if the state did not allow the freedom to exercise *da'wa*, then 'physical *jihad*' by his clandestine armed vanguard is justified. This vision and mission are echoed in the ideology of many modern groups.

Major works

Social Justice in Islam, trans. Hamid Algar and John B. Hardie, North Haledon, NJ: Islamic Publications International, 1999
In the Shade of the Qur'an, trans. Adil Salahi and A. Shamis, 9 vols, Leicester: Islamic Foundation, 2004.
Milestones, Chicago: Kazi Publications, 2003.

Further reading

While there is little available that details the life of Sayyid Qutb, there are many works on the Muslim Brotherhood and Islam in modern Egypt.

Bari, Zohurul, Re-Emergence of the Muslim Brothers in Egypt, New Delhi: Lancers Books, 1995.
Donohoe, J. and Esposito, J. (eds), Islam in Transition: Muslim Perspectives, Oxford: Oxford University Press, 1982.
Esposito, John L., Unholy War: Terror in the Name of Islam, Oxford: Oxford University Press, 2002.

Kepel. Gilles, *Muslim Extremism in Egypt: The Prophet and Pharaoh*, transl. from French by Jon Rothschild, Berkeley, CA: University of California Press, 1985.

MUHAMMAD TAHA (1908–1985)

Sometimes referred to as 'the Gandhi of Africa', Muhammad Taha's contribution to Islamic thought is extremely influential, both within his homeland of Sudan and throughout the Islamic world, particularly as he engages in one of the most thorough-going attempts of the late twentieth century to reconcile Islamic beliefs with the challenges posed by modernity. He was not only a significant intellectual figure, but was also a political activist from the mid-1940s until his execution in 1985.

Mahmud Muhammad Taha was born in 1908 in the town of Rufa'a, which is south-east of the capital Khartoum near the Blue Nile. The Sudan, at the time, was ruled over by an Anglo-Egyptian alliance, although the British were the inevitable dominant partner and Taha, like many of his contemporaries, was educated in an English-language school system established by the British and run on British lines. He then went to study engineering at Gordon Memorial College – which subsequently became the University of Khartoum – where he graduated in 1936. His studies included not only modern science but he also took it upon himself to familiarise himself with Western social and political ideas. He developed an interest in politics and, in 1945, he founded the Republican Party which was the first political party in Sudan to call for the establishment of a national republic, as well as being the only party which engaged in direct, although non-violent, confrontation with the British colonial power. It was a consequence of such confrontations that Taha was imprisoned twice by the British in 1946; the first time for fifty days, the second for two years. The reason for the second longer spell in prison was a result of his public protests against the British attempts to ban the practice of female circumcision. In fact, Taha himself was against the practice, for it is not Islamic but a cultural phenomenon, but his protests were rather against the British attempts to impose laws upon the Sudanese. And so the demonstration, known as the 'Rufaa Incident' was actually more of an anti-colonial demonstration which he organised. One participator at the demonstration was the 14-year old **Hasan al-Turabi** who was to become the head of the Sudanese Muslim Brotherhood.

After Taha was released from prison in 1948, he imposed upon himself seclusion from the world until late 1951. Although during this period the Republican Party was largely redundant, Taha himself spent this time developing the religious, social and political ideas that he was to consistently propagate throughout the rest of his life. The Sudan had been an independent republic since 1 January 1956. The first parliamentary elections had taken place in 1958, and the Umma Party won a majority and formed a government. However, after only eight months, it was overthrown by Lieutenant-General Ibrahim Abboud, the commander-in-chief of the armed forces. Abboud dismissed parliament, suspended the constitution, declared martial law, and established a Cabinet with himself as the prime minister. In 1958, the Republican Party renamed itself the Republican Brotherhood following the military takeover, although throughout this period the Republicans were largely ignored by the other political groups. In 1960, however, three Republican students were dismissed from the Omdurman Institute for Religious Studies (now Omdurman Islamic University) on the grounds of apostasy. The dean of the Institute branded Taha's ideas deviations from Islam. In 1964, the 'October Revolution' occurred, causing President Abboud to resign and he was replaced by a supreme council of state. Sudan was now plunged into a civil war between the north and the south, the latter demanding more autonomy. During this time the Republicans' status improved somewhat, however, when the Sudanese parliament attempted to outlaw the Communist Party in 1967. Taha spoke up in defence of the Communists' right to freedom of expression. In the same way that Taha protested against the British attempt to ban female circumcision while at the same time disagreeing with the practice himself, he protested against the attempt to ban the Communist Party while disagreeing with the Communists themselves. What mattered was the principle. However, the Muslim Brotherhood perceived this as supporting communism, despite the fact that the Republicans frequently opposed the Communist Party, and the Brotherhood, in 1968, argued that Taha should be tried on grounds of apostasy. A trial did take place but Taha himself refused to attend on the basis that the Sudanese government, being secular in outlook at that time, could not judge on a religious issue in a secular court. However, the trial nonetheless took place and took just three hours to reach a verdict, during which it is said that a variety of evidence was heard against Taha, some of it involving a misrepresentation of his views. Taha was declared guilty of apostasy, a view supported in subsequent rulings by Cairo's authoritative Al-Azhar institution and the Muslim World League. The Republicans, and Taha, were now banned from political participation. While the Muslim Brotherhood's political organisation, the Islamic Charter Front (ICF) was relatively small, in its role as a pressure group it was able to push the issue of an Islamic constitution up the agenda and, if it had not been for the military coup in 1969, further measures against the Republicans would no doubt have taken place.

This coup was led by Gaafar Muhammad al-Nimeiry, who at this point was a Colonel in the military. Al-Nimeiry seized power and set up government under a revolutionary council. Initially, the Republicans, while not participating in government, still gave support for the Nimeiry regime in the hope that it would restore democracy on a less sectarian and more tolerant basis. These hopes began to seem well placed when elections occurred in 1971, for which al-Nimeiry was elected president, and his government negotiated an end to the long-running civil war with the rebels in southern Sudan. The 1970s was not a stable time, however, with a number of coup attempts and a huge influx of refugees from other countries such as Eritrea, Uganda and Chad which put a strain on the Sudan's limited resources. At first, al-Nimeiry was pro-Communist, as he looked to the Soviet Union and Libya for support. In 1971, he established the Sudanese Socialist Union as the sole legal political party. However, in 1971, there was a 'national reconciliation' and the regime attempted to broaden its power base by bringing into government the Umma Party, under Sadiq al-Mahdi, and the National Islamic Front (NIF), under Hasan al-Turabi. In 1978, al-Turabi was appointed to the Central Committee of the Sudanese Socialist Union and he headed a committee for the examination of laws to make them compatible with *shari'a*. However, the economic situation became increasingly worse in the late 1970s and al-Nimeiry looked towards the NIF and northern Islamic sentiments to strengthen his position. Al-Nimeiry himself had undergone a change in attitude and he adopted a more Islamic policy orientation and, in 1983, Taha and forty leading Republicans were detained. All were released without charge in December 1984.

In September 1983, Nimeiri had introduced the *shari'a*-based 'September laws', which were given the support of the Muslim Brotherhood. While this programme may be partly a result of al-Nimeiry's own inclination towards Islam, it is also indicative of the fact that he had by this time less support in government and was seeking legitimisation. However, the introduction of *shari'a* was one of the major reasons for the resumption of the civil war in the mainly

animist and Christian southern Sudan around this time. Consequently, in 1984, al-Nimeiry was compelled to impose martial law.
Taha published a pamphlet entitled *Either this or the Flood* which
warned of impending disaster for Sudan unless the sectarian policies
were repealed. Taha argued that the *shari'a* laws introduced were
actually distorted and not accurately reflecting Islam at all. Ironically,
al-Turabi of the Muslim Brotherhood largely agreed, but maintained
the view that it was better to have some kind of *shari'a* than none at
all and, in time, the reform of *shari'a* could take place.

In early January 1985, Taha and four close associates were arrested
and charged, once again, with apostasy. Taha, as with the previous
trial, refused to recognise the legitimacy of the court and it took only
two hours for the verdict. On 18 January, Taha was hanged in Kober
prison in Khartoum, and his body subsequently taken away by heli-
copter to be buried at an unknown location. Taha could have
'repented' and avoided the death penalty, but refused to do so. His
four co-accused, however, did repent and were spared. The execution of Taha, who was 76 at the time, caused anger and revulsion
among many, not only in Sudan itself but abroad. The Arab Human
Rights Organization declared January 18th to be Arab Human Rights
Day in memory of his death. If the act was intended to give al-
Nimeiry more popularity it failed to do so. A popular uprising in
Khartoum in April 1985 finally led to al-Nimeiry's overthrow in a
bloodless military coup.

Taha's teachings are essentially, like so many reformers, a response
to the occupation of the British colonial power, with the resultant
move towards technology, pluralism, and other aspects of modernity,
and the resulting effect on the culture, traditions, politics and religion
of Sudan. Reformers respond very differently to this perceived threat.
Some adopt the view that if you can't beat them, join them and
adopt a secularist approach, separating state and religion. The alternative conservative approach was the total rejection of Western values
and a call for a return to what was perceived as the pristine Islamic
values that existed during the time of the Prophet **Muhammad** as
well as to look to the traditions of the Islamic scholars, especially the
jurists, of the past. However, Taha adopted a middle view suggesting
that Islam can be accommodated to the ideas of secular nationalism,
but for this to be the case *shari'a* has to be a flexible body that is
prepared to exercise independent reasoning (**ijtihad**) to react to a
changing, modern world. To achieve this it was required for educated
Muslims to go back to the original sources, the Qur'an and the
hadith, rather than simply imitate the rulings of the major law

schools. In this way, Islamic law can be reconstructed from first principles rather than being weighed down by the rulings of the medieval era.

However, Taha went further than many other reformers in appealing to what he called the 'Second Message of Islam'. He argues that the standard position of *naskh* should be abandoned. *Naskh* is the accepted principle that earlier verses in the Qur'an are abrogated in favour of later verses, thus resolving the problem of possible contradictions. However, Taha actually argues that *naskh* should be *reversed*. He states that the notion of *naskh* is in any case weakly supported in the Qur'an (2:106) and that quite a few classical and modern scholars reject the concept. While the traditional view is that the earlier Meccan verses are abrogated by the later Medinan ones, Taha argues that the Medinan revelations are more historically specific than the Meccan ones which involve a more general calling of mankind to Islam. The Meccan verses contain the universal core of Islam, the 'second message of Islam', and so the Medinan verses should yield to the Meccan.

By focusing on the more general Meccan suras, Islam is essentially freed from the more restrictive, culture-specific, regulations that are seen as offensive to the modern liberal conscience whereas the early Meccan verses are concerned more with such things as mercy, forgiveness and welfare. However, one can see why many were suspicious of this and accused Taha of apostasy, for the Qur'an, in principle, is not a 'culture-specific' entity for it is the word of God and, therefore, universal. Aside from his writings in the *Second Message*, he also expounds a detailed theology and cosmology in an attempt to integrate his understanding of orthodox Islam with its mystical aspects. He attempts a reconciliation between Islam and modern science and, at the political level, presents detailed proposals for the organisation of government.

Taha was a strong supporter of individual freedom of conscience and believed that people should be free to join or disassociate themselves from their religious traditions should their conscience dictate. He was particularly against the move towards religious sectarianism that was occurring in his own country, believing that all religions should have equal freedom to practise and proselytise. Economically, he espoused a form of socialism based on co-operative ventures, rather than central government control. He was particularly critical of communism, which he believed necessarily led to despotism and a loss of personal freedom. It is too early to say what long-term effect his views, most originally on the 'second message' of Islam, will have on Islamic thought. However, his legacy certainly can be traced to his stand against religious and political intolerance at the expense of his own life.

Major works

The Second Message of Islam, trans. AbdAllahi Ahmed An-Na'im, New York: Syracuse University Press, 1996.

Further reading

An-Naim, A.A., 'Mahmud Muhammad Taha and the Crisis in Islamic Law Reform: Implications for Interreligious Relations', *Journal of Ecumenical Studies* 25(1) (1988).
Kurzman, C. (ed.), *Liberal Islam: A Source Book*, Oxford: Oxford University Press, 1998.

EL-HAJJ MALIK EL-SHABAZZ ('MALCOLM X') (1925–1965)

El-Shabazz, better known as 'Malcolm X', was a powerful and influential African-American activist of the twentieth century and defender of black liberation in the United States. His speeches and activities had a significant influence on the black nationalist and black separatist movements during the 1950s and 1960s. He has been many things to many people, from Pan-Africanist, to the father of Black Power, and a socialist. He associated with the Nation of Islam, but later in life he rejected their views in favour of orthodox **Sunni** Islam, taking the name of El-Hajj Malik El-Shabazz, although he did not reject the name Malcolm X. He was murdered just three months before his fortieth birthday.

Malcolm X was born Malcolm Little in Omaha, Nebraska on 19 May 1925. His mother, Louise Norton Little, had the full-time occupation of rearing eight children. His father, Earl Little, was a Baptist preacher and an outspoken promoter of social and economic independence for blacks and a supporter of Marcus Garvey's 'Back to Africa' movement. As a result of his father's outspokenness, the family experienced a number of confrontations with racism. Earl received death threats from the white supremacist Black Legion, forcing the family to relocate twice before Malcolm's fourth birthday. However, in 1929, their house in Lansing, Michigan, was burned down and, two years later, Earl's mutilated body was found across trolley tracks.

The police declared this to be the result of an accident. Malcolm's mother suffered an emotional breakdown several years later and was committed to a mental institution. The children were consequently split up among various foster homes and orphanages.

Malcolm was placed in a foster home and then in a reform school. Malcolm was an intelligent student at junior high school, graduating as top of his class but, according to his autobiography, Malcolm became disillusioned with education when his favourite teacher told him that his dream of becoming a lawyer was 'no realistic goal for a nigger'. Malcolm, as a result, dropped out from school and, at the age of 17, moved to the Harlem neighbourhood of New York City where he committed petty crimes. Known as 'Detroit Red' he was soon coordinating various narcotic, prostitution and gambling rings. At the age of 20 he was arrested and convicted on burglary charges, given a ten-year sentence. However, prison proved to be a place to further his education as he immersed himself in the teachings of the Nation of Islam (NOI), the black Muslim group founded by Wallace D. Fard and led by Elijah Muhammad (Elijah Poole). Elijah Muhammad taught that white society actively worked to keep African-Americans from empowering themselves and from achieving political, economic and social success. Among other goals, the Nation of Islam fought for a state of their own, separate from one inhabited by white people. Unlike traditional Islam, however, the NOI had a racist tendency in that it declared that whites were the 'devil by nature' and that God was black. The NOI predicted that in the near future there would be a great war in which the white people would be destroyed and black people would rule the world under Allah. In preparation for this new order, Black Muslims were required to practise self-restraint, opposing the use of drugs or alcohol.

Malcolm submitted to the strict discipline of the NOI and immersed himself in the Qur'an and the Bible. During his prison spell he became a powerful and persuasive orator and won a debate on capital punishment when he led the prison debating team against the Massachusetts Institute of Technology. When he was paroled in 1952, Malcolm went to Detroit, Michigan and joined the NOI temple in that city. He considered 'Little' a slave name and adopted 'X' to signify his lost tribal name. In 1958, he married Betty Sanders (later known as Betty Shabazz) and they had six daughters. He quickly rose in the ranks of the NOI and, in 1954, Elijah Muhammad appointed him as chief minister of Harlem's main temple. Through national speaking engagements, television appearances, and by establishing the movement's main information and propaganda newspaper, *Muhammad Speaks*, Malcolm X helped put the NOI on the map.

Malcolm X's charisma, drive and conviction attracted many new members and made him a more prominent spokesperson for the NOI than his mentor Elijah Muhammad. In 1952, membership of the NOI was 500, but by 1963 it had increased to 30,000. He was a sharp critic of civil rights leaders, notably Martin Luther King, for advocating integration into white society instead of building black institutions and defending themselves from racist violence. He argued that Western culture, and the Judaeo-Christian religious traditions on which it was based, were inherently racist and declared that non-violence was the 'philosophy of the fool'. As Malcolm X's reputation soared, this caused tension with Elijah Muhammad and other NOI leaders, which was not helped when during the 1950s Malcolm X was critical of the view that white people were literally 'devils' and he also pushed for a stronger political response to racism, whereas the line of the NOI was to act as a religious self-help movement rather than participate in politics.

Tensions between Malcolm X and Elijah Muhammad increased when Malcolm X learned that his mentor was secretly having affairs with as many as six women in the Nation of Islam, some of which had resulted in children. Malcolm X had strictly adhered to the code of celibacy of the NOI until his marriage and he was deeply hurt by the deception of Elijah Muhammad, who asked Malcolm X to keep the matter quiet. Worse was to come when, in 1963, Malcolm X remarked after the death of President John F. Kennedy that it represented 'the chickens coming home to roost'. This comment was, and still is, often taken out of context and was not intended to be disrespectful to the President, but rather that the violent treatment of blacks had now come back to the 'roost' with violence against a white President. However, the remark was seen, at best, as highly insensitive and led Muhammad to silence Malcolm X. Effectively, this was the same as denying Malcolm X as a member of the NOI and, rather than accepting the silence, he left the movement in 1964 and formed the Muslim Mosque, Inc., an Islamic movement devoted to working in the political sphere.

In the same year as his break with Elijah Muhammad, Malcolm X made his first pilgrimage to Mecca. This trip proved to be a transformative stage in his life, as Malcolm met 'blonde-haired, blue-eyed men I could call my brothers'. On his return to the US he renamed himself El-Hajj Malik El-Shabazz (meaning 'Malcolm – Malik – who is from the tribe of Shabazz and has made the *Hajj*'), converted to

Sunni Islam, and announced that he had found the 'true brother-hood' of man, announcing that whites were no longer devils. Although he remained a strong believer in black self-determination, he no longer held racist tendencies towards whites. He formed the Organisation of Afro-American Unity (OAAU), an organisation inspired by the Organisation of African Unity (OAU) which con-sisted of independent African states. This group advocated racial solidarity and Malcolm X planned to submit to the United Nations a petition that documented human rights violations and acts of geno-cide against African Americans. He encouraged blacks to vote, to participate in the political system, and to work with whites and other racial groups for an end to racial discrimination.

Malcolm X began a collaboration with the writer Alex Haley on an account of his life, and in this manuscript – which was later pub-lished as *The Autobiography of Malcolm X* (1965) – he predicted that he might not live to see the book published. This prediction proved to be true. Relations between Malcolm and the NOI were volatile and he had reason to believe he was targeted for assassination. On 15 February 1965, his house in East Elmhurst, New York, was firebombed, although the family escaped without physical injury, and Malcolm X rarely travelled without bodyguards. However, six days after the fire-bombing, three gunmen rushed onto the stage where Malcolm X was speaking and shot him fifteen times at close range. He was pro-nounced dead on arrival at New York's Columbia Presbyterian Hospital. Fifteen hundred people attended his funeral in Harlem. Later that year, his wife Betty gave birth to their twin daughters. Malcolm's assassins, Talmadge Hayer, Norman 3X Butler and Thomas 15X Johnson, were convicted of first-degree murder in March 1966. The three men were all members of the Nation of Islam.

Malcolm X exerted a significant impact on the Civil Rights Movement in the final year of his life. Black activists began to support his ideas on such things as racial pride and black-run institutions. He also gained a small following of radical Marxists, mostly Trotskyists in the Socialist Workers Party (SWP). His autobiography became a standard text for black movements and the legacy of Malcolm X has moved through generations as the subject of numerous doc-umentaries, books and movies. A tremendous resurgence of interest occurred in 1992 when director Spike Lee released the acclaimed *Malcolm X* movie. The film received Oscar nominations for Best Actor (Denzel Washington) and Best Costume Design. The influence that orthodox Islam had on Malcolm X, as he developed a more universalistic outlook, was never allowed to bear fruit due to his untimely death, although it is an indication of the transformative power that the experience of the *Hajj* can have on an individual. It should be noted that the Nation of Islam, despite bearing the title 'Islam', deviates considerably from the teaching of orthodox Islam and, in fact, many of their principles are in flagrant contrast to orthodox Islamic ideals.

Major works

Malcolm X, aside from his autobiography, wrote a number of letters and articles on political alliances, women's rights, inter-marriage, capitalism, socialism etc., and these are now readily available as collections. The first two of the following are collections of writings and speeches.

Malcolm X: The Last Speeches, California: Pathfinder, 1989.
By Any Means Necessary, California: Pathfinder, 1992.
The Autobiography of Malcolm X, written with Alex Haley, London: Penguin, 2004.

Further reading

Here is only a short selection of what is now a vast corpus on not only Malcolm X, but related issues such as the Nation of Islam, and black activism.

Brisbane, Robert, *Black Activism*, Valley Forge, PA: Judson Press, 1974.
Dyson, Michael Eric, *Making Malcolm: The Myth and Meaning of Malcolm X*, New York: Oxford University Press, 1996.
Friedly, Michael, *The Assassination of Malcolm X*, New York: Carroll and Graf, 1992.
Gallen, David (ed.), *Malcolm A to Z: The Man and His Ideas*, New York: Carroll and Graf, 1992.
Goldman, Peter, *The Death and Life of Malcolm X*, Champaign-Urbana, IL: University of Illinois Press, 1979.

HASAN AL-TURABI (b. 1932)

Hasan al-Turabi is a Sudanese political thinker and activist whose ideas regarding the organisation of an Islamic society have had a profound effect on Sudan especially, but who indirectly has been the inspiration for other movements across the Islamic world. He has effectively been the mastermind behind the development of the Islamic movement in Sudan as well as a scholar well versed in the Islamic sciences.

Hasan Abdallah al-Turabi was born in Kassala near the Sudanese-Ethiopian (now Sudanese-Eritrean) border in 1932. His father, who

had three wives, had eighteen children and al–Turabi was the
youngest son. Al–Turabi is a member of the Bedayriyyah tribe,
counted as part of the Ja'aliyin, which is the largest Arab tribal
grouping in Sudan. He descends from a long line of religious notables, most famously a *Sufi* (the mystical branch of Islam) *shaykh*
(leader) of the Qadiriyya order Wad al–Turabi (d. 1704). Wad al–
Turabi apparently declared that he was a *Mahdi* (eschatological term
meaning the harbinger of paradise on earth) on a pilgrimage to
Mecca. Wad al–Turabi's tomb is at Khartoum and is a recognised
place of pilgrimage. Hasan al–Turabi was only too aware of the pious
heritage of his family and tribe, and his father too had an important
influence on his outlook on life. His father was a judge in the *shari'a*
(Islamic law) courts and, as al–Turabi's mother died shortly after he
was born, it was his father who brought him up, ensuring he received
a good education in the traditional Islamic disciplines.

In his work, his father moved from post to post and so al–Turabi
attended a number of different schools during his childhood, notably
Hantoub Boarding Secondary School, where he was a classmate of
Ja'far al–Nimeiry, who became president of the Sudan from 1971
until 1985. In 1951, al–Turabi entered Gordon Memorial College –
which subsequently became the University of Khartoum – to study
law, and he graduated in 1955. He then studied for a Master's degree
at University College, London, from where he graduated in 1957.
Following a two-year period as lecturer in law at the University of
Khartoum, he began a PhD in law at the Sorbonne, Paris, in 1959,
graduating from there in 1964. Later that year, al–Turabi became
Dean of the Faculty of Law at the University of Khartoum.

Aside from his obvious intellectual abilities, al–Turabi had always
displayed political activism, even since his time at school when he
would take part in school strikes and other activities against British
rule (at the time it was joint Anglo-Egyptian sovereignty, but the
British were inevitably the dominant partner). In 1946, at the age of
just 14, he took part in the 'Rufaa incident', an anti-colonial
demonstration organised by the well-known liberal Islamic thinker
Muhammad Taha. At university, al–Turabi was a rarity among his
peers for whereas there were many Islamist activists, there were few
who were as learned in traditional Islam as he was. At the very least,
there were many young activists looking for a movement to support,
and Communism seemingly presented itself with the strongest ideology. Al–Turabi, however, immersed himself in the study of modern
revivalist Islamic thinkers and, in 1951, he joined an organisation
called the Islamic Liberation Movement. In 1954, this organisation

united with the Sudanese branch of the Egyptian Muslim Brother-hood to form the (Sudanese) Muslim Brotherhood.

While studying in London and Paris, al-Turabi had little influence on the Muslim Brotherhood in Sudan but did keep himself involved with Islamic movements in Europe and, following his return to Sudan from Paris in 1964, he once again became deeply involved in Sudanese politics for the country at the time was in the middle of growing unrest. The Sudan had been an independent republic since 1 January 1956. The first parliamentary elections had taken place in 1958 and the Umma Party won a majority and formed a govern-ment. However, after only eight months, it was overthrown by Lieutenant-General Ibrahim Abboud, the commander-in-chief of the armed forces. Abboud dismissed parliament, suspended the constitu-tion, declared martial law, and established a Cabinet with himself as the prime minister. In 1964, however, when al-Turabi returned to Sudan, the 'October Revolution' occurred causing President Abboud to resign, to be replaced by a supreme council of state. Sudan was now plunged into a civil war between the north and the south, the latter demanding more autonomy. Al-Turabi's involvement in the October Revolution, in which he publicly condemned the military regime, and his ability to articulate broader concerns, meant that by the late 1960s Turabi was the most influential figure in the Islamic movement in Sudan so he resigned as Dean of the University of Khartoum in 1965 to concentrate on his new role as de facto head of the Islamic movement. However, in the 1968 general elections, he failed to gain a seat in his constituency. The Muslim Brotherhood's political organisation, the Islamic Charter Front (ICF) was relatively small, but, in its role as more of a pressure group than a political party, it did manage to push for the issue of an Islamic constitution to be at the centre of a political agenda. The ICFs intention was a gradualist one, seeing the introduction of an Islamic constitution as the start of a process of progressive Islamicisation. However, such intentions were forestalled when, in 1969, a military coup took place.

This coup was led by al-Turabi's old school companion Ja'far Muhammad al-Nimeiry, who at this point was a Colonel in the military. Al-Nimeiry seized power and set up government under a revolutionary council. He became Sudan's first elected president in 1971, and, in 1973 a new constitution was finally put into place. The 1970s was not a stable time, however, with a number of coup attempts and a huge influx of refugees from Eritrea, Uganda and Chad which put a strain on Sudan's limited resources. At first, al-Nimeiry was pro-Communist, as he hoped for support from the Soviet Union and Libya. In 1971 he established the Sudanese Socialist Union as the sole legal political party. In the early 1970s, al-Turabi had spent time in prison because of his protests against the regime but, in 1977, there was a 'national reconciliation' and, in 1978, al-Turabi was appointed to the Central Committee of the Sudanese Socialist Union and he headed a committee for the examination of laws to make them compatible with *shari'a* (Islamic law).

Al-Nimeiry himself had undergone a change in attitude and he adopted a more Islamic policy orientation so that al-Turabi was able to introduce a number of Islamicising measures in education, law and economic institutions. In September 1983, Nimeiri introduced the *shari'a*-based 'September laws', although by this stage al-Turabi was less involved and the laws were somewhat hastily constructed by younger lawyers who were not as well versed in the intricacies of *shari'a* as al-Turabi was. Nonetheless, al-Turabi and the Muslim Brotherhood gave full support to the programme, believing the details could be ironed out at a later stage. While this programme could be partly a result of al-Nimeiry's own inclination towards Islam, it is also indicative of the fact that he had by this time less support in government and was seeking legitimisation. However, the introduction of *shari'a* was one of the major reasons for the resumption of the civil war in the mainly animist and Christian southern Sudan around this time. Consequently, in 1984, al-Nimeiry was compelled to impose martial law.

The acceptance of al-Nimeiry's September Laws by al-Turabi and the Muslim Brotherhood was unusual in that previously the policy of the Brotherhood was that an Islamic state would result from a gradual Islamicisation of society through education, welfare, and so on. For example, the introduction of *shari'a* included the contentious *hudud* punishments of amputation, flogging, and stoning. Al-Turabi and others in the Brotherhood had argued that *hudud* punishments would only be introduced once an Islamic state existed where, for example, poverty had been abolished. If such was the case, then the situation would not arise whereby, for example, a poor and starving person stole a loaf of bread and was then punished by having the offending hand amputated, for there would be no poor and starving people. However, in this case, the *hudud* laws were introduced immediately in a society in which there was great poverty and corruption. It was not so much the issue of whether or not *hudud* laws were prescribed by Islam, but rather the conditions in which they should be applicable.

By supporting al-Nameiry, al-Turabi was opening himself up to the criticism that he supported what was gradually becoming an unpopular dictatorship; however, it also meant that the Brotherhood – which up until now had been a small player in Sudanese politics – was given relative freedom of operation. Al-Turabi felt that having Islamic law, however flawed, was better than having none or little and he campaigned to reform the existing Islamic laws rather than argue against their existence. By 1985, however, Sudan was in the grip of famine and people were revolting against the regime. Al-Nemeiry, in an attempt to deflect the blame from himself, turned against the Islamists, and al-Turabi was thrown in prison. In the same year the Muslim Brotherhood joined forces with a number of Sufi groups to form a new political party, the National Islamic Front (NIF). A popular uprising in Khartoum in April 1985 finally led to Nimeiry's overthrow in a bloodless military coup. After a year of military rule, Sadiq al-Mahdi, leader of the Umma Party, was elected prime minister in the first free election in 18 years and the NIF managed to get 17 per cent of the vote, although this would have been considerably lower if the non-Muslim southern Sudanese had voted, but voting proved impossible there because of the civil war. Al-Turabi was freed from prison.

Yet another military coup, headed by Brigadier Omar Hassan al-Bashir, occurred in June 1989, but this brought to power a group of officers who were prepared to follow al-Turabi's advice and the NIF, in the guise of the Revolution of National Salvation (RNS), were given *carte blanche* to implement a comprehensive Islamic programme of social and political reform. Al-Turabi was successively Minister of Education, Attorney General, and Deputy Prime Minister. It was at this point, however, that the idealisms of al-Turabi came into sharp conflict with the realities of maintaining government of a country stricken by poverty and civil war. As a result, the concerns of the RNS were more directed to government and maintaining order – which turned out to be authoritarian and repressive – than to reinterpreting Islamic law. Consequently, al-Bashir removed al-Turabi from his official post as speaker of the parliament in 1999. In February 2001, he was placed under house arrest, accused of conspiring against the Sudanese government. He was freed in October 2003, but was arrested once more in March 2004, accused of plotting a coup.

Al-Turabi is a supporter of equal rights for women, arguing that it is in accordance with Islamic teachings contained in the Qur'an, the Traditions of the Prophet Muhammad, and the Islamic community during the life of the Prophet. Al-Turabi states that women, in the early days of Islam, were independent and fully responsible who converted to Islam as individuals and took an active role in public and political life, as well as sometimes fighting in battle. He argues that women have the right to propose and refuse marriage, to have control over their own property, and to take a full part in society. He states:

> The verdict of Islamic jurisprudence is just the practical expression of the dictates of faith. Women, according to *shari'a*, are counterparts of men. And in Islamic jurisprudence, there is no separate order of regulations for them ... The underlying presumption in the *shari'a* is that sex is immaterial.[1]

His views on women, leaving aside the questionable historical accuracy of some of his assertions, resulted in a radical move of the Muslim Brotherhood away from its focus on just Islamic men and rather to encompass the rights of all Muslims so that the movement has, as a result, received a lot of support from educated women in its attempts to promote legal and social reforms. It is interesting that only two women were elected to the People's Assembly during the 1985–1989 period and both of those were NIF candidates.

The other main concern, although obviously related to his views on women's rights, of al-Turabi was the establishment of an Islamic state, and on this he has been fairly consistent:

> An Islamic state cannot be isolated from society, because Islam is a comprehensive, integrated way of life. The division between private and public, the state and society, which is familiar in Western culture, has not been known in Islam. The state is only the political expression of an Islamic society. You cannot have an Islamic state insofar as you have an Islamic society. Any attempt at establishing a political order for the establishment of a genuine Islamic society would be the superimposition of laws over a reluctant society.[2]

While al-Turabi would have preferred the Islamisation of society, he has been pragmatic enough to fall into the camp of state first, Islamic society next. In this, he disagreed with the intellectual father of the Brotherhood movement, Sayyid Qutb, who argued that existing states are unbelieving and opposition obligatory. It is far too early to say what legacy al-Turabi will leave. However, he has always championed the view that democracy and gender equality are traditional

Islamic principles and this has inspired movements elsewhere. His writings are widely read, although his political activities are little known outside Sudan itself.

Major works

'The Islamic State', in John L. Esposito (ed.), *Voices of Resurgent Islam*, Oxford: Oxford University Press, 1983.
'Principles of Governance, Freedom and Responsibility in Islam', *American Journal of Islamic Social Sciences* 4(I) (1987).
Women in Islam and Muslim Society, London: Milestones, 1991.

Further reading

There is a lot of exciting material not only on al-Turabi but on the religious and political situation in Sudan at present.

El-Affendi, Abdelwahab, *Turabi's Revolution: Islam and Power in Sudan*, London: Grey Seal, 1991.
Hamdi, M.E., *The Making of an Islamic Political Leader: Conversations with Hasan al-Turabi*, Boulder, CO: Westview Press, 1999.
Lowrie, Arthur L. (ed.), *Islam, Democracy, the State and the West: A Roundtable with Dr Hasan Turabi*, Tampa, FL: World and Islam Studies Enterprise, 1993.
Sidahmed, A.S., *Politics and Islam in Contemporary Sudan*, New York: St Martin's Press, 1996.

Notes

1 *Women in Islam and Modern Society*, p. 11.
2 'Principles of Governance, Freedom and Responsibility in Islam', p. 1.

ALI SHARIATI (1933–1977)

Shariati is regarded as the ideological father of the 1979 Iranian revolution. His writings were certainly revolutionary, as well as being modern in style and radical in his approach to how Islam can address what he regarded as the oppression and alienation experienced by Muslims under the Pahlevi regime in Iran. His writings combined Islamic concepts with Western political philosophy. He was politically active and died in exile, quite possibly the result of an assassination by the Iranian secret service.

Ali Shariati was born in Mazinan in eastern Iran in 1933. He was initially educated in Mashhad when his father, Muhammad Taqi

Shariati, a one-time cleric who chose to become a teacher, established the Centre for the Spread of Islamic Teachings to propagate the progressive element of Islam. His father was an intellectual who believed that Islam and modernity were compatible, while rejecting the secularism that was beginning to prevail in the country. The Centre recruited youths who were against left-wing anti-religious intellectualism but were also opposed to the *Shi'a* conservativism represented by the religious scholars, the *ulama*, of the time. In such an atmosphere, this could not help but influence the young mind of Ali Shariati. In fact, he has written of the importance his father played not only in teaching him to think but also in encouraging him to read. At an early age, Ali Shariati became an active member of his father's Centre.

He studied not only Iranian but also foreign literature, poetry and philosophy. He graduated from Mashhad's Teacher Training College in 1952 and began teaching at a high school nearby. He also started writing, publishing *Tarikh-e takamol-e falsafa* (*A History of the Development of Philosophy*) in 1956. In that same year he enrolled as an undergraduate at the University of Mashhad. His teachings, together with his studies at the university and his activities for his father's Centre, meant that Ali Shariati had many contacts with disillusioned Iranian youth. His early writing at this stage displays a concern with Islam's encounter with the West and how it might respond to this. He argued that Islam is a distinct school of thought that had been weakened as a result of its encounter and amalgamation with other cultures, while acknowledging that it had also been enriched by them in terms of giving the Islamic world (and more specifically Iran) such variety of ethnicities. Western colonialism especially had weakened Islamic identity, he believed. Ali Shariati argued that Iranian intellectuals had done Islam or their country no favours by buying into concepts of modernity or Marxist visions of a communist utopia. From his own personal experiences he found that the youth of Iran, at least in his own currently limited geographical sphere, were far more open to looking to Islam for answers to issues raised by modernity, whereas his teaching colleagues were, on the whole, far too conservative. Shariati correctly identified a spiritual vacuum among the youth of Iran which was not helped by the quietist attitude adopted by the *ulama*.

Iran during this period was a place of great political conflict of interests: on the one hand, the interest of Britain and the USA and their stake in the oil of Iran, and, on the other, the determination of Prime Minister Mossadegh to nationalise the oil industry. The USA and the UK, for their part, supported the Shah in dismissing the Prime Minister in 1953. These events had a marked impression on Shariati who coined the term *Zar-o Zoor-o Tazvir* ('wealth, coercion, deceit') to describe the capitalist elite, the intrusions of the USA and Britain, and the obscurantist policies of the official clergy.

Shariati's studies of Persian literature at the University of Masshad gave him a reputation as a brilliant scholar and, in 1960, he was given the opportunity to do graduate studies at the University of Paris. He found Paris to be both attractive in terms of its intellectual enlight- enment and repulsive in terms of its Western decadence. The intel- lectual environment, however, allowed him to explore the revolutionary writings of French sociology and philosophy. This was in a period of intense student radicalism and he was particularly influenced by Third World movements. He attended lectures by Louis Massignon as well as other Marxist scholars. During this period Shariati realised that Western thought could prove to be a useful tool in terms of its methodology as a critique of Muslim society, while maintaining that Islam was self-sufficient in terms of possessing its own radical ideology, political culture and systems, notions of responsibility, and social functions. In fact, he argued, Shi'a Islam especially could offer much more than any secular ideology in that it possessed such additional dimensions as love, redemption, reward, resurrection, and eternity.

Shariati did not keep his philosophical and political meanderings to himself. He was politically active during this period, supporting Algerian and other liberation movements, joining the Confederation of Iranian Students and the (Iranian) National Front, and becoming editor of its newsletter 'Free Iran'. His proclamations reflected the writings of such revolutionary militants as the French West Indian political theorist Frantz Fanon. He advocated revolutionary armed struggle against the Iranian regime and he supported the uprisings that took place in Teheran in 1963 against increasing capitalism and corruption. Despite his own criticisms of the *ulama*, Shariati acknowledged the contribution to the struggle made by one cleric by the name of **Khomeini**. For his part in the riot, Khomeini was exiled to Turkey then Iraq.

Shariati returned to Iran in 1964, having completed his doctoral studies, but was immediately arrested because of his anti-government activities. Shariati was sent to Khoy prison in Azerbaijan for nearly two months. On his release he applied for various teaching positions for some two years but inevitably was turned down. He did, how- ever, eventually succeed in gaining a position teaching history at the

223

University of Masshad in 1966. It did not take long for Shariati to become something of a star at the university, being the most popular teacher and he was mobbed by students at various talks he gave. No doubt his reputation had come before him, but he was certainly a charismatic speaker, although marred somewhat by a lack of expertise in Islamic sciences which clerics were quick to pick holes in.

He made frequent lecture trips to Teheran, particularly to a debating institution known as the Husayniya-yi Irshad. *Husayniyas* (centres for religious education) were common institutions in Iran. They are usually located next to a mosque and, whereas the mosque was usually restricted to congregational prayers and other more formal religious practices, the *husayniyas* welcomed speakers on often controversial religious issues. The term '*husayniya*' derives from the martyred Imam Husayn (see **Ali ibn Abi Talib**) and, therefore, these institutions have frequently been centres for the instruction on the events of that time, often rousing feelings of strong emotion and associated feelings of oppression and injustice among Muslims. For this reason, the government was very wary of such institutions. Shariati's lectures had a huge impact and it is no surprise that he was arrested once again in the summer of 1973, and the Husayniya-yi Irshad was closed down. He spent the next eighteen months in prison and his books were banned. After he was released his movements were restricted, being forced to remain in his hometown of Mazinan. In June 1977 he was allowed to leave for Europe but he died in Britain in the same month under suspicious circumstances. The British coroner reported that he had died of a massive heart attack, while his supporters blamed SAVAK, the Iranian secret police.

While acknowledging the popular appeal of Marxist ideology he criticised it for treating people as units of production rather than possessing human values. Islam, he argued, was always inherently a mass movement but possessed humanistic values that Marxism lacked. Shariati placed great emphasis on the role of Man as God's vice-regent on earth. In other words, God had given Man the responsibility of ruling the earth and, by 'man', this did not mean, for Shariati, a small minority or a caliph, but all people. Therefore, God's vice-regency was synonymous with power to the masses, to *al nas* (the people). The **umma** is a classless society for which only God's will can reign. While Shariati's ideas owe much to the revolutionary values of Marx and the existential values of Sartre, he also takes a great deal from the works of the mystical Muslims such as **Ibn Sina** and **Sadr al-Din Shirazi** ('Mulla Sadra'). In his well-known work *The Sociology of Islam,* Shariati writes of the 'theomorphic man':

a 'Perfect Man' who possesses the qualities of truth, goodness and beauty, a rebellious spirit who combines the virtues of Jesus, Caesar and Socrates. This concept of a 'theomorphic being' owes much to **Ibn Arabi**'s concept of the Perfect Man and draws upon *Sufi* concepts of the Perfect Man (*insan-i-kamil*) that were also developed by the Indian poet and reformer **Muhammad Iqbal**. In fact, much of Shariati's writings on science and nature are reminiscient of Iqbal, for he also regarded the Qur'anic view of nature as close to the scientific view of the world and, perhaps surprisingly, Shariati sees Iqbal, a *Sunni* Muslim, as typical of the kind of Perfect Man.

In practical terms, Shariati argued in a pamphlet entitled *What is to be Done?* that the coming revolution would be undertaken by a militant band of intellectuals rather than the *Mullahs*. He would often cite the paradigm of Ali and Husayn as the great fighters against oppression. While the conservative *ulama* found much offence in his teachings, Khomeini, without openly acknowledging his debt to Shariati, would also frequently employ slogans created by Shariati which gave the impression among his followers that Khomeini was far more liberal in his outlook than he turned out to be.

In his latter years, no doubt affected by the time he had spent behind bars, Shariati became more concerned with issues related to freedom. In his work *Khud-sazi-e enqelabi* (*Revolutionary Reconstruction of the Self*), he states that total freedom is to be equated with Islamic emancipation. His concept of freedom was not of the liberal democratic kind, but rather freedom of the self, which is not only political in the need to break away from oppression and dictatorship, but also a personal response to one's condition in liberation from ignorance and evil. Therefore, political liberation was closely tied to a mystical enlightenment of the self which can be achieved through reflecting upon the non-material aspects of life.

Shariati's writings are attractive in their prose style, although not intellectually rigorous. He is very selective in his approach, picking on aspects of Western and Islamic thought that he found suitable while ignoring other elements that are crucial to a clear understanding of the concepts involved. For this reason, he could be easily criticised at an academic level. Nonetheless, his popularity rests more with his intuitive approach and his charismatic style which resulted in tapes of his lectures passing from hand to hand in the streets of Teheran. The only other figure who had a similar impact during his own residence in Paris was Khomeini. Undoubtedly, Shariati proved to be a constant threat to the oppressive Pahlevi regime and, even in death, his charisma remained, as evidenced by his images and slogans that were displayed in the streets of Teheran during the revolution of 1979.

See also: **Ali ibn Abi Talib**; **Abd al-Karim Soroush**

Major works

Shariati's writings are, on the whole, short and incisive. Good translations demonstrate his poetical way with words and reading a few of his pamphlets should help one to understand his appeal.

On the Sociology of Islam, trans. H. Algar, Berkeley, CA: Mizan Press, 1979.
Marxism and Other Western Fallacies: An Islamic Critique, trans. R. Campbell, Berkeley, CA: Mizan Press, 1980.
Man and Islam, Berkeley, CA: Mizan Press, 1981.
Hajj, Berkeley, CA: Mizan Press, 1984.

Further reading

The Rahnema is a sympathetic and in-depth study of Ali Shariati.

Dabashi, H., *Theology of Discontent: The Ideological Foundation of the Islamic Revolution in Iran*, New York: New York University Press, 1992.
Rahnema, A., *An Islamic Utopian: A Political Biography of Ali Shari'ati*, London: I.B. Tauris, 2000.

HASAN HANAFI (b. 1935)

Hasan Hanafi is an Egyptian philosopher and social scientist who is recognised internationally as a public critic and spokesman of modernity and its relationship to Western and Muslim civilisation. In the contemporary debate between modernity and Islam, Hanafi has provided great insight and imagination, combining his knowledge and understanding of Western culture and thought with his knowledge of the Islamic heritage. While he talks of an Islamic revolution, he is not of the militant tendency and nor does he associate himself with any particular Islamic group, 'secret' or otherwise.

Hasan Hanafi was born in Cairo, Egypt in 1935. In 1952 he joined the Muslim Brotherhood which had been founded by Hasan **al-Bana** in 1928, and Hanafi became a very active member while continuing his studies at the University of Cairo. To understand Hanafi's life which he himself identifies in his autobiography as the development of a 'national consciousness', we have to place him within the national context of the events in Egypt that formed his character. Like his predecessor al-Bana and **Sayyid Qutb**, he lived through a time of self-referential questioning of what it meant to be both Egyptian and Muslim, largely as a result of the fact that Egypt during much of this time was under British dominance and suffering from poverty (contrasted to that experienced by the British colonialists especially), spiritual vacuity, low morale and humiliation. Egypt had been under British occupation since 1882 and a British protectorate since 1914. The outbreak of the First World War led Britain to declare Egypt a protectorate and to sever all ties with Turkey (Egypt was still nominally part of the Ottoman Empire) which had entered the war on the side of Germany. The war caused considerable hardship and resentment among the *fellahin*, the Egyptian peasants, who were conscripted to dig ditches and had their livestock confiscated. Hanafi himself was forced to leave Cairo as a child due to German bombing raids.

By being allied to the British, Egypt suffered a great financial drain on its resources and so Britain, in return for this contribution, promised that Egypt would be allowed self-determination once the war was over. However, although Egypt was declared an independent monarchy in 1922, the British still reserved the right to intervene in Egyptian affairs if their own interests were threatened. In Egypt a new nationalist movement was set up, the *Wafd* ('Delegation') Party, but it was often considered to be too closely tied to British interest to attract the more anti-British, Islamic radicalist elements. To this end, al-Bana founded the Muslim Brotherhood (*al-Ikhwan al-Muslimun*, also translated as the 'Society of Muslim Brothers') in March 1928. This soon became the main expression of Islamic radicalism although, during al-Bana's lifetime, it was not a political party as such but, initially, a collection of small benevolent groups with the aim of alleviating the ills of Muslim society by providing welfare, education and a purpose for many disaffected young Muslims. These small groups of benevolent societies were not an uncommon feature in Egypt at that time. It is notable that membership of such groups consisted mostly of laypeople and young religious students. Generally, the **ulama** (the religious scholars) were absent from their ranks. In 1929, the Brotherhood had only four branches, in 1938 three hundred branches, and by 1948 there were 2,000 branches with a total membership of some two million.

After the Second World War, disenchantment with the British increased even more as well as the 'disaster' (*al nakhbah*) of 1948 when five Arab armies were defeated against Israel, and this led many to resort to terror for results. The Brotherhood was often blamed for terrorist actions and, by 1949, some 4,000 members were in prison and, in the same year, al-Bana was shot dead in the street. It was during these turbulent times that Hanafi was growing up and developing his own religious and national consciousness. He regularly took part in demonstrations as a student and was particularly critical of the communist movement which he considered to be immoral and deviant. Like his predecessors, he looked for a distinctly Islamic perspective rather than foreign solutions to the problems Egypt faced. However, unlike many of his colleagues in the Brotherhood, he did not believe being a good Muslim meant that you could not, for example, converse openly with women (which he liked to do) or enjoy Western classical music! Intellectually he studied all the great Muslim reformers, such as al-Bana, Qutb, **al-Ghazali**, and **Mawdudi** and, according to his autobiography, he began to feel that Islam could undergo a renaissance. He became particularly interested in philosophy, although he found these classes at university rather pedestrian and medieval. As a result, he would often come into conflict with his professors and was brought before a disciplinary board which resulted in him losing his honours status.

In 1956, he set off to study in France, the same year that the Suez War was declared and France joined Britain and Israel in attacking Egypt. In France, and Paris in particular, Hanafi had arrived when philosophical activity was beginning to thrive and would reach its apex during the 1960s and 1970s. It was an exciting time to be in Paris and Hanafi plunged himself into the contemporary philosophical debates that were taking place. He also familiarised himself with and, to varying extents, embraced such philosophical systems as idealism and existentialism. He submitted a doctorate thesis on 'The General Islamic Method' which, although it expressed his aim to formulate Islam as a general and comprehensive system for individual and social life, was considered – quite rightly one suspects – by the faculty to be too broad and ambitious. Consequently Hanafi focused on the study of the roots of Islamic legal thought (*usul al-fiqh*) in an attempt to create a new methodology and he was helped in his studies by a professor in philosophy at the Sorbonne and leading Roman Catholic modernist Jean Guitton (1901–1999). Guitton not only taught Hanafi about Western philosophy, but also aided him in research methodology and public speaking, providing Hanafi with the confidence to participate in what was a very competitive intellectual atmosphere in Paris at the time.

For his doctorate he produced an extended essay entitled *Les Méthodes d'Exégese, Essai sur la Science des Fondement de la Compréhension*

'Ilm Usu al-Fiqh (The Methods of the Science of the Fundamentals of Understanding in the Discipline of Usul al-Fiqh). Here Hanafi applies Western philosophical methods of analysis to the traditional approach of Islamic legal methodology. While he enjoyed Western intellectual thought, he was also critical of Western politics especially and was eager to return to Egypt. In 1966, he was able to take up a teaching post at the University of Cairo as well as engaging in such public activities as lectures and contributing contentious essays to magazines. During this time he did not attach himself to any particular political grouping but his critical public speaking nonetheless roused suspicions among the government authorities and even the rector of the university advised him to tone down his public image and accept an invitation to lecture in the US where he would be well away from Egyptian security forces. In 1971, Hanafi took up the offer and became a visiting professor at Temple University in Philadelphia.

During his years in the United States in the 1970s he moved away from philosophy and devoted his studies more to the social sciences, especially sociology of religion. He was also particularly interested in the principles behind liberation theology and speculated as to how these might be applied to Islam. During the 1980s Hanafi was now an international public figure who, although maintaining close contact with the University of Cairo, held visiting professorships at universities throughout the world including Kuwait, Morocco, Japan and the UAE. He continues to maintain his independence from any particular political or ideological stance, although he has been criticised by certain Muslim factions for being anti-Islamic which has raised concerns for his safety. He is currently Professor of Philosophy in the Department of Philosophy at Cairo University.

A number of themes can be identified in the vast library of works Hanafi has now written. First of all is his concern with 'heritage and renewal' (*al-turath wa al-tajdid*) which involves creating a delicate balance between tradition and modernity. While on the one hand Hanafi wants to assert the essence and universalism of Islam, he is also critical of how that has been expressed as an historical entity in Islamic societies. By 'heritage' (*turath*), then, Hanafi – in line with many Muslim scholars – understands this to mean the 'Islamic element' in culture and history but this may not be something that is static and prescribed in the Traditions, rather, it can be an evolving phenomenon. It is, in the hermeneutical sense, the transformation from Logos to Praxis, the transformation from revelation to the particulars of everyday human life. The need is expressed, not uncommon to the **salafiyyah** movement, to break away from the burden of history and look to the essence of Islam as axioms of renewal. Renewal is not a purely theoretical phenomenon, but is part of political and social action which Hanafi refers to as the Islamic Left and which he sees as a combination of Islamic heritage and the modernist vision of Nasser.

Hanafi is opposed to violence, but he does speak of revolution. He sets out a blueprint of a theology of liberation that can act as an effective opposition to oppression and poverty. The theological element requires a close re-examination of what Islamic theology actually consists of and to see it as not so much a sacred science but a social science. Similar to such early Islamic modernists as **Muhammad Abduh**, Hanafi sees no conflict between reason and revelation, but he would go further by incorporating a third element of a tripartite equation: reason, revelation, and reality. This reflects his liberation theology, for it is in reality – that is the social and political environment of the time – that humans must act to fulfil the demands of reason and revelation. Theology provides a theoretical basis for revolutionary action and Hanafi stresses the importance of the masses to be educated in Islamic heritage if they are to lead by consensus.

In his study of philosophy and religion Hanafi not only sets out to revolutionise Islamic thought, but also it is an attempt to understand the Western world-view. He sets out to create a science for the understanding of the West which he refers to as Occidentalism – an obvious dig at the Western science of Orientalism. He made a point of studying and teaching Western civilisation including medieval Christian thought as well as more modern Western thinkers. In line with the writings of Edward Said on Orientalism, Hanafi sees it as a vehicle used by the West to enforce its power over its colonies. Occidentalism, however, comes at a time of the liberation of the colonised and is able to present a critique of Western civilisation as well as presenting its own independent world-view. He sees Occidentalism as a shift in the balance of power as well as the emergence of a new social science which, on the one hand, is critical of Western methods of social science but, on the other, replaces it with new methods and concepts.

Hasan Hanafi represents a relatively new breed of Muslim intellectual that is not in any way militant, but is nonetheless revolutionary both in an intellectual way but also coupling this with activism. As a philosopher and social scientist he has learned the Western traditions while not giving up on his own Islamic heritage. Like many of his contemporaries he is engaged in the difficult and controversial task of marrying the need for revolution and evolution when faced with the challenge of modernity while not giving up on

what is the essence of Islamic belief. To this end he has had his critics, most notably among the more conservative elements of the
ulama.

Major works

Only the following work is currently available in English.

Islam in the Modern World, 2 vols, Cairo: Anglo-Egyptian Bookshop, 1995.

Further reading

A lack of material at present, aside from the following journal article and an
entry by Esposito.

Akhavi, S., 'The Dialectic in Contemporary Egyptian Social Thought: The
    Scripturalist and Modernist Discourses of Sayyid Qutb and Hasan Hanafi',
    International Journal of Middle East Studies 29(3) (August 1997).
Esposito, John L. and Voll, John O., 'Hasan Hanafi: The Classic Intellectual',
    in *Makers of Contemporary Islam*, Oxford: Oxford University Press, 2001.

RACHID GHANNOUSHI (b. 1941)

The Tunisian, Rachid Ghannoushi, is a controversial political and
social activist who represents the generation following that of the
Salafiyyah (although considered modernist, the movement 'looks
back' to the time of **Muhammad** and his **Companions** as a guide to
the right way to live). While maintaining essential Islamic values, he
sees no contradiction between the values of a multi-party system,
pluralism and women's rights, for example, and that of Islam. He has
been a public opponent of the oppressive regimes in Tunisia and this
has resulted in imprisonment and exile for him.

Rachid al-Ghannoushi Khriji was born in 1941 in southern Tunisia in the province of Qabis. He comes from a small village and his
father was a pious Muslim who had four wives and ten children.
Although he was not in a position to provide his children with a
thorough or broad education, his father did ensure that all his children studied the Qur'an. Ghannoushi's mother came from a more
cosmopolitan merchant family. It was because of her that her children
were able to receive a formal education and break away from the
narrow world of agriculture. This was by no means an easy thing to
do and Ghannoushi was not able to attend primary school until the
relatively mature age of 10. However, he could already read and
write by this point and enthusiastically engaged in the study of Arabic

and French. Unfortunately, his father took him out of the school after only a few years, partly because he needed extra hands on the farm, but also he resented the teaching of French which he perceived as the language of Tunisia's colonists. However, it was not long before the family gave up farming and moved to the village, and Ghannoushi set off in 1956 to study at a religious school in the city of Gabbas where he gained a diploma in theology.

The diploma, which followed a formal Islamic curriculum, allowed Ghannoushi, in 1962, to attend university in Tunis to study the Qur'an and Islamic law (*shari'a*) as well as more modern subjects. However, Ghanousshi found the system and content of teaching archaic and out of touch with the realities of the modern world. For example, the study of Islamic law was more concerned with practices that occurred many hundreds of years previously rather than what was happening in the modern world. Consequently he did not complete his studies and instead became a primary school teacher. In 1964 he left teaching and went to Egypt where he studied agriculture at Cairo University. However, this also proved to be a short period for, after just four months, the President of Tunisia, Bourguiba, ordered all Tunisian nationals to leave Egypt, fearing they might be tainted by Nasser's brand of Arab socialism. So Ghannoushi transferred to the University of Damascus in Syria and was able to stay there long enough to attain a bachelor's degree in philosophy. Despite the Tunisian president's efforts, Ghannoushi was attracted to Arab socialism and joined the Syrian Nationalist Socialist Party (SNSP).

While Ghannoushi at this time could not be considered a particularly devout Muslim, his encounter with socialism did not result in giving up his religion. Even his studies in philosophy were mostly concerned with Islamic philosophy rather than Western. As a university student he travelled across Europe over a seven-month period and this experience made a strong impression on him, but not in a positive sense. In fact, what he saw of Europe convinced him that it was not the happy and prosperous place he had previously believed it to be. He also began to question his allegiance to Arab socialism and saw it as a foreign import that could not resolve the ills of Islamic society. It was then he looked inwards at Islam itself and became more involved with the Muslim Brotherhood and it was here that he saw a new face of Islam, so very different and more alive than the Islam he had studied formally. He started reading the works of contemporary Muslim reformers and was especially influenced by **Muhammad Iqbal**'s *Reconstruction of Religious Thought in Islam* and **Muhammad Qutb**'s *Man between Materialism and Islam*, as well as the writings of **Hasan al-Banna** (founder of the Muslim Brotherhood), **Sayyid Qutb** and **Mawlana Mawdudi**. In these works, Ghannoushi found the answers that had been troubling him, notably the uncertainties with such political theories as socialism coupled with his sense of Islamic heritage. He found that Islam did have a strong and contemporary side after all. A crucial turning point in Ghannoushi's life was the Six Day War in 1967 when Damascus was bombed by Israeli planes and the Arabs looked to a strong ideology to withstand the shame of the loss to the Israelis. Many at this time turned to Islam rather than socialism. In 1968, Ghannoushi moved to Paris to study for a Master's degree at the Sorbonne. Paris at the time was a place thriving with intellectual activity, including Islamic political groups. Ghannoushi found it difficult to fit in with a culture that was going through a period of individualism and sexual liberation. He turned towards Islam even more and attached himself to a group called the *Tablighi Jamaat* which originated in Pakistan. The *Tablighi* were an apolitical Islamic missionary society consisting of preachers who would travel around the world calling (*da'wa*) Muslims to be more observant in their religious practices and not to stray. Ghannoushi's attachment to this group gave him both a sense of purpose and a community he felt more at home with. Ghannoushi became a very active member, engaging in missionary activities among, especially, the poor North African Muslim immigrants and he eventually was given the position of *imam* (leader of prayers) at a small (it was a converted storefront) mosque in Paris. For Ghannoushi, this was a time that in a spiritual sense was fulfilling, but he found such a responsibility a difficult one.

In 1970 Ghannoushi returned to Tunisia to visit his mother but while visiting a mosque he encountered some *Tablighi* members who invited him to stay in Tunisia and preach in a mosque in Tunis. He agreed to do this and became both a preacher and an activist. He took up a teaching position in philosophy at a secondary school, joined the Qur'an Preservation Society and actively engaged in giving lectures and offering lessons in Islam to, especially, Muslim youth. As he himself noted, 'in those years it was difficult to find a young man praying, especially if he was from the so-called educated people ... The system had taken the precaution of indoctrinating the youth – the materialistic tendency rendered them useless and servile.'[1] Ghannoushi attracted large crowds at his public talks, especially from the young working class, but also many students. His main theme was to blame the current ills of Tunisian society – and more generally of Arab Muslims – on the lack of identity. In the case of Tunisia the country had for a number of years pursued a socialist policy under Bourguiba which had resulted in high unemployment and a failing economy. Ghannoushi argued that the people needed to look to Islam as a political and social alternative:

> I remember we used to feel like strangers in our own country. We had been educated as Muslims and Arabs, while we could see that the country had been totally moulded in the French cultural identity. For us the doors to any further education were closed since the university was completely Westernised. At that time, those wanting to continue their studies in Arabic had to go to the Middle East.[2]

During the late 1970s Bourguiba became increasingly oppressive, using the military to crush any public demonstrations, and Islamic movements became more politicised. One group in particular, the Islamic Association (*Jamaah al-Islamiyya*) was founded in 1979 with the specific intention of engaging in political and social action rather than merely discussion. The leader of this organisation was Ghannoushi. Being the leader of a group that, by its nature, would be in opposition to Bourguiba was a dangerous enterprise, but it also resulted in it being very popular as it was perceived as genuine opposition to the government. In 1981 the Association changed its name to the Islamic Tendency Movement (MTI) and became a political party but this just caused greater resentment from Bourguiba who could tolerate Islamic movements so long as they did not emerge as genuine political opposition. In the same year as MTI's foundation as a political party, Bourguiba arrested and imprisoned Ghannoushi and many of its other leaders. The MTI was forced to go underground where it continued to develop its organisation to nurture a new generation of young Muslim activists. Ghannoushi was given amnesty in 1984, but Bourguiba continued in his oppressive policies and, in 1987, Ghannoushi was once again arrested which resulted in street battles and demonstrations. Bourguiba's tactic was to attempt to discredit the MTI by accusing it of plotting to overthrow the Tunisian government with the support of Iran. He argued that the MTI constituted an 'Islamic threat' and labelled them 'Khomeinists' (see **Khomeini**).

Bourguiba pushed for the death penalty against Ghannoushi. However, in 1987, Bourguiba was declared medically unfit to govern, and Prime Minister Zine al-Abidine Ben Ali assumed the presidency. While retaining the secret police, Ben Ali freed political prisoners, legalized most opposition parties, and eased restrictions on the press. To promote his legitimacy he also appealed to the country's Islamic heritage and even went on a pilgrimage to Mecca. The MTI was promised official recognition as a political party and changed its name to the Renaissance Party (*Ennahda*), although Ben Ali reneged on his promise and refused its recognition, claiming that religion and politics should be kept separate. No doubt Ben Ali was concerned that the Renaissance Party could well take power. In fact, Ben Ali went further and adopted the same tactics as his predecessor in imprisoning and harassing Muslim activists, claiming that they presented a fundamentalist threat to political stability.

The main thesis of all of Ghannoushi's teaching is best presented by Ghannoushi himself:

> While we should try to keep this [Tunisia's Islamic civilisation] identity, we do not refuse to interact and learn from other civilisations. We should do this while also keeping our own identity. The way to civilisation is not to completely follow the Western way or become completely Westernised. We have our own identity and we learn from modern life and science and try to improve within the framework of Islamic civilisation.[3]

Hence, Ghannoushi is not against change and modernity, but believes it must be rooted in Tunisia's Islamic and Arabic heritage, and he believes that the attempts to impose socialism upon his country have proven disastrous. Islam, for Ghannoushi, is self-sufficient; it has its own world-view with its own set of principles and values and so does not need to import other values that are alien to it. He is against a wholesale rejection of the West, as the above quote demonstrates, but this does not mean that the West should be blindly imitated either. While acknowledging the universality of Islam, he also sees it from a multidimensional perspective and so the distinctive cultural, historical and political identity of Tunisia also has to be taken into account. Even when it comes to other Muslim scholars, Ghannoushi says they are not spokesmen of Islam, for there can be no one specific ideology. Islam must evolve in the same way societies do.

In terms of values, Ghannoushi argues that what is at fault with Islam, at least in his own society, is its failure to identify itself with the impoverished working classes and with women. Islam should be seen as a liberating force, not an oppressive one, and he sees no necessary contradiction between democracy and Islam. In fact, he argues that democracy originates in Islam and the Western concept was inherited from Islamic civilisatioin during the Middle Ages. For Ghannoushi, a state that upholds such values as human rights, the rule of law, a multi-party system and freedom of speech is in effect a Muslim state, regardless of its secular credentials and, he argues, he would rather live in a free secular state than any state that imposes an oppressive version of Islam. As his paradigm he cites Andalusia (Muslim Spain) as a time when Islam embraced diversity and pluralism and thrived on it.

Major works

'The Battle against Islam', *Middle East Affairs Journal* 1(2) (Winter 1992).
'Secularism in the Arab Maghrib', in *Islam and Secularism in the Middle East*, New York: New York University Press, 2000.

Further reading

The Tamimi is particularly recommended as he has had virtually unrestricted access to Ghannoushi.

Esposito, John L. and Voll, John O., 'Rashid Ghannoushi: Activist in Exile', in *Makers of Contemporary Islam*, Oxford: Oxford University Press, 2001.
Tamimi, Azzam, *Rachid Ghannouchi: A Democrat within Islamism*, New York: Oxford University Press, 2001.

Notes

1 'Nobody's Man – but a Man of Islam', in *The Movement of Islamic Tendency: The Facts* (London, 1987), p. 82.
2 Ibid., p. 80.
3 Quoted from Esposito (2001), p. 107.

ABD AL-KARIM SOROUSH (b. 1945)

Abd al-Karim Soroush is regarded by many of his contemporaries as perhaps the principal Iranian and Islamic philosopher and theologian to have emerged in the past twenty years. Some Western commentators, in a not unusual effort to anchor non-Western figures within a Western context, have compared him, misleadingly, with Martin Luther. This, one suspects, is partly because of his efforts to synthesise religious authority with that of political liberty, but also because of his revolutionary credentials.

Soroush is the pen name of Hosayn Dabbagh who was born in Tehran in 1945. He attended the Alavi High School where he was able to study both the religious fields and the scientific, which, in fact, paved a way for his life-long interest in the relation between the two fields. He went on to study pharmacy at university in Tehran and, having graduated, he spent his two years 'military' service as Director of the Laboratory for Food Products, Toiletries and Sanitary Materials. He left Iran to continue his studies in England in the mid to late 1970s. This period proved to be a time of incredible upheaval in the history of Iran. When Soroush left the country, it was a prosperous state ruled by a Western-orientated Shah. When Soroush returned in 1979, Iran had undergone a revolution and was ruled by the Islamic clergy. Despite the growth in prosperity in Iran during the 1970s there were many anti-government demonstrations, especially among students and intellectuals. The Shah responded with increased oppression and, in 1978, riots broke out in many Iranian cities led by the *Shi'a* clergy who wanted the nation governed by *shari'a*. The principal ideologue behind this was Ayatollah **Khomeini**, who at the time was directing the demonstrations from his refuge in Paris. By late autumn of 1978 Iran was virtually in a state of civil war and, in January of 1979 the Shah fled abroad. Soon after that Khomeini returned to Iran as their new hero.

During this time, Soroush continued to study, first an MSc in analytical chemistry at the University of London, and then to Chelsea College where he researched the field of history and the philosophy of science. What seemed an unremarkable career, however, was affected by the events in Iran. Although Soroush was absent during this period, he kept a careful eye on events and was politically active in London. Soroush developed a deep interest in the teachings of various Iranian religious activists, such as **Ali Shariati**, and he became active in Muslim groups in London, publicly condemning Iranian leftist and Marxist movements. He became a public figure through his lectures, some of which were published in his first work *Tazed-e dialektiki* (*Dialectical Antagonism*) which was a criticism of leftist ideology. His second work, *Nahad-e na-aram-e jahan* (*The Restless Nature of the World*), looked at the foundations of Islamic philosophy. These works were published in Tehran and, on his return to Iran, he was already a well-known figure, becoming Director of the Islamic Culture Group at Tehran's Teacher Training College as well as being appointed by Khomeini personally to the Advisory Council of the Cultural Revolution. The Council had initially been responsible for the closing down of Iran's universities and the restriction of free speech, although Soroush's remit seemed to be to reopen the universities. However, he resigned this post after four years due to professional differences, although it remains unclear what they were.

Although Soroush was initially perceived by many of the ruling clergy as an ideologue of the Iranian Republic because of his anti-Marxist writings, this status was not to last as the Republic became more oppressive particularly, for Soroush, in connection with intellectual discourse. In 1983, Soroush transferred from the Teacher Training College to the Institute for Cultural Research and Studies, where he served as a member of the research staff until he was forced to leave in 1997. For some time after that he taught Philosophy of Science, as well as giving lectures on philosophy of religion and the empirical sciences. However, since 1995 his teaching activities have been restricted and he has been prevented from lecturing in the mosques.

Soroush's familiarity with Western philosophical and political ideas, coupled with his knowledge of the Islamic sciences and modern trends in Islamic intellectual thought, has resulted in him being a figure of great intellectual force in the sphere of Islamic revivalism. There are three specific themes that can be identified in all his writings: (1) ethics and social criticism; (2) philosophical anthropology and political theory; and (3) the epistemology and sociology of knowledge. The latter subject was particularly the focus of perhaps his best-known work, *The Hermeneutical Expansion and Contraction of the Theory of Shari'a*. In this work he is concerned with a favourite topic of his; the relation between science and religion. He raises the issue of the role of religion in the modern world and argues that Islamic society can conceivably be secularised as it undergoes modernisation without sacrificing its Islamic culture or denigrating core Islamic values. By 'secularism', Soroush means that which is rational or scientific rather than seeing it in its usual sense of that which is opposed to religion for, Soroush would argue along with many other Islamic scholars, Islam is neither irrational nor non-scientific. The growth in science and knowledge more generally does not come at the expense of religion, but rather they work together in helping us understand religion and its proper place in society.

Soroush's use of the science of hermeneutics is a growing trend among Muslim thinkers today, perhaps most notably in the controversial Egyptian Nasr Hamid Abu Zayd (b. 1943). Not surprisingly, Soroush's views have also proved to be controversial for the conservative clergy. Soroush argues that while the Qur'an, as the word of God, is pure, absolute and therefore unchanging, this does not alter the fact that its revelations were delivered to a society that, by the nature of all societies, is subject to change and evolution. Revealed texts possess both objectivity and subjectivity. While the word of God does not change, the interpretation of it does, or at least should. Therefore, no interpretation is fixed and unchanging and no one culture, group, time period, or individual has a monopoly on what is the right or wrong interpretation of the sacred sources. Soroush does not deny the importance of Islamic scholarship for an understanding of the sources, but he does believe that all people have the right to attempt interpretation. It must be remembered that Soroush was addressing an audience of **Shi'a** Muslims, not **Sunni**. In Shi'a Islam especially there is greater emphasis on the view that religious knowledge is effectively 'inherited' and privy to the elite clergy, whereas Soroush is presenting a much more democratic rendering which would amount to virtual heresy among many Shi'a clergy.

For Soroush, religious knowledge is effectively no different from knowledge in general: it is an evolving phenomenon that operates with fairly general parameters that make it 'religious' as opposed to scientific, historical, and so on. Religious knowledge is given a human, worldly, as opposed to a divine, other-worldly character. The parameters of knowledge overlap, so that it really does not make sense to speak of religious knowledge as something different from, say, scientific knowledge. Progress in one form of knowledge inevitably affects another; they do not exist in separate bubbles. Soroush, however, is not a relativist in terms of knowledge. Far from non-religious scientific knowledge undermining the fundamental and unchangeable truths of religion itself, it assists in establishing what those truths are. Knowledge of *shari'a* is a flexible thing rather than a list handed down from one generation to the next without ever changing or one being frightened to change it.

Soroush offends the traditional clergy further by questioning the validity of the contentious concept *vilayat-i faqih* ('guardianship by the clergy') which was the central teaching of Khomeini's political philosophy. Khomeini argued that in the absence of the Imam the clergy should do more than simply advise the government on how Islamic their legislation is; rather, they should rule directly. This doctrine, however, had little Qur'anic support. Since Soroush argues that the knowledge of the jurists is human rather than sacred, he sees no reason why they should be allowed to possess such a claim to infallible authority. Instead of obeying the dictates of the ayatollahs, or any person claiming a monopoly in religious knowledge, the student of religion should struggle to determine their own understanding of the body of religious knowledge through dialogue and questioning. Soroush's democratic approach to knowledge encourages people not to imitate or obey previous rulings but to search for themselves, otherwise jurists will become power-hungry and hypocritical.

What Soroush meant by 'expansion and contraction of the *shari'a'* was that Islamic law should be seen within a broad framework of knowledge *per se*, and thus our knowledge of *shari'a* will be expanded. If it is contained within a narrow framework, it limits the potential to understand. His theory asserts three principles: (1) the principle of coherence and correspondence (any understanding of religion bears on the body of human knowledge and tries to be in coherence with the latter); (2) the principle of interpretation (a contraction or expansion in the system of human knowledge may penetrate the domain of our understanding of religion); and (3) the principle of evolution (the system of human knowledge is subject to expansion and contraction). *Shari'a*, for Soroush, should not be understood as merely rules dictated by the clergy for others to obey, but is rather a part of a much greater framework of all Islamic knowledge, including science, mathematics, medicine, philosophy, and so on.

In his work, *Let Us Learn from History*, he adopts an empirical approach to history, arguing that it generally shows that mankind is, in a Hobbesian sense, weak. It is only a fantasist who believes that mankind is innately good, and to have faith in man to do good merely opens the gates to those who wish to do evil. He nonetheless argues for the liberal values of reason, liberty, freedom and democracy for, he believes, they are not in opposition to Islamic values. In particular, he has championed the cause of democracy on the basis that Islam cannot thrive unless such a political system exists. People must be free to believe or not, and Islam, or any religion, cannot be imposed upon a people from above

One can understand why Soroush in recent years has come into conflict with religious authorities in Iran. Soroush, for his part, has not been shy in directing his criticisms at the clergy, accusing them of sacrificing the basic values of Islam and assigning privileges to themselves. Importantly he has stressed that clerics have no *a priori* right to rule, but rather rulers should be elected on merit. Soroush, in fact, supports a view that has always had a supporting faction within the clergy itself: that when clerics work in the service of the state, their independence, loyalty and integrity are compromised. However, perhaps few clergy will go as far as Soroush in arguing that they should not therefore receive financial support from the state.

Soroush is important in today's climate as he remains a vocal proponent of democracy in Iran and as a result has braved many death threats to travel across Iran to give his speeches. In fact, he keeps a collection of his shirts that have been shredded during attacks on him by pro-regime militants. In 2004, Soroush was awarded the prestigious Erasmus Prize. The Erasmus Prize is awarded annually to a person or institution that has made an exceptionally important contribution to European culture, society or social science.

Major works

'The Evolution and Devolution of Religious Knowledge', in Kurzman (ed.) *Liberal Islam*, Oxford: Oxford University Press, 1998.
Reason, Freedom and Democracy in Islam: Essential Writings of Adbolkarim Soroush, trans. and ed. with a critical introduction by M. Sadri and A. Sadri, Oxford: Oxford University Press, 2000.
A good website, in English, for his lectures, articles, etc. is: http://www.drsoroush.com/English.htm

Further reading

Boroujerdi, Mehrzad, *Iranian Intellectuals and the West: The Tormented Triumph of Nativism*, New York: Syracuse University Press, 1996.
Dabshi, Hamid, *Theology of Discontent: The Ideological Foundations of the Islamic Revolution in Iran*, New York: New York University Press, 1993.

GLOSSARY

Abbasids   One of the great dynasties of classical Islamic civilisation (750–1258 CE).

Bid'a   'Innovation', meaning heresy in the context of Islamic law and teaching.

Caliph   Arab '*Khalifa*' meaning 'successor' or 'deputy', especially of the Prophet. Caliph usually understood as ruler of Muslims, but can apply to all Muslims as 'vice-gerent' of earth.

Companions   Those followers of the Prophet who were closest to him during his lifetime and strove to assimilate his teachings.

Falsafa   Arabic for 'philosophy'.

Fatwa   A legal opinion produced by a *mufti* (jurisconsult).

Fiqh   'Understanding' of the law, and so therefore jurisprudence.

Fitnah   'Trial' or 'testing'. In Islamic history, these 'trials' refer to the early civil wars.

Five pillars   The five principal categories of worship that represent the minimum level of religious observance for pious Muslims.

Ghayba   'Occultation'. Mysterious concealment which, in Imami Shi'a Islam is the belief that the twelfth Imam is 'concealed'.

Hadith   'Report', or 'event'. The literary form that communicates the Prophet's sayings and deeds (*sunna*).

Hijra   'Emigration' especially of the Prophet from Mecca to Medina in 622.

Ijtihad   Independent reasoning engaged in by a *mujtahid*.

Ikhwan al-Safa   'Brotherhood of Purity'. A secret society founded around 951 in Basra, Iraq.

Imam   'Leader'. In Shi'a Islam, Imam are vested in infallible guidance by God, although an imam can also be a religious teacher or prayer leader.

Ismaili   A major branch of Shi'a Islam which takes its name from the sixth Imam, Ismail.

Jahiliyah   The term for the time of the pre-Islamic era: the 'age of ignorance'.

242

Jihad 'Striving' or 'exertion', especially in the religious path or in holy war.

Ka'ba The 'cube' that is the main sanctuary in Mecca.

Kalam 'Speech' or 'discourse' especially on religious matters, hence theology.

Kharijite 'Seceders'. A strict sect of early Islam.

Mahdi 'Guide' or 'leader'. Messianic figure who will appear at the end of the world.

Madhhab Literally, 'a direction'. Specifically referring to the different schools of law.

Mujtahid One who exercises *ijtihad*.

Mullah Persian form of '*mawla*' (master) of religious sciences. Member of the *ulama*.

Murji'ite 'Postponers'. An early school of *kalam* who left punishment for God to decide.

Mu'tazalite The 'rationalist' school of *kalam*.

Naskh 'Abrogation' of certain Qur'anic verses by others.

Qadi Islamic judge.

Qur'an 'Recitation'; especially the Islamic scripture.

Rashidun 'The Rightly-Guided', reference to the first four Caliphs of Islam.

Salafiyyah A movement deriving from the early twentieth century founded by al-Afghani and Muhammad Abduh.

Shari'a Islamic law.

Shi'a 'Party', 'faction' or 'sect'. Deriving from those who followed Ali who believed that the Prophet had chosen him to be his heir. There are a number of different Shi'a groups.

Shirk Idolatory. Considered an unforgivable sin.

Successors The immediate generation that came after the Companions.

Sufi An Islamic mystic.

Sunna 'Custom', especially that of the Prophet Muhammad, which is then transmitted in the literary form known as *hadith*.

Sunni Popular name for the Muslim majority.

Tafsir 'Commentary', especially of the Qur'an.

Taqlid 'Imitation'. Accepting the legal decisions of previous scholars without question, so opposite to *ijtihad*.

Tawhid God's unity. A central tenet of Islamic doctrine. To worship any other god is *shirk*.

Ulama The learned class of religious scholars.

Umayyad The first Muslim dynasty (661–750).

Umma   The Muslim community although, more generally, a reference to any community that shares a common religion.

Zimmi   A member of the 'People of the Book' and so includes Jews and Christians who are therefore given protection status by Muslims.

INDEX

INDEX

Islam: The Basics

Colin Turner

With nearly 1500 rich years of history and culture to its name, Islam is one of the world's great faiths and, in modern times, the subject of increasingly passionate debate by believers and non-believers alike. *Islam: The Basics* is a concise and timely introduction to all aspects of Muslim belief and practice. Topics covered include:

- The Koran and its teachings
- The life of the Prophet Muhammad
- Women in Islam
- Sufism and Shi'ism
- Islam and the modern world
- Non-Muslim approaches to Islam

Complete with a glossary of terms, pointers to further reading and a chronology of key dates, *Islam: The Basics* provides an invaluable overview of the history and the contemporary relevance of this always fascinating and important subject.

0-415-34106-X